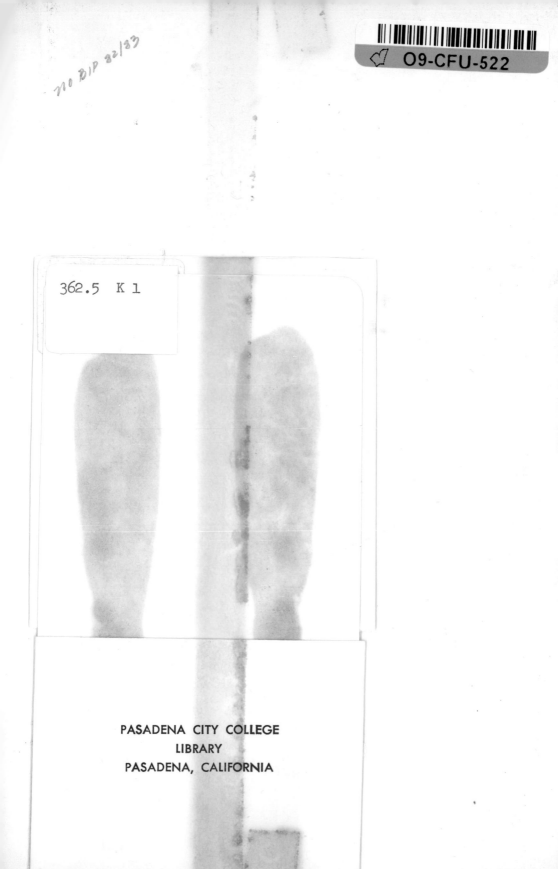

DOWN AND OUT IN THE USA

If you think that living on welfare
Is all sugar, cherries and honey,
You're wrong, because there is too much month
Left at the end of the money.

— *National Welfare Rights Organization* Welfare Fighter, 1972

WITHDRAWN

FRANKLIN WATTS, Inc.
New York | 1973

DOWN AND OUT IN THE USA

A HISTORY OF SOCIAL WELFARE

LUCY KOMISAR

Also by the author:
The New Feminism

Library of Congress Cataloging in Publication Data

Komisar, Lucy, 1942–
  Down and out in the USA.

  Bibliography: p.
  1. Public welfare—United States—History.
I. Title.
HV91.K64   362'.973   73–8951
ISBN   0–531–02647–7
ISBN   0–531–05560–4 (pbk.)

Book Design by Rafael Hernandez

ACKNOWLEDGMENTS AND THANKS:

To the New York Public Library for allowing me to use the Frederick Lewis Allen Room. It was invaluable.

To the staff of the Center for Social Welfare Policy and Law, who shared their expertise and knowledge on current happenings in welfare law; thanks are due especially to librarian Barbara Rios and to the Center's attorneys.

To Elizabeth Wickenden, administrator and consultant on welfare to national and international organizations for 40 years; to Henry Rosner and Arthur Schiff, both Assistant Commissioners of the Human Resources Administration, New York City; and to Steve Antler, Associate Professor of Social Welfare, School of Social Welfare, State University of New York at Stony Brook, L.I., for reading the manuscript and making important contributions.

To Dorianne Lee, who gave me peace and quiet in her Paris apartment so I could write.

To Dave and Frances and Vic and Larry

TABLE OF CONTENTS

INTRODUCTION

Newspapers write editorials about the "welfare crisis," local officials cry that their treasuries are being squeezed dry, politicians take to the platform to denounce the shiftless who don't want to work, and lawmakers struggle with efforts to alter the law in the midst of philosophical differences so immense that they produce a stalemate.

The proponents of welfare reform seek to change not only a particular law that dates from 1935, but a philosophy about work and people that was as much a part of western civilization in the 1600's as it is today. They seek to overturn beliefs that were born along with capitalism, the Industrial Revolution, and the Protestant Reformation. They are trying to alter ideas that literally were brought to America on the Mayflower and which became a central part of the American character.

This book traces the development and philosophy of public welfare from the Middle Ages and Elizabethan England through the colonization and settlement of America, the poor laws of the 1800's, the programs and problems of the Depression, the "welfare crisis" of the past few decades, and, finally, the new proposals for change.

One of the chief reasons for social organization has been mutual protection, and there have always been people — the sick, disabled, aged, children, widows, and others — who have not "made it" in the economic system and have had to be supported in some other way.

Nevertheless, people have always resisted dealing with the problem of supporting those who cannot support themselves. "They have had to be coerced by religious exhortation or taxes, and still, people have continued to look for ways to reduce their obligation," says welfare expert Elizabeth Wickenden.

They have done this:

• by deliberate harassment: "We won't let people starve, but we'll try to discourage them from seeking help." Midnight searches and inquisitions into personal lives are part of this tactic;

• by shifting the responsibility to someone else: In the past, relative-responsibility laws reached to grandparents and grandchildren;

• by the work test: forcing people into degrading make-work and substandard jobs;

• by categorizing people—and deciding to give aid only to certain groups: The federal welfare program does not aid adults without children unless they are aged, blind, or disabled;

• and sometimes they have done it the way it ought to be done—by preventing need before it occurs by a program of social insurance and the creation of real jobs.

The attitude toward public welfare has hardly changed in four centuries. It continues to be based on the notion that aid to the destitute must be deliberately low or else people will refuse to work, a formula that is applied to the helpless as well as the able-bodied; to children as well as adults; and in times of mass unemployment as well as prosperity.

Shortly before this book went to press, the U.S. Supreme Court issued a decision that brings us full circle to the days of the workhouse philosophy.* It upheld a New York State law that required "able-bodied" welfare recipients, including mothers with young children, to take jobs supplied by the local state employment office. If no jobs were available, they would work off the amount of their welfare checks at part-time jobs for the local government. Those not working would have to report to the state employment service every two weeks.

The opinion in the seven to two decision said that the work rules sought to "promote self-reliance and civic responsibility," to make sure that welfare money was spent for those who were really in need, and to cope with the financial problems local governments were suffering. The ruling bolstered work programs in twenty-two other states.

Lest one think that things were always so, the book begins with a look at welfare in the Dark Ages.

---

* New York State Department of Social Services v. Dublino, decided June 21, 1973. (See pages 170–172.)

DOWN AND OUT IN THE USA

When families were organized into clans and tribes, they produced their food and other needs communally. Every member of the group had an obligation to care for the others. Communal child-rearing meant that the death of one parent did not require the other to cease working or find child care, and the old, the sick, and the disabled shared in the tribal wealth even when they could not work.

In medieval times, in the twelfth and thirteenth centuries, people lived on the land, either as serfs on feudal manors or peasant farmers in small villages.[1] Feudal lords were bound to care for their serfs, and people who lived and died in the villages where they were born felt the same loyalties and obligations as members of a tribe.

Those who needed help received it from individual almsgivers or from the Church. Its right to collect tithes made the Church itself a public institution. Canon law required that the clergy be hospitable "and not miserly to the poor,"[2] and a third of the income of the parish church was earmarked for charity. Monasteries gave food and lodging to anyone who asked. A request by a person for aid was enough to make him eligible.

The Church set up hospitals and poorhouses run by religious orders or lay brotherhoods, and parish priests distributed church funds to the needy of their towns. Money was not given indiscriminately to those who could work, but aid was a right of those who needed it. The property of the Church belonged to the people, and the people had an ob-

1

THE HERITAGE OF EUROPE

ligation to provide for the poor. A poor person could stand up in church and denounce the rich man who had refused to give him alms.

Poverty was not a disgrace. In fact, giving alms was seen as a way of getting into heaven: the poor provided the wealthy with an opportunity to exercise the virtue of charity and thereby obtain salvation. Great lords who gave their serfs bare subsistence in life sought a sure way to heaven by writing wills that left money to the Church for the care of the poor. Sometimes pennies were distributed at their funerals, and thousands flocked to the last rites of the very rich. The object of almsgiving was the well-being of the giver's soul, not the relief of the destitute.

It was hardly necessary to investigate the claims of the needy in small communities where the priest knew everyone. Yet even so, a fourth-century priest, St. John Chrysostom, found it necessary to admonish: "Let us have no more of this ridiculous, diabolical, peremptory prying."[3]

Catastrophe and Disruption

Then three major occurrences completely disrupted the system of Church aid to the poor and altered the concept and philosophy of the poor law. They were the ravages of the bubonic plague that swept Europe in the fourteenth century, the enclosures of common farmland for sheep in England in the fifteenth century, and the seizure of all Church property by Henry VIII in the sixteenth century.[4]

The Black Death swept through Europe in the mid-1300's. One of every four persons died of it, and the sudden loss of population resulted in a critical labor shortage. Workers demanded higher wages and peasants on the land sought to escape their servitude and earn better livings as paid workers on farms or in the towns. Many took to the roads to look for work in other communities. They were joined by the soldiers who had returned home after serving in the battles of the Hundred Years War between England and France.

The government of England responded by passing the Ordinance of Laborers in 1349. Its aim was to prevent workers from leaving their jobs to find better pay and to prevent them from leaving the land and the feudal manors to find better jobs in an economy of growing trade and crafts industries and scarcity of labor.

The law required "all persons able to labour and without other means of support to serve any master at the rates customary prior to the pestilence."[5] Giving alms to able-bodied beggars was against the law and punishable by imprisonment. Even those who were not able-bodied (they were called "impotent") were not allowed to wander about seeking alms. A law of 1388 declared that impotent beggars could seek alms only at their present residence, in a neighboring town, or at their place of birth. Punishment for violators included branding on the forehead.

However, people did wander about, and some took to robbery and violence. In the minds of those in power the beggar became virtually synonymous with the vagrant and the criminal. People looking for work at better wages were considered just as criminal as the highwaymen who menaced travelers.

The Enclosures

The enclosures of common farmland aggravated the problem. Increased foreign demand caused a growth in England's woolen industry, and in the 1400's, land that had been used for farming was fenced off for sheep. Peasants could no longer use the common lands that had been available to all, and agricultural unemployment increased as landowners fired farm workers, turned out tenants, and started raising sheep. The enclosures sometimes led to the eviction of the populations of entire villages.

In the past, the destitute had been the widowed and the old and the ill who remained in their villages to be cared for by their neighbors. Now people were forced out of their homes and villages and left to seek work in the larger towns and cities. And the problem of giving aid to the destitute became increasingly mixed with the need to act against lawless vagrants who threatened life and property.[6] Also, it was more difficult to determine who did not want to work, who were willing but unable to find work, who had left their jobs for better wages and conditions, and who needed temporary assistance between jobs.

Church law had said to "keep hospitality" but in a manner that did not encourage the able-bodied to accept alms instead of work. Now that people no longer lived in their own little villages, it became virtually impossible to distinguish the "worthy" from the "unworthy."

Another cause of poverty was the new and growing factory system with its uncertainty, so characteristic of capitalism. Workers were no longer sure of working at the same farm year after year where they could at least eat the food they grew. Now they were dependent on cash and the ups and downs of the new capitalism in which a company suddenly could fail, where production could be halted or cut, all because of developments elsewhere in the world of credit and trade. Workers were not "bound" to the factory as they were to the manor, but that meant that they lacked the minimal security they had known as serfs.

Regulation of Beggars

In the next century, Henry VIII continued an oppressive poor-law policy by establishing laws to regulate and punish beggars. A statute of 1531 empowered justices of the peace to issue licenses to the impotent poor allowing them to beg in certain areas. Those who begged without a license were to be whipped or set in the stocks for three days with nothing to eat but bread and water. Able-bodied beggars were to be tied to the end of a cart, driven through town, and whipped.[7]

A statute of 1536 said that parish churches were to make regular collections for the support of the poor. The money was to be used to aid the "poor, impotent, sick and diseased people being not able to work" and to provide work for "such as they be lusty or having their limbs strong enough to labour."[8] However, the surplus of labor meant that there were no jobs to be provided.

In that same year, Henry VIII began to seize the lands of the Roman Catholic Church. He confiscated the property of the religious foundations and dissolved the monasteries, including some 460 that had been giving aid to the poor.

With that action, the principle established a few years before, that the parish (which was the smallest unit of local government) was responsible for the care of the poor, became the basis for all future measures dealing with the poor. Parish-church wardens and "substantial householders," who served without pay, became the "overseers of the poor," responsible for the administration of local charity.[9]

In the beginning, they had no power to tax. They simply determined how to distribute the alms that were deposited voluntarily in the church poor box. However, this system did not work, and slowly they were given the power to tax those who did not give according to their means. By 1563, under Queen Elizabeth, there was a compulsory tax called the poor rate; those who did not pay it could be imprisoned.[10]

Now that local parishes were responsible for their poor, they were concerned about the possibility of being forced to take care of "someone else's poor" as well. In 1572, a statute required the justices of the peace to make registers of the names of the poor of each parish and to provide for them out of the funds collected through the poor rates. Each month, the mayor and high constable were to make a search for indigent strangers and send them back to their own homes.[11]

A law in 1575 said that "stores of wool, hemp and iron" should be kept ready to provide work for the able-bodied poor in the houses of correction or workhouses to which they could be committed.[12] The law also set a fine of twenty shillings for aiding or harboring a beggar.

The Elizabethan Poor Law

Over the years, a succession of statutes had been shaping a public philosophy of dealing with the poor. The culmination came at the turn of the century, at the time of a severe economic depression, when the threat of famine led to bread riots. The law established then, to be known as the Elizabethan Poor Law, became the basis of poor relief in England for centuries and was the foundation of the poor-relief system that was developed in the American colonies and the United States and which exists to this day, altered in form but not philosophy.[13]

The Act of 1601 divided the poor into three classes:
• the lame, impotent, old, and blind and others unable to work;
• the able-bodied poor — "sturdy vagabonds" and "valiant beggars";
• poor children.

Overseers of the poor were to be appointed in each parish by the justices of the peace. They had the power to raise funds by taxes to aid the impotent poor, to set up workhouses for the able-bodied, and to bind out the children of the poor as apprentices. The punishment for anyone who refused to do work ordered by the overseers was imprisonment.

Parents were responsible for the support of their children and grandchildren, and children were liable for the care of their unemployable parents and grandparents. Vagrants were to be returned to whatever town they had lived in last for at least a year, and aid was provided either in cash or in kind (food or coal).

The statute established three lasting principles: local responsibility for the poor, the requirement that people provide support to their poor relations, and the idea that towns were liable only for and to their own residents.

However, towns could choose to look after their poor through voluntary charity rather than taxation if that were possible, and voluntary charity continued to be the major source of assistance to the poor. Such funds were given to aid the poor in their homes and to set up almshouses.

The 1600's saw the beginning of new attitudes about the poor tied to the development of Protestantism and capitalism. Calvin quoted St. Paul: "If a man do not work, neither shall he eat." Poverty became a sign that a person had displeased God, and dependency was an indication of moral failure. Under capitalism, riches became a reward for thrift and virtue, a sign of God's favor. Destitution was the lot of the idle and immoral. The poor were sinners in need of reform or punishment.

Residence Requirements

The next step in the development of the English poor law came as the result of these ungenerous attitudes, and it too was a principle that remained in English and American law for centuries. It was the 1662 Law of Settlement and Removal.[14] A person without property who was not living in his own parish and who could not guarantee that he would not become a public charge in the future could be sent back to his original place of "settlement"—to his legal residence. The parish where he had "settlement" was legally required to give him aid when he needed it.

The preamble to the act said that large numbers of the poor were moving to those rural areas where public assistance policies were more liberal. In fact, most of the migration was to London where there appeared to be more job opportunities but where many people ended up destitute nonetheless.

The settlement law was not rigidly enforced. It was often cheaper to give a family aid than to send it back to its legal residence. However, about fifteen thousand persons a year were sent back to their homes. Sometimes parishes made agreements to take back their own legal residents if they became "chargeable" while living elsewhere.

The establishment of workhouses was another economy measure that attempted to discourage people from applying for relief and sought to get some work out of those who did.[15] Parishes could set up workhouses and refuse help to anyone who would not enter them. Workhouses represented "indoor" as opposed to the "outdoor" relief given people in their own homes. However, the workhouses did not break even since the majority of their inhabitants, the old, the sick, mothers and children, could not do the work provided.

In the years that followed, public opinion and social philosophy continued to object to the idea of public aid to the poor, asserting sometimes that it was a violation of natural law and that, in fact, poverty was a necessary factor in human life. Adam Smith, who published *The Wealth of Nations* in 1776, believed that the poor law was an artificial and evil arrangement. He wrote that there is a fixed amount of money in the economy for the support of the masses. When public aid to the poor is subtracted from this sum, it merely results in less money for distribution as wages to everyone else.[16]

The Reverend Joseph Townsend wrote, "It seems to be a law of nature that the poor should be to a certain degree improvident, that there may always be some to fulfill the most servile, the most sordid, and the most ignoble offices in the community." He said, "When hunger is either felt or feared, the desire of obtaining bread will quietly dispose the mind to undergo the greatest hardships, and will sweeten the severest labors."[17]

Separating Out Employables

The next development in the British poor law was Gilbert's Act of 1788. It set up poorhouses for the old and sick and for unwed mothers and their children. The able-bodied poor were to be given work near their homes, and their wages were to be supplemented by poor relief.[18] The chief purpose of the act was to separate employables from unemployables.

Local officials could find work for the poor by offering tax reductions to employers or by setting up public works projects. Under this act, there was better treatment of the "deserving" poor, and the work was intended to be useful, not just make-work to force people to pay for the charity they received.

Toward the end of the eighteenth century, the children of families who went on relief were bound out to the growing textile industry. Youngsters of four and five went to work in factories, and manufacturers ordered dozens at a time from the poorhouses. They were shipped wherever they were needed, given only room and board as pay, and forced to remain until their indentures were up at twenty-one. They were a very stable source of labor. One reformer, Sir Robert Owen, limited the work period of children in his factories to thirteen hours a day, a liberal act in that time.[19]

Many full-time workers earned such low wages that they could not support themselves and their families. When the wars with France led to increases in food prices, there was unrest and violence. Sometimes workers burned the haystacks of farmers who failed to pay living wages. Riots were suppressed by the army.

Aiding the Working Poor

In 1795, a group of magistrates met in the town of Speenhamland to discuss the problem of low wages, and they came up with the idea of supplementing workers' incomes when they fell below a level of subsistence figured on the price of bread and the size of the worker's family. A large majority turned down a proposal to establish a minimum wage based on the price of grain.

The next year, Parliament made the Speenhamland proposal law.[20] In some cases, an unemployed person would be sent from house to house looking for work. Whoever employed him would provide food and sixpence a day. The parish would add another four. In other cases, the overseers of the poor auctioned off the unemployed to the highest bidders and paid the needed supplements. Or the town could allot a certain number of the jobless to each farmer and require him to either employ the workers or pay higher taxes.

However, after the crisis passed, the system was not used widely. One of the influences against it may have been the kind of thinking expounded by people like Thomas Malthus whose theories are considered responsible for the next major change in the British poor law.

Thomas Malthus

Malthus, who published his "Essay on the Principle of Population" in 1798, declared that starvation, disease, celibacy, and war were the only means of keeping the population reduced to the point where the existing food supply could feed it. Since there was not enough food for all, if the poor had enough money for food at present prices, that would simply increase competition for the scarce supply and force up prices.

Even worse, the poor laws had permitted the impoverished to marry and have children, increasing the number of poor to be aided.

The poor laws thus depressed the condition of the poor by increasing the population without increasing the food supply. As food was distributed among the poorest, the labor of the worker bought less, and he too was forced to ask for assistance.

He added that the poor laws had cut down the will to save among working people. They spent their money at the ale house instead of saving it for hard times and old age.

Malthus called for the gradual abolition of the poor law, beginning with the declaration that the poor have no *right* to support. He proposed that "no child born from any marriage taking place after the expiration of a year from the date of the law and no illegitimate child born two years from the same date should ever be entitled to parish assistance." Under Malthus' plan, marriages and births would diminish and death would increase so that the balance between food and population would be restored.

In the meantime, "dependent poverty," he said, "ought to be held disgraceful." The poor person should be taught "that he had no claim of *right* on society for the smallest portion of food, beyond that which his labour would fairly purchase; and that if he and his family were saved from feeling the natural consequences of his imprudence, he would owe it to the pity of some kind benefactor, to whom, therefore, he ought to be bound by the strongest ties of gratitude."

The worthy poor would be cared for by private charity. However, even there, Malthus said one must "restrain the hand of benevolence from assisting those in distress in so indiscriminate a manner as to encourage indolence and want of foresight in others."[21]

The Workhouse Test and Less Eligibility

The last major contribution to the English poor law came with the Reform of 1834. It was provoked by rising poor rates that had tripled in two generations. A royal commission set up to investigate the situation decided that the increase of "pauperism" (the support of the destitute by public funds) would have to be curbed. The poor law, it said, was "a bounty on indolence and vice." The enacted reforms established two principles: the "workhouse test" and "less eligibility."

The law abolished outdoor relief and required all who wanted aid to enter the workhouse. This was the "test" of real need. The commission said: "Into such a house none will enter voluntarily; work, confinement, and discipline will deter the indolent and vicious; and nothing but extreme necessity will induce any to accept the comfort which must be obtained by the surrender of their free agency, and the sacrifice of their accustomed habits and gratifications.[22] "Thus the parish officer, being furnished an unerring test of the necessity of applicants, is relieved from his painful and difficult responsibility; while all have the gratification of knowing that while the necessitious are abundantly relieved, the funds of charity are not wasted by idleness and fraud."[23]

English statesman Benjamin Disraeli said after the law was passed: "It announces to the world that in England poverty is a crime."[24]

The principle of "less eligibility" meant that the condition of the person on poor relief "shall not be made really or apparently so eligible as the situation of the independent laborer of the lowest class."[25] That meant that the poor, regardless of their needs or the size of their families, should not be given as much money or as decent living conditions as those of the lowest-paid worker. Since there were many workers who earned below subsistence, poor relief, on principle, was to provide below-subsistence living. The principle of less eligibility was proposed to prevent the able-bodied poor from accepting poor relief instead of working, but it was applied as well to those who could not work or who could not find jobs.

The proponents of the law figured that it would save money. Even though the cost of supporting someone in the workhouse was higher than aiding him at home, people would not apply for aid unless they were in dire necessity. However, the act did not reduce costs or end outdoor relief. To begin with, although critics of public aid spoke as if most of those on relief were employable, most were actually the aged, disabled, or children, and half the so-called able-bodied poor were in need because of illness.[26]

In many localities, the boards that administered the law refused to break up families, and they gave outdoor relief and wage supplements. Most of those receiving this kind of aid were widows and the aged. During the depressions of the 1840's, social unrest and militance among the poor led to increased outdoor relief. Only some 200,000 of the nearly $1\frac{1}{2}$ million receiving aid were in workhouses.[27]

In some cases where there was a lack of space in the workhouse, the "able-bodied worker" of the family would enter while the rest got outdoor relief at home. In the workhouses, husbands and wives were separated and sent to live with members of their own sex.

Suffering in Workhouses

Many of those condemned to the workhouses suffered greatly. One critic, Samuel Roberts, published a tract in 1839 called *Mary Wilden, A Victim of the New Poor Law.* It was the pitiful tale of an old woman who had died in the workhouse, with evidence that she was an epileptic who had been cruelly beaten and left helpless, ridden with lice, dressed in rags, with the folds of her clothes stuck in her open wounds.

The author charged that the law condemned the poor to "close imprisonment" and "to famishing and disease—to brutal violence—to horrible filth—and to premature death."

He said, "We have laws to protect brute beasts from such horrible cruelty, but it seems none to protect the most piteable of all human creatures."[28]

William Gaspey in 1842 published a volume called *Poor Law Melodies and Other Poems.* One verse declared that:

> Tears! tears! tears! are the portion of the Poor,
> For the heartless fain would see how much they can
> endure;
> And to prove *their* pity never fails,
> They have built the wretched, Union* gaols,
> Where King Starvation reigns supreme
> And plenty is—a pauper's dream!
> And 'mid this mockery of life,
> Lingers the pale, yet lovely wife,
> Torn from her first and dearest tie,
> In this abode of gloom to die.

and

> Oh! glorious was that mortal's skill
> Who first devised the Poor Law Bill,
> To teach in these enlightened times,
> That Poverty's the worst of crimes.[29]

Charles Dickens was the most noted literary critic of poor-law evils. He aimed his satirical barbs at the overseers of the workhouse in *Oliver Twist,* which was published in 1850:

The members of this board were very sage, deep, philosophical men; and when they came to turn their attention to the workhouse, they found out at once what ordinary folks would never have discovered—the poor people liked it! It was a regular place of public entertainment for the poorer classes; a tavern where there was nothing to pay; a public breakfast, dinner, tea, and supper all the year round; a brick and mortar elysium, where it was all play and no work. 'Oho!' said the board, looking very knowing, 'we are the fellows to set this to rights; we'll stop it all, in no time.' So they established the rule that all poor people should have the alternative (for they would compel nobody, not they) of being starved by a gradual

*workhouse

process in the house, or by a quick one out of it. With this view, they contracted with the waterworks to lay on an unlimited supply of water, and with a cornfactor to supply periodically small quantities of oatmeal, and issued three meals of thin gruel a day, with an onion twice a week and half a roll on Sundays.

It was rather expensive at first, in consequence of the increase in the undertaker's bill, and the necessity of taking in the clothes of all the paupers, which fluttered loosely on their wasted, shrunken forms, after a week or two's gruel. But the number of workhouse inmates got thin as well as the paupers, and the board were in ecstasies.[30]

In actual fact, thousands of poor people died as a result of poor food and inhumane treatment in workhouses.

Extent of "Pauperism"

The poor law touched large numbers of people, though few at any one time. Although only 2 or 3 percent of the population applied for relief in any year, and at the beginning of the nineteenth century there were some one hundred thousand people in workhouses out of a population of 9 million, up to a third of the population lived with such low pay and meager job security that most of them were forced to become paupers at one time or another.[31] Still, in 1909, another royal commission issued a report based on the premise that people became dependent on public aid because of defects in their character.[32]

The principles of the Elizabethan Poor Law of 1601 and of the Law of Settlement and Removal issued some sixty years later became the bases for the public relief established by the colonists who came to America in the seventeenth and eighteenth centuries. Later, even after an independent nation had been established, citizens and lawmakers looked to England ✓/ as a model, setting up workhouses, binding out children, giving outdoor relief to worthy widows, adhering to the principle of less eligibility, and looking on relief as a stigma and on paupers as lazy or immoral or evil people who hardly deserved the largesse of the working public. And Malthus had his adherents in America as well as in England.

THE HERITAGE OF EUROPE

From the moment they landed in the New World, the American colonists established a system of relief based on the British model. To begin with, they acknowledged their obligation to support the poor; in 1642, the lawmakers of Plymouth ruled that each town had to support its own indigent. At the same time, they established strict residence requirements. Later, they provided ways to make sure the poor worked for whatever they got.[1]

The First American Poor Law

The Plymouth poor law established money allowances, gave people help in building homes, and provided for town cows and grazing land. It was a common practice to place a poor or sick person with a family, and sometimes the person moved from one family to another at a dizzying pace. The town meeting of Hadley, Massachusetts, in 1687, voted that the Widow Baldwin would go "round the town," spending two weeks with each family that could take her.[2]

The statute also provided "that those that have relief from the towns and have children and do not employ them, that it shall be lawful for the township to order that those children shall be put to work in fitting employment according to their strength and abilities or placed out by the town."[3]

People were prohibited from bringing into town, without official consent, anyone who was liable to become a public charge in the future.[4] There were strict rules about enter-

2
EARLY AMERICA

taining strangers. One needed the permission of local authorities to offer hospitality to nonresidents. Otherwise, if they needed aid, the host had to reimburse the town. Often, before people left on trips, they would obtain letters from the officials of their home towns promising that the town would pay for their support if they became needy while traveling elsewhere.[5]

The captains of ships that landed at Plymouth were made chargeable for any of their passengers who became needy, and they were required to return such persons to their place of origin.[6]

"Warning Out"

In 1655, Massachusetts passed a law giving towns the right to decide who could settle there, and the British custom of "warning out" was used to avoid supporting immigrants, many of whom arrived at the colony ill from their long voyages. It generally took from five to ten years to attain permanent residence and during that period, people could be ordered out if officials decided that they were likely to need public aid in the future. In Connecticut, towns had three months to "warn out" anyone who became needy because of sickness or disability.[7]

Sometimes people could remain in town if they offered security against their becoming paupers. Other times, those who stayed were subject to fines. And no one who had been told to leave could later claim public assistance.

The poor law passed in Pennsylvania in 1682 was similar to those of New England. The poor were cared for by funds raised by county taxes and distributed by the courts. There were strict residence requirements. Sometimes settlers had to post bond with the town as security against their becoming dependent. Those children whose parents could not support them were sent out to work or apprenticed to artisans or tradesmen by the overseers of the poor.[8]

Auctioning Off the Poor

During the 1700's, a popular method of aiding the poor was to contract with private individuals to care for them. People might be "auctioned off" at town meetings to the lowest bidder, the person who agreed to take them at the least expense to the town.[9] The bid generally depended on how much work the pauper was capable of and how little he or she might have to be fed. Often the people who bid for the care of the poor were barely above the poverty line themselves. The system became especially widespread after the Revolution.

Sometimes the poor were given relief in kind while they lived at home. In 1740, Boston sold grain to the poor at 10 percent of the cost. Towns bought cows and provided pasture land for the indigent.[10] Many towns reduced the taxes poor people were required to pay. The town might also pay for the addition of a room on someone's house so the family could care for aged parents. Contracts were made with doctors, to care for the poor of the town, and there were the familiar complaints about doctors overcharging the towns for their services.[11]

In 1660, Boston built the first almshouse in America,[12] but almshouses were not used widely until the 1800's, because the country was too sparsely settled to make them practical. In cases where the need was temporary, a person still might be granted a weekly or monthly allowance and allowed to live at home. However, officials were not adverse to breaking up families; if a man could not work, the town would indenture his children and also put his wife out to service.

The Workhouse

An increased demand for assistance resulted from the large immigration of Germans and Irish in the mid 1700's, and in 1749 an act authorized the overseers of the poor in Philadelphia to give work to the able-bodied poor so that they would contribute toward their support.[13] The law was meant to include both those in almshouses and those receiving outdoor relief. Some years later, in 1771, a new law ordered overseers to employ the poor in houses stocked with hemp, flax, thread, and other materials. It was the beginning of the workhouse in America.[14]

Then a bill in 1798 authorized the counties of Pennsylvania to buy farms, set up buildings on them, and send the poor to work the land.[15] They were the poor farms. The first poor farm, in fact, had been established in Philadelphia in 1773. The notion that those dependent on public aid ought to work for it was institutionalized in the workhouse and the poor farm.

American poor relief also developed under the philosophy that pauperism was a sign of laziness, immorality, and unworthiness, and that paupers deserved to be stigmatized and degraded. A Pennsylvania law of 1718 provided that every person who received relief, including children, had to wear the letter *P,* for pauper, on the shoulder of his right sleeve. Anyone who refused would be denied aid or committed to the house of correction to be whipped and put to hard labor for up to twenty-one days.[16]

Benjamin Franklin expounded the common belief about poor relief when he visited London in 1766. He said, "There is no country in the world in which the poor are more idle, dissolute, drunken and insolent. The day you passed that act [the Elizabethan Poor Law of 1601] you took away from before their eyes the greatest of all inducements to industry, frugality and sobriety by giving them a dependence on somewhat else than a careful accumulation during youth and health for support in age and sickness."

He advised: "Repeal that law and you will soon see a change in their manners."[17]

Laws Against Beggars and Vagrants

With the philosophy that the poor and jobless are a species of criminal, the poor farms and workhouses became places of punishment for the "idle," the "vagrant," and the drunkard as well as for the thief. Colonies passed laws prescribing punishment and forced work for such persons. Beggars and vagrants often were whipped before they were jailed. In a few large towns, the unemployables were put in almshouses, the able-bodied were sent to workhouses, and the criminals were kept in jails or houses of correction. Elsewhere, they were thrown in with widows, children, the aged, the sick, and the insane.

In 1699, Massachusetts provided for the suppression and punishment of "rogues, vagabonds, common beggars and other lewd idle and disorderly persons" in houses of correction that were in fact workhouses. They could also commit "stubborn servants or children."[18]

An act of 1766 authorized construction in Philadelphia of

a workhouse to receive "loose, disorderly, idle and dissolute persons" as well as "rogues and vagabonds" and to put them to hard labor under rigid discipline.[19]

Illegitimacy was also treated as a crime, with the punishment visited upon the children. Churchwardens in Virginia in 1769 were instructed to bind out the children of unwed free white women. The children of unwed indentured servants were required to serve their mothers' masters. All black children, of course, were slaves like their parents. Children of parents who led an "idle, dissolute and disorderly course of life" also could be bound out to work.[20]

Complaints of High Taxes

In spite of the strict laws of settlement, towns complained that they were being forced to pay for outsiders. In 1735, Boston asked for aid from the colony of Massachusetts asserting that a third of the people in the city's almshouses had not been *born* in Boston.[21] In 1791, the freeholders of Moyamensing township complained that they were paying heavy taxes for the poor coming into Philadelphia. They asked the assembly to establish a separate poor district for them, and this was done. Philadelphia, on its part, complained that it was forced to bear the burden for all the colony since it was the main port of entry.[22]

In some cases, the colony reimbursed the towns for caring for "unsettled" poor. There were numerous disputes and court cases between towns arguing over who had the responsibility for a particular poor person or family. Often the costs of such cases were far above the cost of aid to the individuals involved.

Meanwhile, the states strengthened their restrictions on settlement. Pennsylvania instituted fines for people who did not report the names of their guests to the overseers of the poor within ten days of the guests' arrival. Philadelphia required notice within three days.[23] A Massachusetts town in 1790 warned out about a third of its population.[24] Warning out was especially prevalent in rural towns that forced new immigrants back to the port cities where they had landed.

The fact that people were required to return to their original residences meant that they could not travel freely to look for work when there was none at home. One of the lures of the West must have been the lack of settlement laws and warning-out practices, at least until a town was set up and established its own poor law based on the eastern model.

The change in the status of the towns and provinces from colonies of England to independent states of a new nation had no effect on the system of public assistance that had been developed. By the beginning of the nineteenth century, the states had laws that provided for outdoor relief to the poor in their own homes, binding out the poor as apprentices or indentured servants, care in almshouses, farming out individual paupers to the lowest bidder, and a new development—farming out all the poor of one locality to a single contractor who would set up a workhouse or poor farm for his own profit.

In the Territories

The system spread to the new territories and states as they were settled. A law of 1795 in the Northwest Territory said that overseers of the poor would contract out the care of the poor, apprentice poor children, and provide places where the poor could work to pay for their support. Anyone who brought into the town a person who might become chargeable could be punished, and poor people without legal residence could be ordered out if they sought the aid of the town. Later, such persons were warned out but allowed to remain if they furnished bond as security.[25]

The Territory of Michigan in 1809 set penalties of up to three hundred dollars for anyone bringing in paupers or those likely to become so. There were provisions for the removal of paupers who had no legal residence and for the recovery of the costs of their temporary relief. Later, in 1825, the territory passed a law barring aid to nonresidents and to people who had not lived there since the time of the British surrender.[26]

The care of the poor was contracted out, children were bound to service, and others were sent to the poorhouse. Some direct aid was allowed in cases of temporary need. There was also a provision requiring support by relatives.

The legislature of the Missouri Territory provided that if

there were no poorhouse in a county, its overseers were to advertise each April for sealed bids for the maintenance of the poor. They could make temporary arrangements for people who were added to the poor lists during the year.[27]

Binding Out Children

The Missouri Territory's provision for binding out children was used widely, and not just for paupers. The court could bind out poor orphans, children who begged, children whose parents were poor and whose fathers were habitual drunkards, or any fatherless child whose mother was considered of bad character and who had no visible means of support.

Boys could be apprenticed until the age of twenty-one and girls to sixteen; later the age limit for boys was reduced to eighteen. They were not allowed to leave the territory during the apprenticeship, and after their years of work, they were given a new Bible, two suits of clothes, and $10. The law was not repealed until 1935.

In a famous case in 1881, a Kansas family was forced to sue to get back a child of eight who had been bound out under this law. The parents had become ill, had lost their crops, and were forced to seek aid from the county poor farm. When the father, J. H. E. Ackley, got well, he got work and left the poor farm to try to make arrangements for his family. Without his knowledge or his wife's consent, the superintendent of the poor farm and the local judge had bound out the boy as an apprentice, with indentures lasting, as was usual, to eighteen.

The rest of the family went back to the farm, and Ackley filed a claim to recover his son. The court decided that the lack of the parents' consent or their ignorance of the plan did not invalidate the apprenticeship. Since the child was then a county charge, it said the judge had the right to bind him out. The court suggested that the father try informally to get back his son.[28]

People in the western territories held the same view of relief as those in the East. In Montana, aid was stopped if a doctor found that the recipient had "sound mind and body."[29] One taxpayer brought a suit against the county commissioners, because there were more than a hundred people receiving aid in their homes while there was room for thirty additional people at the county poor farm. In that case, however, the court ruled against him, declaring that some people believe "being committed to the poor farm carries with it a stigma of disgrace, and many indigent persons prefer to retain what they term self-respect and independence by remaining in their own homes, however inadequate these homes may be to their comfort."[30]

Evils of Almshouses

Still, the general opinion forced more and more people into the almshouses which, in the 1800's, became a popular method of aiding the poor. Reports by lawmakers in Massachusetts and New York in the 1820's emphasized the evils of outdoor relief and recommended almshouses as the best means of frightening the able-bodied into going to work and of discouraging people from applying for aid.

The chairman of the Massachusetts state committee wrote that "of all the modes of providing for the poor, the most wasteful, the most injurious to their morals and destructive to their industrious habits is that of supply in their own families." He declared that "the most economical mode is that of Alms Houses; having the character of Work Houses, or Houses of Industry, in which work is provided for every degree of ability in the pauper; and thus the able poor made to provide, partially, at least for their own support; and also to the support, or at least the comfort of the impotent poor."[31]

A report by the legislature of Pennsylvania in that same period declared that public aid for the poor could only increase the evil it intended to relieve, demoralize the working classes, promote idleness and licentiousness among the poor, destroy thrift and industrious habits, and throw the burden of maintaining the idle and spendthrift upon those who worked hard and saved.[32]

Yet, according to the legislators of Massachusetts, even the almshouses did not deter the poor from throwing themselves upon the bounty of the state. In 1833, a report declared, "Almshouses are their inns, at which they stop for refreshment. Here they find rest, when too much worn with fatigue to travel, and medical aid when they are sick. And as they choose not to labor, they leave these stopping places, when they have regained strength to enable them to travel; and pass from town to town *demanding* their portion of the State's allowances for them as *their right*."

The legislators declared, "These unhappy fellow-beings often travel with females, sometimes but not always their wives," and "nearly all of them are able, and if kept from ardent spirits, and compelled to work, would show themselves to be able to earn their own subsistence."[33]

Actions Against Nonresidents

Attempts to keep paupers out of the states increased. In 1822, New York State spent $13,500 for court appeals, enough to care for 450 people in almshouses for a year. The money spent in court and for the removal of nonresidents amounted to one-ninth of the relief budget.[34]

In 1837, Massachusetts ordered that a bond of $1,000 be required from all aliens arriving at a state port who appeared likely to become public charges. A head tax of $2 was collected from shipmasters for the support of the foreign poor. Other seaboard states adopted the same head tax until the Supreme Court ruled it unconstitutional some forty years later.[35]

In 1847, a group of Massachusetts citizens petitioned for the complete repeal of all public-relief laws saying that immigrants were coming directly to the almshouses.[36]

In spite of all the talk about setting the paupers in the poorhouse to work, based on the common opinion that most of them were quite capable of employment, the goal was unrealizable. Most were not able-bodied, but sick, disabled, too old, or too young. In fact, during the summer, most poor farms had to hire farm labor from the community. One study of a Philadelphia almshouse in 1848 showed that only 12 percent were capable of working.[37] The almshouses were so miserable that it is not surprising that all but the most desperate and helpless found some way to avoid them.

Succeeding reports by New York State legislative committees in 1838 and 1856 described large numbers of people crowded in unhealthy conditions, with the insane, the feeble-minded and the sick, including those with contagious diseases, living with healthy women, children, and aged persons.

Nearly twenty years after the first report, the second

committee condemned the fact that in any county house could be found "the lunatic suffering for years in a dark and suffocating cell, in summer, and almost freezing in winter — where a score of children are poorly fed, poorly clothed, and quite untaught — where the poor idiot is half starved and beaten with rods because he is too dull to do his master's bidding — where the aged mother is lying in perhaps her last sickness, unattended by a physician, and with no one to minister to her wants. . . ."[38]

A newspaper publisher protested against the intolerable conditions in a Kansas almshouse in 1894. He criticized "the method of farming out the paupers to the lowest bidder, than which no plan could be more shameful — more productive of evil results. The price paid is $1.50 per week, and the contract until recently contained a proviso that, in the case of the birth of illegitimate children, the price is to be reduced to $1.25! It is upon such terms as these that lessees are to provide the inmates — the cripples, the idiots, and the insane — with food, raiment, and with proper care, making such percentage of gain out of this miserable business for themselves as they may."[39]

At another poor farm, there was no conversation permitted between inmates except that which concerned their work. The unruly were deprived of their meals or sent to punishment cells. Everyone slept crowded together on cots.[40]

Outdoor v. Indoor Relief

The debate about outdoor versus indoor relief continued, although practical considerations — lack of space and the higher costs of almshouses — meant that large numbers of the poor were able to get aid in their own homes. Between 1830 and 1860 in New York State, as much as half the money spent in any year for relief went for temporary assistance outside the almshouse. Southern states particularly, which did not subscribe to the New England Calvinist notion of the virtue of work over idleness (they had slaves to do *their* work), took a more humane view of (white) peoples' needs, and South Carolina law provided that even in areas with indoor relief, the local officials might decide it better to give aid to the poor who were living with friends or relatives than to force them into the poorhouse.

However, the states of the Northeast were more likely to agree with that attitude of the Guardians of the Poor of Philadelphia which in 1827 opposed outdoor relief as "calculated in an especial manner to blunt and ultimately destroy that noble pride of Independence, the birthright of every American citizen on which the very pillars of our republic, have their basis — as its consequences are to create a dependence on the bounty of others, rather than excite the laudable ambition of creating resources of our own, it cuts the sinews of Industry and of consequence promotes idleness and not infrequently crime, its having become common has made it fashionable. . . ."[41]

In 1827, the country was in a period of economic recovery after the recession of 1815–1821. Thirty years later, it was suffering from financial panic brought on by the failure of the New York branch of the Ohio Life Insurance and Trust Company. The panic lasted for a year and a half. The mid-1800's was also a time of increased immigration, especially from non-English speaking countries.

Thus, in 1857, the mayor of Philadelphia spoke out in favor of outdoor relief, asserting that sending people to the almshouse would make those in temporary need less self-reliant.

A new president of the board of the Guardians of the Poor declared that outdoor relief was more humane and less costly than almshouse care.[42]

The same year, a New York State Senate committee issued a report in favor of outdoor relief, declaring, "Worthy indigent persons should, if possible, be kept from the degradation of the poor house, by reasonable supplies of provisions, bedding, and other absolute necessaries, at their own homes. Half the sum requisite for the maintenance in the poor house would often save them from destitution and enable them to work in their households and their vicinity sufficiently to earn the remainder of the support during the inclement season when indigence suffers most, and when it is most likely to be forced into the common receptacles of pauperism, whence it rarely emerges without a loss of self respect and a sense of degradation."[43]

It was common to give temporary grants, pensions, grocery orders and food baskets, supplies of wood or coal, and secondhand clothing and bedding, especially in winter. Often supplies rather than money were given on the theory that the poor would not know how to spend cash wisely.

Generally, the people who got outdoor relief tended to be widows with young children, the old and ill whose relatives could house them but not pay for their other needs, and disabled or sick workers and their families.

Effects of Depressions

Investigations of "pauperism" were more likely to focus on the growth of the relief rolls than on the treatment accorded the poor. Several business depressions during the 1800's led to increased numbers of people on relief, and to a rise of criticism of the system for promoting laziness and poverty. There were efforts to cut back spending for the poor ⌣ and to make them work for the aid they received.

In 1873, Iowa allowed people to choose between a $2-a-week outdoor-relief grant and the poorhouse. (The average weekly wage was under $9.) In 1880, overseers could require labor from any applicant or member of the family who could work.[44] Transients and others who sought relief were often put to work on the roads or other public works. There were soup kitchens and private charity drives for food and clothing. States added laws increasing the number of relatives responsible for the poor, from parents and children to brothers, sisters, grandparents, and grandchildren.

At one point, toward the end of the century, outdoor relief was completely abolished in New York, Washington, San Francisco, Philadelphia, Baltimore, St. Louis, and Kansas City.

The penchant for giving the poor good advice and moral uplift instead of money went well with the prevailing philosophy that giving cash actually harmed them and that making public assistance agreeable would encourage dependency.

In 1818, the New York Society for the Prevention of Pauperism said about public charities, "Is not the partial and temporary good which they accomplish, how acute soever the miseries they relieve, and whatever the number they may rescue from sufferings or death, more than counterbalanced, by the evils that flow from the expectations they necessarily excite; by the relaxation of industry which such a display of benevolence tends to produce; by that reliance upon charitable aid, in case of unfavourable times, which must unavoidably tend to diminish, in the minds of the labouring classes, that wholesome anxiety to provide for the wants of a distant day, which alone can save them from a state of absolute dependence, and from becoming a burden to the community."[45]

There was a particular danger, according to the critics of public aid, in regarding relief as a right rather than an act of benevolence for which the poor should feel grateful.

The Attitude of Charities

Societies concerned with the poor believed that instead of focusing on money, one should provide spiritual assistance. The New York Association for Improving the Condition of the Poor prepared instructions to its own "friendly visitors" in 1845: "The evils of improvidence can never be diminished, except by removing the cause; and this can only be done by elevating the moral character of the poor, and by teaching them to depend upon themselves."

It told the visitors "to encourage deposits in savings banks for rent, fuel and winter supplies" and added the message of the principle of less eligibility that had been adopted in England less than a dozen years before: "The rule is, that the willingly dependent upon alms should not live so comfortably with them as the humblest independent labourer without them."[46]

The AICP kept a woodpile where able-bodied men who sought aid could demonstrate that their need was not due to a disinclination to work.[47]

The problem was that even when many people worked full-time, they did not earn enough to support themselves and their families. One economist figured out that the wages of a construction worker in 1833 were too low to support a family of four even if the worker had employment all through the year. The wages of shirtmakers, who were women, were even lower.

In addition to living in misery, paupers should, many people believed, be denied ordinary civil rights like the vote. A Massachusetts law of 1874 provided that people on relief could not vote, and there were efforts to extend this to include men who had received public assistance at any time during the year before the election.[48] (Women could not vote in any event.)

As late as 1934, the constitutions of thirteen states said that recipients of public relief could not vote or hold office. Inmates of poorhouses were denied the vote in Louisiana, Missouri, Oklahoma, and Pennsylvania, and other welfare recipients were ineligible in Delaware, Maine, Massachusetts, New Hampshire, New Jersey, Rhode Island, South Carolina, Texas, and Virginia. However, such restrictions against voting were generally not enforced.[49]

Social Darwinism

That period of the last quarter of the nineteenth century was influenced by Social Darwinism, which was popularized in England by Herbert Spencer and in the United States by sociologist William Graham Sumner. Spencer argued for the abolition of the poor laws, saying that the "unfit" then would be eliminated according to the plan of nature and the principle of natural selection. "The poverty of the incapable, the distresses that come from the imprudent, the starvation of the idle, and those shoulderings aside of the weak by the strong," he called "the decrees of a large farseeing benevolence."[50]

Sumner declared that " 'the strong' and 'the weak' are terms which admit of no definition unless they are made equivalent to the industrious and the idle, the frugal and the extravagant." He asserted that "if we do not like the survival of the fittest, we have only one possible alternative, and that is the survival of the unfittest. The former is the law of civilization, the latter is the law of anti-civilization."

He suggested, "Let every man be sober, industrious, prudent, and wise, and bring up his children to be so likewise, and poverty will be abolished in a few generations."[51]

The contrast in the treatment of the "undeserving" poor, who were presumably the unfit, and the "deserving" poor, who were merely the (often middle-class) victims of circumstances beyond their control, was marked. Numerous states gave relief at the times of natural disasters like droughts and insect plagues. Sometimes there were loans to enable farmers to buy seed grain and coal.

Yet even then, the states were penurious. The Kansas

legislature in 1874, the time of a grasshopper plague, authorized counties to issue bonds for money to buy food to sell to the poor. The victims of the disaster would sign notes, payable in one year at 10 percent interest, and the county would take liens on their property in the interim.[52]

In Montana, when there were crop failures due to drought or other natural causes, at least one hundred needy freeholders could petition the county to issue bonds to provide seed loans.[53] At various times in the 1800's, Congress appropriated money for emergency relief for the victims of floods, fires, cyclones, earthquakes, Indian raids, grasshopper plagues, epidemics, and drought. However, attempts by some congressmen to get legislation to aid the victims of the depression of 1893 and later of the depressions of 1914 and 1921 were unsuccessful.

Special Rules for Soldiers

The only victims of man-made disaster who received assistance without stigma or degradation were veterans and their families and the widows and orphans of soldiers. Civil War veterans were exempt from the laws that applied to other paupers. County boards of supervisors made special appropriations for them, and the law in numerous states provided that no veterans or widows or dependents of soldiers could be sent to the poorhouse. In Iowa, the alternative to the poorhouse was aid of $2 a week; generosity had its limits. Many states later provided aid for veterans of the Mexican, Indian, and Spanish-American wars and for veterans of America's intervention in China during the Boxer Rebellion.

After the Civil War, homes were established for soldiers' orphans; other children went to the poorhouse. When the numbers of soldiers' orphans declined, other children were allowed in. However, in 1898, the governor of Iowa noted that counties were sending children under ten to reform schools as criminals rather than to the soldiers' orphans' home, because support of the reform school was a state expense while the counties paid the cost of the orphans' homes.[54]

The relief system also provoked criticism in an area which for once was not considered the fault of its recipients. Where so much money was involved, so were efforts to use the programs for political advantage. Often almshouse managers or the individuals who won local contracts for the care of the poor were cronies of political bosses. Sometimes people got relief in return for their votes instead of on the basis of their need.

Seth Low, the reform mayor of New York, described conditions where "the friends of politicians received help whether needy or not," and "families with voters were the first served. The 'outdoor relief' appropriations became a vast political corruption fund," and "the poor did not get the chief benefit of increased appropriations."[55]

In sum, by the turn of the century, the American system of public assistance was firmly based on the notion, borrowed from the British, that the poor were idle, immoral, improvident creatures who had failed to work or save for their needs, who needed moral preachings to improve their character, and who should be kept alive at the least cost to the community and with concern that the amount of aid did not encourage them or invite others to live for very long on the bounty of the state.

The proponents of the almshouses argued that they saved money because they deterred people from becoming paupers, they got work out of those who entered them so that recipients helped pay the cost of their keep, and they instilled work habits in those who must have been idle.

Advocates of outdoor relief pointed out that almshouses were in fact more expensive than allowances, that they were miserable and degrading, that they broke up families, and that they threw into total dependency those who might have been able to live with only minimal help from the town.

It was a debate that would not be resolved until the Great Depression.

The American welfare system is not based on the principles of Social Darwinism that were so popular during the period of the "robber barons" of the late 1800's. However, during that period, another movement took hold, based on principles that on their face were altruistic, but which in fact reflected the same ideology permeating poor relief since the time of Elizabeth. The Charity Organization Society movement became extremely powerful by the turn of the century, and much of its philosophy and practice was inherited by those who developed the social casework theories that underly the present welfare system.

Charity Organization Society

The first Charity Organization Society (COS) was founded in Buffalo in 1877, modeled on a movement that had already begun in England, and the groups spread to other cities in America. The first purpose of the COS was to serve as a registry, to compile a list of the needy poor, and to prevent duplication and the chance that someone might be collecting from two agencies at once. The investigations that were conducted before anyone was added to the registry insured that only the "worthy" would be helped. The COS movement specifically excluded blacks from aid, and since it often established the lists used by public agencies, blacks were denied government assistance as well.

3
CHARITIES AND ALMSHOUSES

The philosophy behind the COS movement was that pauperism was the result of personal inadequacy, laziness, drinking, lack of thrift, extravagance, and sexual immorality. The altruism of these societies consisted in their commitment to reform the poor and help them end the evil ways that had brought them to destitution.

The movement believed that indiscriminate almsgiving was an evil to be corrected. One of the Society's leaders, Josephine Shaw Lowell, declared that "relief should be surrounded by circumstances that shall . . . repel everyone, not in extremity, from accepting it." She believed that outdoor relief did great "moral harm because human nature is so constituted that no man can receive as a gift what he should earn by his own labor without a moral deterioration."[1]

There was a sharp contrast between the attitudes of the charity organization leaders and the founders of the settlement-house movement who were more committed to social change and, like Jane Addams, were often socialists and feminists.

The COS lobbied for the abolition of outdoor relief. In some cities it succeeded and even did away with winter distributions of food and coal.

Charles R. Henderson, a speaker at the National Conference on Charities and Corrections in 1891, declared that outdoor relief

> *tends to excite hostility to the state itself. First, relief educates a large class to look to government for help; and when this is received the feeling of dependence increases. The poor man has become a pauper, a beggar. A willing pauper is near to being a thief. As the State excites hope which it cannot fulfill, a time comes when the pauper is a public enemy. It is in this class that the worst foes of order are found, the only real proletariat that we have.*
>
> *As the State cannot distribute its funds fairly, discontent is aroused in the neighborhood where aid is given. One poor man cannot see why he is not aided as much as his next-door neighbor, since he is quite as poor and has more children. Having been educated by the State to be a beggar, he turns upon the State because it does not recognize his demand for support to be based on "natural rights."*

CHARITIES AND ALMSHOUSES

Henderson pointed out that "none of these considerations weigh against personal and voluntary charity, which is a favor and not a legal obligation, and which may be suspended when the demand is made in the name of right."[2]

COS leaders, like the opponents of outdoor relief before them, noted that forcing people to choose almshouse care would cut the relief rolls. "Aid should be given so as to remove temptation to accept dependence," said a speaker at the 1898 COS national conference. "When public aid, which is looked upon in some way as a public right, is offered in a form which is not deemed desirable, as maintenance in the almshouse, the applicants for public maintenance are reduced to a residuum composed mostly of those who are chronic paupers."[3]

Advice Rather than Money

The COS emphasized casework rather than financial aid in its approach to the poor. The first "friendly visitors" were unpaid volunteers, mostly graduate students.

This was a period when the role of such volunteers was to promote the Protestant Ethic, to uplift the poor, and to exhort them to adopt the middle-class values of saving money and being clean. In return for whatever meager payment a poor person received, he or she had to listen to well-meant advice on how to become a better person.

However, Charity Organization officials generally were disappointed with the failure of "ladies and gentlemen of the community" to donate their time to the task. Soon, paid workers were sent out. (The beginning of professional social work coincided with other changes like the standardization of time zones and the establishment of national commercial and financial arrangements that reflected the needs of industrial society. It was at this time that the first social work school was founded—the New York School of Philanthropy, now the Columbia School of Social Work.)

The social workers "diagnosed" the problems of the impoverished person or family and worked out plans for "rehabilitation." They told people what they should eat, where they should live, and how they should relate to their families, friends, and neighbors.

If an individual asked for money for coal or clothing or to buy medicine or pay the rent, the caseworker would proceed as if this indicated a failure of character. Caseworkers investigated every aspect of their "clients'" lives and established close supervision. Families generally were given aid in kind, but if money was provided, they had to account for every penny spent.

The COS believed that although public relief tended to promote dependence and pauperism, private aid given according to charity organization rules could be used to build the character of the poor, encouraging them to be industrious and to practice thrift.

There were, of course, some who denied the notion that people seeking relief were employable but shiftless. In 1890, the secretary of the Massachusetts State Board of Charities declared that, "that mythical class, the 'able-bodied poor'" was "scarcely found in this country in public establishments, except for a few months in the cold season, when the number of employments, both for men and women, is considerably reduced by Nature herself."[4]

Amos G. Warner, who had headed the Baltimore COS and the public charities of Washington, D.C., wrote that poor health and sickness were the most common factors that caused people to seek relief. He said that "most of those out of employment are not capable in any complete sense of the term." He noted the high incidence of industrial disease and accidents.[5]

The COS and Morality

The COS movement set certain moral standards for recipients of its aid. No assistance was given to a drunkard or to his family. The wife could get aid for herself and her children only if she left her husband; then she was considered a widow. However, women whose husbands had left *them* were not treated as widows, because that would only encourage men to leave their families so they could get help.[6]

If a husband did desert, the COS advocated that the family be broken up, with its members placed in institutions.

If a family was found eligible for aid, the COS first turned for contributions to relatives, friends, neighbors, churches, fraternal organizations, and former employers. It was a sure way of informing everyone acquainted with the applicant that he or she was now a pauper.

The aid was offered under the principle of less eligibility. The COS believed that no one would work without the threat of starvation, and to discourage malingerers, the amount given was at the lowest possible level.

However, others at the turn of the century began to point out that even full-time workers often did not earn enough to keep them from want. Robert Hunter, the author of *Poverty,* published in 1904, estimated that although 4 million people, some 5 percent of the population, were getting public assistance, there were another 6 million poor getting nothing. He figured out a budget for five which set the poverty line at $460 a year in the Northeast and Middle West and $300 a year in the South. Then he pointed out that railroad workers earned less than $375 a year in the North and under $150 in the South, that cotton millhands in the North were paid under $300 and less than $235 in the South, and that nearly a third of the workers in the middle Atlantic states earned under $300.[7]

However, supplemental aid to full-time workers was not contemplated by the leaders of public or private charity. The next major change in the relief system was the development of aid to certain categories of the "deserving" poor: widows, the aged, and the blind.

Aid to Widows

The move to give assistance to widows was based on the belief that it was harmful and wrong to take children away from their mothers solely because the women did not have enough money to care for them. An initial unsuccessful attempt to avoid breaking up families in this way was made in New York in 1898. The city, working with the Society for the Prevention of Cruelty to Children, would have taken such children out of institutions and paid their families the same amount of money it was paying the institutions for their care. The bill passed the legislature, but voluntary charitable agencies lobbied against it as outdoor relief that would "pauperize" its recipients, and the governor vetoed the bill.[8]

However, the issue was raised again by the White House

Conference on Dependent Children called by President Theodore Roosevelt in 1909. The conference declared that "home life is the highest and finest product of civilization" and that "children should not be deprived of it except for urgent and compelling reasons," and certainly not because of poverty. However, the White House Conference stated clearly that the aid for such "children of parents of worthy character" should come from private charity, not from the public.[9]

Nevertheless, one of the results of the conference and the issues it raised was the mother's pension movement. The first mother's pension laws were adopted in Missouri and Illinois in 1911 and other states followed. The laws provided for monthly payments for poor widowed, divorced, or abandoned mothers for the partial support, up to the legal working age, of their children living at home.

There were no payments until investigation proved the worthiness of applicants; there were the usual residence requirements, and the amounts paid were set either by the legislature or the courts, but they were a pittance, often limited by law to $2 per week per child.

The Kansas Mother's Pension Act of 1915 required that applications for aid include the affidavits of two householders of the township or city who certified to the woman's character and fitness to have custody of her child.[10]

In Montana, she had to present a petition bearing the signatures of ten taxpayers. Notices were posted in three places, and anyone who wanted to argue against her grant could do so at a public hearing.[11]

The laws usually were administered by the courts or by child welfare boards, not by the usual poor-relief officials. District court judges or juvenile officers determined whether mothers were mentally, morally, and physically fit to bring up their children.

New York succeeded in passing a mother's pension act in 1915 after a state legislative commission reported, "The unskilled widowed mother is unable to support herself and her family at a reasonable standard of living by taking work into the home or going out into the broader fields of industry. The work available to such women outside of the home inevitably breaks down the physical, mental, and moral strength of the family and disrupts the home life through an inadequate standard of living and parental neglect, due to the enforced absence of the mother at the time the children most need her care. The work available in the home results, equally inevitably, in the prevention of normal family life, by causing overwork, congestion, child labor, contagion, and a dangerously low standard of living."[12]

Under the prodding of the U.S. Children's Bureau, which was set up after the 1909 conference, most states enacted mother's aid laws. However, they were largely voluntary. The local community had the right to implement the legislation and to pay for the assistance. Only a few states shared the costs. Many localities did not institute the program at all.

Only a small portion of the families that needed help ever got it, and they did not receive very much. Although the grants often were called "pensions," they were not administered as such. The women were thoroughly investigated for evidence of their need and worthiness, and they were required to accept the ministrations of caseworkers. "Worthy" meant, for the most part, widows as opposed to unwed, abandoned, or divorced mothers. It also meant white and often Anglo-Saxon as well.

Discrimination

A study by the Children's Bureau in 1922 discovered that in a quarter of the agencies investigated, Mexican, Italian, and Czechoslovakian families were given smaller grants than Anglo-Saxons. One agency added 10 percent to the food budgets of "high type" families. Another study in 1931 of half the recipients in the country showed that 96 percent of the mothers were white. North Carolina and Florida each had one black family on the rolls. Houston, Texas, and Indianapolis, Indiana, with black populations of 21 percent and 11 percent, had no blacks on the rolls at all.[13]

In addition, the required standards of social and sexual conduct were so strict that in California, mother's aid recipients were called "gilt-edged widows."

The grants were meager. In 1926, the average monthly grant went from maximums of $20 in states like New Jersey, Texas, Colorado, and Maine to $70 in California, Connecticut, Indiana, Kansas, and Michigan. The period was the 1920's, a time of prosperity, but the grants were at subsistence or below-subsistence levels.

The low payments forced many mothers to work, although the "suitable home" requirements and rulings in some areas said they could not spend more than three days a week away from home. That meant that many could not get regular jobs. Often, the district judge was required to rule that a job away from home would not interfere with giving proper care to the children. Thus women often took in laundry to do at home.

In any case, most women in the general workforce held the lowest-paying unskilled or semiskilled jobs in agriculture, manufacturing, or domestic or personal service, and even when they performed the same jobs as men they commonly received less pay.

Two other new programs were also started at about this time: aid to the blind and the aged.

Aid to the Blind and Aged

Aside from veterans, the only groups ever considered "worthy" recipients of public assistance have been the aged and the blind. However, there again the laws were voluntary. Counties could adopt, and pay for, the programs. A handful of states provided aid to the blind, beginning with Ohio in 1898. Arizona and Alaska passed the first aid-to-the-aged laws in 1915 but by 1929, only eleven states had such legislation. There were strict residence requirements. Montana said the applicant had to be a resident of the state for the preceding fifteen years, and benefits did not begin until a person was seventy.[14]

Old-age assistance laws were declared unconstitutional in Pennsylvania and Arizona, but finally they were upheld. However, mandatory old-age assistance laws were not passed until after the crash of 1929, and even then, by 1934, only twenty-eight states had them. The refuge of most of the aged poor—and of the blind—remained the poorhouse.

Following Sigmund Freud's visit to the United States, the early 1920's saw an emphasis on a psychiatric view of poverty that tied it to individual pathology, especially the existence of "dependent personalities." Under this theory, it was harmful to give too much assistance to the poor. Since it was thought that they had dependent personalities to begin with, such aid would only make them more dependent.

CHARITIES AND ALMSHOUSES

By the beginning of the Depression of the 1930's, care in almshouses was still a basic method of providing for paupers. Ten states did not provide for outdoor relief at all; a third used outdoor aid in special and emergency cases; and less than half the states considered it as important as the almshouse in the care of the poor. Several states, at the time of the 1929 crash, still had laws that provided for contracting out the care of the poor, and some still permitted the apprenticing of children.

The states also maintained their residence requirements, which ran from as little as six months to as long as ten years. Anyone who left South Dakota for thirty days lost residency. A majority of the states provided emergency relief to non-residents until they were returned to their home towns.

Relative-responsibility laws also continued in most places, and people who failed to support poor relations could be prosecuted.

The American Poor Farm

An extensive critique of the almshouse system was written by Harry Evans and published in 1926. *The American Poorfarm and its Inmates* was the result of a study proposed by the U.S. Secretary of Labor and carried out by the Loyal Order of the Moose, which published the book, the Ladies of the Maccabees, the Woodmen of the World, the Security Benefit Association, and a dozen other fraternal organizations that were hardly radical critics of America.

Evans charged that "the poorfarms and their helpless inmates are part of the political spoils of the community. The superintendent, manager or overseer of the poor is usually appointed because he is influential in politics or because he will take the job for less pay than anyone else, and not because of his special fitness for the work."[15]

In fact, one of the difficulties encountered in making the study was "the almost universal illiteracy of almshouse superintendents. The reports of state inspectors often included notations that the "superintendent can read or write a little."[16]

One of the basic faults of the system, aside from poor physical conditions in the almshouses, was that the sick, the feebleminded, the blind, the deaf, the aged, widows, children, criminals, drunkards, drug addicts, and people with contageous diseases all were housed together.

Evans said, "The poor farm is our human dumping ground into which go our derelicts of every description. Living in this mess of insanity and depravity, this prison place for criminals and the insane, are several thousand children and respectable, intelligent old folks, whose only offense is that they are poor."

He added, "Many of the intelligent, already weakened in body and morale, break mentally under the strain. Daily association with the idiotic and the feeble-minded, many of whom are incapable of caring for their bodies and are filthy beyond belief, is enough to drive a healthy person insane."[17] Officials estimated that some 75 percent of the inmates of almshouses were feebleminded. It was common for feebleminded women and girls to be made pregnant by other inmates or by attendants.

The Contract System

Evans condemned the contract system in which a person operated the poor farm, owned its produce, and cared for the inmates for a specified amount per person. "The more cheaply the paupers are maintained, the more profit to the contractor," he said. Some state laws required public auctions to determine who would care for the poor.

Evans described how that worked:

The local papers announce that the Board of Supervisors, on a certain day, will auction off the position of superintendent of the poor farm. This is notice to prospective bidders, who proceed to inventory the poor farm and its inmates. They find there are, say forty inmates; ten of them can do a fair day's work; another ten can do some work; the rest are helpless.

So the shrewd bidder figures that he will get so much labor out of the inmates; perhaps they can do all the work of the farm. If so, there will be no paid employees. The only outlay will be for food, fuel, clothing, doctor bills and medicine. In short, the amount of the bid per inmate is determined by the inmates' working capacity. The bidder is buying the time and labor of the inmates. Perhaps there are a few feebleminded huskies among the forty paupers who can moil and toil in the fields. Perhaps there are a few strong feeble-minded women who can wash dishes and scrub. There will be profit from their labor. So he carefully examines all paupers and makes his bid accordingly.

Evans called this "a species of slavery . . . exploitation of one of the weakest units of our population. Without reason to know his rights, without mental capacity to arrange the terms of his employment, the labor of the pauper is put on the auction block and sold."[18]

He also condemned the squalor and dangerous conditions that existed in the almshouses and poor farms: "Dangerous unsanitary conditions prevail at most poor farms. The rule is water from wells, outdoor, filthy privies, no sewerage or cesspools. Sanitation cannot be maintained among a group of feeble-minded paupers, huddled together, some of whom cannot care for their own bodies, practically all of them given to slovenly habits, without running water and sewerage. Slop and garbage are thrown out the kitchen door, or dumped in piles about the yard. The drain from the grounds and privies contaminates the well water. Often there is no hot water to wash bedding and clothing."[19] He described most of the houses as shacks and firetraps.

Danger to Children

Evans attacked the practice of sending children to the poor farms. He noted also that, "There are still agencies in the east that pick up the street gamins and ship them west. This practice is not so prevalent as it was some years ago. The writer once saw a train of eastern pauper children at Ames, Iowa—one hundred of them. They were dumped on the prairies of Iowa and Minnesota."[20]

Sometimes, as a method of deterring applications for relief, paupers were sent to convict camps. Evans wrote that in Terrel County, Georgia, "some years ago the increase in applications for county aid became so numerous that the county commissioners abandoned outdoor relief to the poor and adopted the plan of sending applicants to the convict farm. Since then there have been few applications." He added,

"There are three crude shacks at the prison farm for paupers, with three inmates. One old pauper abandoned his shack and sleeps with the convicts."[21]

Some states sent short-term criminals — petty thieves, tramps, drunkards, and prostitutes — to serve their terms at the poor farm. Evans noted ironically, "It may be the plan is also a deterrent to crime. He is a hardened criminal, indeed, who does not feel it a disgrace to live at a poor farm."[22]

He gave chilling examples of conditions around the country, of "the silence, the repression, the gloom, the despair, the loneliness, the degradation, the desolation" and the miserable physical conditions of the poor farms.

The Poor Farms Report

In Sandusky, Ohio, he reported: "Building very old and dilapidated; walls in terrible condition; no screens; swarms of flies everywhere; no comfortable chairs; rooms very dirty; inmates do the work; food very poor. The so-called hospital building is a miserable place, more like a prison. An imbecile woman's only bed is an old box filled with straw and a dirty quilt. She was very unkempt, barefooted, covered with flies. Concrete, filthy floors. A disgraceful place."[23]

In Bent County, Colorado, from a 1920 report of the state board of charities: "Building an old church condemned five years ago as unfit for habitation; walls unsafe and falling in; little protection from cold; old floors cracked and dirty; miserable beds and bunks; a bedridden inmate with tubercular hips who has been in this bed since September (three months before) and has not had a bath . . . in another dilapidated room sits a woman in rags, past 90, over an old stove trying to keep warm."[24]

In Rensselaer County, New York: "Four days a week breakfast consists only of bread and coffee; rolled oats and syrup are added the other three days; six days a week supper consists only of bread and tea; prunes are added on Sunday; meat and a vegetable for dinner — no butter or milk any time."[25]

In North Carolina: "For several years an uncontrollable blind man lay on a pallet with one end of a chain around his ankle and the other stapled to the floor."[26]

In Tioga County, New York: "Everybody lives together — the blind, the feeble-minded, the intelligent, the children, the epileptic, the contaminated, the noisy—and the flies and vermin."[27]

Evans was able to find only one exception to the lot. The state infirmary of Rhode Island was "well-equipped, officered with trained nurses, skilled therapeutists and vocational teachers, in contrast to institutions governed locally." He said there were "schools for children and their illiterate mothers and shops where inmates are given vocational training." He described the place as "clean and comfortable; there is music and entertainment and religious services; there are lawns and gardens; it does not have the sordid appearance of a poor farm; something is found for every inmate who is not bedridden to do."[28]

He decried the insensitivity of the country's citizens and public officials. "The unconcern of so many local officials is amazing. It discloses a lingering strain of brutality, a hangover from the dark ages of the inquisition." He cited the case of a poor farm in Stone County, Missouri, which had a monthly appropriation of $5.41 per inmate. When money ran out one winter, the desperate overseer left the farm "and became a beggar himself—begging for the abandoned paupers. Meanwhile, the paupers subsisted on swill from the slop barrel. If any of the good people of Stone County interested themselves, it is not of record."[29]

Evans thought the chief reason for the conditions of people at the poor farms was that: "They cannot protest. They cannot fight for their rights." He said, "If these unfortunates had the capacity to organize, the capacity and opportunity to speak, to print, to vote, their conditions would be relieved. Because they are mute, they are neglected."[30]

Such was the condition of thousands of America's poor only three years before the Depression.

When the stock market crash came on October 10, 1929, it shattered a myth as well as the economy. A popular cartoon showed a squirrel asking a man on a park bench why he had not saved for a rainy day. "I did," he replied.

Up until 1870, half the workers of the country had been independent farmers; large numbers of others were local tradesmen and artisans. With the rise of industrial capitalism, individual workers were more dependent on business cycles and factors involving currency, markets, credit, and foreign trade than on their own thrift or industriousness. Now, the crash not only threw millions out of jobs, three million in the winter of 1929, but wiped out the savings of those who had dutifully adhered to the admonitions about saving for their old age. The banks had failed.

Private charity proved totally inadequate. It had been contributing only a fraction of the funds distributed in relief anyway; often it merely gave out money that had been appropriated by local governments. The localities, which were responsible for providing assistance, were swamped. They had never before had so many demands for relief. Often half the town was in need; in one-industry communities, like mill and mining towns, virtually the whole town might be shut down. With no local taxes, the town could hardly give assistance. Many communities tried to float bonds, but there were constitutional limits on the amounts of money they could raise and practical limits on the credit their tax bases afforded.

4
DEPRESSION

One old debate that suddenly became irrelevant was the question of outdoor relief versus almshouses. Aside from the fact that the new poor were "deserving," there were just too many of them to send to the county farms. Sometimes food and fuel were given instead of cash, and there were vouchers people could use in local grocery stores.

How the Poor Coped

People stayed in bed to save fuel — or when they had no fuel. They lost their homes when they couldn't pay the mortgages, or they were forced to sell them at sharply deflated prices in order to eat: cities generally would not give relief to anyone who owned a home. People moved in with relatives or lived in shacks. Some slept in fields or empty iron pipes. "Hoovervilles" of tin huts appeared on empty lots.

Communities opened soup kitchens and breadlines. People scrounged for food on docks, picking up what had fallen off the trucks. They looked in garbage cans; they begged day-old bread from bakers. Children in school were listless from hunger. Some teachers fed them from their own pockets, and occasionally even gave them showers when the water was turned off at home. Men who were temporarily called back to a steel mill were so weak from hunger and malnutrition that they could not do the work.[1]

By the winter of 1930–31, there were 4 to 5 million jobless; by the next year the figure had reached 8 million, one in six of the working population. By 1931, most cities had passed laws to prevent married women from working in the local government, and women teachers were fired by most school systems when they wed.[2] Since the women often were the sole breadwinners in their families, the move was irrational and cruel as well as discriminatory.

Hoover's Plan

President Herbert Hoover seemed to want to solve the crisis by cheering on everyone else. He said the federal government must not encourage or allow local governments to abandon their "precious possession of local initiative and responsibility" and declared in a 1931 message to Congress, "Our people are providing against distress from unemployment in true American fashion by a magnificent response to public appeal and by action of local governments."[3]

The chief task of Hoover's Emergency Committee on Employment was to encourage business to "spread the work" and to "coordinate" local efforts. The head of the committee, Colonel Arthur Woods, wanted the President to ask for a large public-works appropriation from Congress, but Hoover said that additional federal spending for public works would not be financially prudent.

Congress defeated bills to appropriate 25 million dollars for drought and unemployment relief to be distributed by the Red Cross. John Barton Payne, chairman of the Red Cross, spoke against the bill himself. He thought that the receipt of government money would ruin his own fund drive. "Why should the Government be dealing in this sort of thing when the people have plenty of money?" he asked.[4] The Red Cross, he believed, could deal with the drought relief, because that was a disaster due to an "act of God," but not with unemployment which was the result of acts of people.

Hoover declined to distribute some sixty thousand bushels of wheat the government had in its storehouses, although feed was made available to keep cattle alive. When people pointed to the number of workers selling apples on the streets, Hoover explained, "Many people left their jobs for the more profitable one of selling apples."[5]

Republicans and Businessmen

Republicans and businessmen backed Hoover's approach to the growing relief crisis. The Republican governor of Rhode Island supported the President's opposition to federal relief aid with a telegram saying, "Rhode Island is not unmindful of the heritage of self-reliance and of courage and of thrift bequeathed by the founders."[6]

Walter Gifford, chairman of the President's Organization on Unemployment Relief and president of American Telephone and Telegraph, said that federal aid would encourage individuals to stop giving private charity, and business would stop trying to spread the work and help former employees. Local communities would spend less money for relief, and in the end, the jobless would be worse off than before.[7]

A top executive of U.S. Steel said in a radio speech in

1931, "While the number of unemployed is considerable, the number in real distress is relatively few, because the masses have been provident and are caring for themselves and each other. We should not overlook the fact that there are always some unemployed in each community, and this normal number should not be taken to swell the appearance of unusual distress at this time."

And he added, "We had almost reached the point where the many, and not the few, had concluded that they could live without work, and by their wits alone. This cannot be done. The first step for the individual is to accept that employment which lies at hand, no matter what it may be, and by his efforts and diligence and ambition to raise himself, as has been possible for others, to a better and more remunerative position."[8]

There were then 8 million unemployed.

When Henry Ford was reminded of the homeless boys who had taken to the road, riding freight cars from town to town and looking for work, he replied, "Why, it's the best education in the world for those boys, that traveling around. They get more experience in a few months than they would in years at school."[9] Health experts said the boys were also getting diseased and malnourished and were suffering from accidents and exposure.

At a public hearing where a U.S. senator noted that people could not live on wages of one or two days' work a week, the president of the National Association of Manufacturers declared, "Why, I've never thought of paying men on the basis of what they need. I pay men for efficiency. Personally, I attend to all those other things, social welfare stuff, in my church work."[10]

When unemployment was up to at least 10 million and Hoover vetoed the Emergency Relief and Construction Act in 1932, the NAM issued a statement saying that "public doles tend to continue and exaggerate the evil by subsidizing uneconomic factors in industry."[11]

Businessmen had some specific suggestions about the kind of relief that ought to be given the poor. Just after the crash, one Wall Street executive suggested that, "Families in need of shelter, food and clothing should be cared for in quarters provided by the municipality in which they reside in order that a careful check may be kept on their actual requirements until they are able to secure work and become self-supporting. Single men, unable to secure work, should be enrolled at our military posts and required to drill each day. Those who are physically unable to drill should be required to perform camp labor suitable to their age and condition of health."[12]

An Oklahoma gas-company official proposed to his friend, the Secretary of War, that restaurants save their leftovers to be picked up each morning by trucks with barrels labeled "meat," "beans," "potatoes," "bread," and "other items." He added that diners would have to be urged to take care not to drop cigarette or cigar ashes on their unfinished food. The unemployed would work for these scraps by chopping wood.

He noted, "We expect a little trouble now and then from those who are not worthy of the support of the citizens, but we must contend with such cases in order to take care of those who are worthy." And he added, "God placed them here and it is our duty to see that they are taken care of in a Christianlike manner."[13]

The Secretary of War discussed the plan with Colonel Woods. It was not put into effect. At that time, the government was still storing 60 thousand bushels of surplus wheat.

Congress Proposes Relief

Members of Congress introduced numerous measures for the relief of the unemployed. They read into the *Congressional Record* a list of thirty-one federal appropriations that had been made between 1803 and 1921 for emergency and disaster relief from floods, fires, earthquakes, cyclones, and droughts. They pointed out that the federal government gave aid to states for highways and for agriculture.

Senator Robert LaFollette noted that Congress had recently appropriated over $2 billion for the relief of those who owned property and stocks in banks, railroads, insurance companies, and industry. He asked whether the danger of destroying individual initiative was not just as great in those cases.[14]

The Secretary of Agriculture favored loans to farmers for fertilizer, feed, livestock, and tractor fuel, but said money for food for the farmers and their families would establish a dangerous precedent and "constitute a dangerous step toward the dole system in this country." He thought the Red Cross should take responsibility for feeding people since it got its funds through voluntary contributions.[15]

Senator LaFollette made a survey at the beginning of 1932 and discovered that almost every city and town in the country was near bankruptcy, that relief payments were being given on a starvation basis, and that they were about to stop altogether.[16] Families in New York, for example, were getting $2.39 a week (the average worker's wage had been about $50 a week), and only half the eligibles were getting anything. Across the country, only one in four of the unemployed was getting relief. And grants were being cut as funds decreased and applicants increased.

The American Friends Service Committee, conducting relief work in the coal mining areas of West Virginia and Kentucky, had such limited funds that it decided to weigh the local children and feed only those who were at least 10 percent underweight. It soon ran out of money completely.[17]

Public Unrest

Unrest and disorders grew as the unemployed went on hunger marches, confronted relief officials to demand aid, forcibly prevented evictions, and carried back furniture that had been put out on the street. As the jobless grew more militant and more organized, they succeeded in getting more money and goods from relief centers, and the movement spread throughout the country. Thousands also demonstrated in their communities and at state capitals.

A march of several thousand unemployed from Detroit to the Ford River Rouge plant in Dearborn, Michigan, was stopped by the police with tear gas bombs. In 15-degree weather, firemen turned their hoses on the crowd. Police fired on the marchers, killing four and wounding others as they fled.[18]

In the spring, there were riots in the coal mining areas of Kentucky. In June, the Bonus Marchers reached Washington. They were World War I veterans who had numbered three hundred when they began their march in Portland, Oregon. Riding freight trains and camping in the countryside, they arrived in Washington with thousands more who had joined them along the way. The Bonus Marchers had come to demand immediate payment of a bonus that World War I soldiers were scheduled to receive in 1945; Congressman Wright Patman of Texas had introduced a bill to accomplish their aim.

Eight thousand paraded down Pennsylvania Avenue. But the bill was defeated, and President Hoover ordered troops to turn back the demonstrators. Soldiers under General Douglas MacArthur set fire to their shacks and dispersed them with tear gas.

Emergency Relief Passed

Finally, the Democrats succeeded in getting an Emergency Relief and Construction Act passed, and Hoover signed it three months after he had vetoed a similar bill on the grounds that it unbalanced the budget. The act provided $300 million for direct payments and work relief stipends to be lent to the states at 3 percent interest. However, by the end of the year, states had borrowed only $30 million. The loans would have fallen due in July, 1935. (Elizabeth Wickenden says, "There was a banker's mentality: the states didn't want to borrow and the federal government was reluctant to lend.")

In 1932, the government also contracted with the American Red Cross to distribute the stores of wheat and cotton it had in its warehouses. People across the country subsisted on diets like that of one Kansas family which in October got a week's rations of two loaves of bread, a small sack of stale cookies donated by a bakery, a pound of sugar, a pound of lard, two pounds of beans, and a half pound of pork.

By the spring of 1933, when Franklin Delano Roosevelt became President, some 12 to 15 million, a third of the labor force, were unemployed, and wages had fallen by a third to an average of $17 a week.

Shortly after he took office, Roosevelt signed the Federal Emergency Relief Act (FERA) and shattered the centuries-old notion that relief was a local matter. The federal government appropriated $500 million to give the states, half on a matching basis, one federal dollar for every three spent locally, the rest to go at the President's discretion to areas most in need.

Harry Hopkins, who was appointed head of the Federal Emergency Relief Administration, recalled, "From the beginning we strove to make methods of relief differ deeply from practices of local poor relief which still held a heavy hand over many local agencies."[19]

Roosevelt noted, "We are now dealing with people of all classes. It is no longer a matter of unemployables and chronic dependents, but of your friends and mine who are involved in this. Every one of us knows some family of our friends which is or should be getting relief. The whole picture comes closer home than ever before."[20]

The People on Relief

There were 4 million families, some 18 million people, receiving public aid. In some states, 40 percent of the population was on relief, in some counties 90 percent. By the end of 1934, the figure rose to 20 million. Nearly one family in six was dependent.

In the past, the relief recipients had been the unemployables. When the depression hit, the blue-collar workers lost their jobs first. Then came the white-collar workers and professionals. Many of them suffered bitterly the stigma that had always been attached to the poor law. One engineer told a government investigator, "I simply had to murder my pride. We'd lived on bread and water three weeks before I could make myself do it." A lumberman said, "It took me a month. I used to go down there every day or so and walk past the place again and again. I just couldn't make myself go in."[21]

The altered class nature of the unemployed had an effect. Professional workers generally were treated more generously in the stringent financial investigations required as means tests for relief applicants. They were not forced to sell their homes or cars.

The government aid, which was distributed by the state and local governments, was used largely for food. In the beginning, the relief agencies paid one month's rent for families that had been evicted from their old apartments; then they waited for them to be evicted again before providing rent money for a new place. There were allowances for light, gas, fuel, and water. Eventually, more money was given for rents.

The average monthly grant for the country as a whole in 1933 was about $15, but the allowances varied from $33.22

in New York to $3.86 in Mississippi. The next year's national average rose to $24.50 and then in 1935 to nearly $53. Early in the program, there was a federal ruling that people had to be paid in cash, not in script or vendor payments.

Some states provided medical aid for relief recipients, but dental care was restricted to emergency extractions and repairs. There was no money for hospital bills. The principle was that money could not be spent for conditions "that do not cause acute suffering, interfere with earning capacity, endanger life, or threaten some permanent new handicap that is preventable."

Local caseworkers conducted investigations of applicants and paid home visits to make sure their needs were being met and that they were still eligible.

Surplus Foods

The Federal Surplus Relief Corporation was set up to buy surplus foods and distribute them to the needy through public and private agencies. It gave out basic commodities like butter, cheese, cereal, apples, sugar, potatoes, and flour as well as coal and mattresses and blankets made from surplus cotton. States set up commissaries where people on relief could pick up the supplies, and the poor stood in line for hours to claim their allotments. However, the commodities were provided chiefly to take the surpluses off the market, not for the assistance they gave the hungry.

Harry Hopkins ended the use of commissaries, because he thought they put a stigma on the recipients. Instead, they got grocery orders which allowed them to shop at their local stores but which still often specified the amounts and kinds of foods that could be bought. Hopkins later commented, "It is a matter of opinion whether more damage is done to the human spirit by a lack of vitamins or complete surrender of choice."[22]

Often the costs of rent and doctors' bills were paid for by vouchers. Many recipients never saw cash. The federal government preferred giving cash because it got aid to people quickly, it preserved the normal channels of retail trade, and it countered the demoralizing feelings of helplessness and lack of self-respect that unemployment had caused. However, it was up to the locality to choose to give cash or vouchers or supplies.

Public Works Projects

The Civilian Works Administration was established in 1933 by executive order to hire as many people as possible for projects proposed by local authorities. It swiftly took on some 4 million workers who built and repaired schools, worked on roads, taught illiterate adults to read and write, and were responsible for countless civic improvements.

Only half of the CWA workers had to come from the relief rolls. The CWA paid prevailing wages or hourly minimums set by the government. However, the Roosevelt Administration was particularly concerned about getting people off the relief rolls and into jobs.

The President said later, "The lessons of history, confirmed by the evidence immediately before me, show conclusively that continued dependence upon relief induces a spiritual and moral disintegration fundamentally destructive to the national fiber. To dole out relief in this way is to administer a narcotic, a subtle destroyer of the human spirit. It is inimical to the dictates of sound policy. It is in violation of the traditions of America. Work must be found for able-bodied but destitute workers."[23]

The Emergency Work Relief Program adopted in 1934 was run by the Federal Emergency Relief Act and financed state projects that hired people on relief.

The CWA, which lasted for only nine months, had paid regular wages to employees. The Emergency Work Relief Program paid wages based on a worker's "budget deficiency," an amount fixed according to the worker's "needs" rather than a standard wage for the job done. A person would labor only for the number of hours at the "fair rate" needed to earn the amount of relief to which he or she was entitled.

The FERA set a minimum wage of thirty cents an hour, then in 1934 substituted a system of local prevailing rates to be set by community committees representing relief officials, unions, and business or professional groups.

The W.P.A.

The Works Progress Administration replaced the FERA in 1935, and financed construction and other projects. It sought to give people the kinds of work that would fit their skills. It took only people certified by the local relief agencies and paid substandard monthly wages. When unions protested that these rates pushed down private wages, the government paid the workers prevailing rates, but their hours were limited to the number needed to earn the same amount: the "security wage" computed to be what the worker needed depending upon the worker's level of skill and where the family lived. However, the security wage was so low, that many workers still required other assistance.

Even so, businessmen charged that the wages were unfair competition to private industry. In rural areas, where wages of 10 cents an hour were common, especially for black workers, businessmen complained that the workers were being spoiled. Southern plantation owners charged that they could not get blacks to work their fields for what they had been paid in the past.

Georgia Governor Eugene Talmadge sent President Roosevelt a letter he had received from a farmer who wrote, "I wouldn't plow nobody's mule from sunrise to sunset for 50 cents a day when I could get $1.30 for pretending to work on a ditch."

Roosevelt replied, "I take it, from your sending the letter of the gentleman from Smithville to me, that you approve of paying farm labor 40 to 50 cents per day. Somehow I cannot get it into my head that wages on such a scale make possible a reasonable American standard of living."[24]

In most instances, the security wage was below what workers in private industry earned. When the government went from the FERA to the WPA in 1935, the average grant was doubled. However, the hourly rates were cut because of protests by employers who feared it would drive up their own costs.

The purpose was to spread the work and, under the old philosophy of less eligibility, to encourage people to seek private employment. Liberals in Congress pushed through an amendment to pay WPA workers prevailing wages, but Roosevelt killed it.

Wages Not Dole

The WPA also was run on the principle of paying wages to as many workers as the appropriations would cover, rather than taking all the available funds and dividing them among all who needed aid. This was one of the most debated issues at the time: Was it better to give everyone something or to fix a wage and give out as many jobs as one could? Hopkins was insistent on the idea that the security wage was a wage, not a dole.

A third of the WPA money went for bridges and roads, another 20 percent for public buildings, parks, and playgrounds. Workers served hot lunches to school children and repaired library books. Artists, actors, and writers were given work in their fields. However, there were also protests from professionals, white-collar workers and skilled laborers that they were assigned to projects involving unskilled manual labor and that they did not have the opportunity to use their own skills.

In New York the work bureaus were set up entirely separate from the home-relief agencies because of the stigma attached to the dole.

In the first five years, the WPA produced an average of 2 million jobs annually, and at its peak it accounted for about a quarter of the unemployed. A look at the dates on cornerstones of public buildings in any community will give an indication of the extent of the agency's activity.

In addition to administering work-relief programs, many states required that people work for the *direct* relief they received. Communities had recipients cut grass and weeds, trim hedges, rake leaves, clean buildings, collect garbage, and work on roads. Wages were paid on the budget deficiency basis; in effect, people worked for the amount of their relief checks. They were often make-work projects insisted upon by communities that believed no one should get anything for nothing.

The FERA had ruled that full-time workers should not get federal relief, but in 1934, 18 percent of the recipients were employed at wages that could not support their families, and half of them worked full-time. In 1934, the median wage for white workers was $9.30 a week, for blacks $3.50. Women got less than both white and black men, but the exact statistics were not figured until 1939.

The federal government said that recipients could turn down private jobs that did not meet prevailing standards of wages and working conditions. The agency investigated reports of unjustified job refusals, and in 1935 found only twenty out of over six hundred cases. Most recipients appeared willing to take just about any kind of job to get off relief.

Other Work Programs

The first relief program Roosevelt had signed into law was the Civilian Conservation Corps, which put a quarter of a million men (no women were eligible) to work at subsistence wages developing recreation areas, planting trees, and working to prevent floods, fires, and soil erosion in the national forest lands. They were required to send part of their wages to their families.

The Rural Rehabilitation Division of the FERA made loans to farmers for seed, fertilizer, farm tools, livestock, feed, and other supplies. The Resettlement Administration, which took over the functions of the RRD, moved farmers from submarginal to productive land, helped them develop their land, and built housing for workers in rural areas and suburbs.

Young people benefited from the National Youth Administration, which began in 1935 and offered vocational education and funds for jobs for high school and college students.

Most state laws that set up programs for distributing relief required recipients to be state residents; often local agencies insisted they be local residents as well. The FERA ran a transient program to help some 300,000 of the more than a million and a half homeless people wandering from town to town. It gave aid to the states to care for transients and set up transient centers and camps. Many towns set up what Hopkins called "thinly disguised flophouses" for single men. He explained that they were "regarded as cheaper than ordinary poor relief." And, "Communities felt more secure in having the still distrusted transients gathered in one place."[25]

In 1932 alone, over a quarter of a million people lost their homes when they could not meet mortgage payments. In 1933, the Home Owner's Loan Corporation was set up to refinance mortgages and provide money for taxes and repairs. Loans were given to one out of ten of the country's homeowners, largely members of the middle class.

The FERA also had a Division of Self-Help Cooperatives

that aided groups set up to provide goods and services for use and barter rather than for profit. Some thirty-five thousand families were involved in projects that grew food, produced dairy products, raised poultry, caught fish, made cloth and soap, did plumbing and carpentry, repaired shoes and automobiles, and cut wood for fuel. The State Relief Commission of Ohio set up the Ohio Relief Production Units, Inc., and leased a dozen factories in which jobless men and women made dresses, overalls, furniture, and stoves for their use and for exchange with relief agencies in other states.

Attacks on Relief

There was constant criticism of the federal relief programs, both from those who thought the government was doing too much and from those who thought it was not doing enough. When the FERA legislation was first passed, conservative congressmen and businessmen charged that it would destroy the basic traditions and principles of the country. One congressman asked, "Is there anything left of our federal system?" and another charged, "It is socialism. Whether it is communism or not, I do not know."[26]

Robert E. Wood of Sears, Roebuck asserted, "While it is probably true that we cannot allow everyone to starve, although I personally disagree with this philosophy and the philosophy of the city social worker, we should tighten up relief all along the line, and if relief is to be given, it must be on a bare subsistence allowance."[27]

A banker named Frank A. Vanderlip declared, "Our present efforts in the direction of relief have broken down self-reliance and industry. I profoundly believe that society does not owe every man a living."[28]

Ex-President Hoover also attacked the Roosevelt program for weakening the country's "moral fiber." Harold Ickes, who ran the CWA, commented that when Hoover had been President he had not hesitated "to weaken the moral fiber of banks and insurance companies and manufacturing and industrial enterprises" by giving them millions of dollars in aid.[29]

Some businessmen said that the ability to go on relief prevented many workers from sincerely looking for work.

In 1934, the Chamber of Commerce and the National Association of Manufacturers demanded that the control of relief be returned to the states. However, of thirty-seven governors interviewed on the proposal only Governor Talmadge agreed with it.

There also was opposition to the CWA for providing jobs to people not on relief as well as to those on relief and for paying regular wages. In 1934, the CWA was abolished and its projects transferred to the FERA which hired only those on relief and paid substandard wages.

Businessmen charged repeatedly that work relief competed with private enterprise. Mattress manufacturers objected when the FERA workshops used surplus cotton to make mattresses for people on relief. There were protests when the FERA obtained cattle that would have died from the drought and used them to provide canned beef and shoes for reliefers. Shoe manufacturers refused to rent the machinery the government needed. They did not accept the government's contention that the people who were to receive the goods had no money to buy them on the regular market.

Business also protested against the self-help projects. They charged that they represented the opening wedge of socialism, and they forced limits on the amount of money FERA gave to the cooperatives which were finally phased out, beginning in 1935.

Workers' Protests

Workers also had complaints about the program. They said wages were inadequate. And they demanded work relief for all who needed it. Hopkins agreed that the wages were not enough, but Congress was unwilling to appropriate the money needed to raise the rates or make more jobs available. The FERA and the WPA recognized the right of relief recipients to organize and complain and appeal to higher authorities. Local and state groups established the Workers' Alliance in 1935, and grievance committees went to relief offices to protest the inadequate grants, the failure of relief agencies to pay rents, the humiliating methods used by investigators, the use of commissaries and grocery orders, and the conditions under which work relief was performed. (In the beginning of the program in the South, work-relief recipients were treated almost as if they were members of pauper chain gangs.)[30]

There were hunger marches, demonstrations, and work-relief strikes. Often the protesters were able to win larger grants and end objectionable practices. Protests against rent evictions frequently led to clashes with the police and to arrests. When federal funds for Colorado were cut off because of the state's failure to appropriate matching funds, the jobless rioted in relief centers and food stores and in the state legislature. An appropriations bill was passed quickly.

When the city of Chicago tried to cut food allowances by 10 percent, the unemployed held a large demonstration and the city council rescinded the cut. When Illinois failed to appropriate matching funds for relief, federal funds were cut off, and demonstrations were held until the legislature voted the necessary amount. By 1937, the Workers' Alliance claimed some sixteen hundred local groups with a dues-paying membership of 300,000.[31]

There was supposed to be no discrimination in relief or public works programs, but local customs prevailed, and blacks and other minorities were victims of the same bias they had suffered in private employment. There were also segregated "women's projects." Women worked at sewing clothes, serving school lunches, and staffing health clinics, and many people thought married women should not be given jobs at all, in public or private employment.

Radical Relief Plans

Several critics of the Roosevelt program won widespread support for their own proposals for government aid. In 1934, writer Upton Sinclair ran as the Socialist party candidate for governor of California on a plan to End Poverty in California (EPIC) by turning the empty factories and farmland over to the jobless to work for use instead of profit.

His opponent in the race endorsed the Townsend Plan, a proposal to give everyone over sixty years of age $200 a month on the condition that he or she stop working and agree to spend all the money in a month. There were some 11 million people over sixty and the plan would have cost $24 billion a year, half the national income. Some 25 million people signed petitions endorsing the plan, and there were several thousand Townsend clubs in the country.[32] When the proposal was introduced in the House in 1934, nearly two hundred congressmen stayed away from the vote, and the others turned it down without a roll call.

The House Labor Committee recommended passage of the Lundeen Bill, a plan proposed by a Farmer-Labor representative from Minnesota who called for unemployment compensation to everyone over eighteen who was out of work through no fault of his or her own, including the self-employed, such as farmers, storekeepers, and professionals.

The causes of unemployment could include illness, disability, old age, and maternity as well as economic factors. Benefits would equal the prevailing wage, with a minimum of $10 a week and $3 for each dependent. With at least 10 million unemployed, the plan would have cost about $10 billion.[33]

The money was to be raised by taxes on inheritances, gifts, and incomes of over five thousand dollars a year, and it would be administered by bodies elected by workers' and farmers' organizations. The Roosevelt Administration prevented the measure from coming to a vote. The American Federation of Labor also opposed it. When it was offered as an amendment to another bill, it got fifty-two votes.

Louisiana Senator Huey Long's "Share the Wealth" plan would have given everyone a homestead worth $5,000, an income of $2,000 a year, and pensions for the aged, free college educations for the young, and a radio, washing machine, and automobile for every family. The money was to come from taxing the rich. The "Share the Wealth" movement ended with Long's assassination in 1935.[34]

Social Security

The plan the government adopted to deal with the needy on a permanent basis differed from all of these schemes. The government programs focused on certain specific reasons for dependence, and was built both on practices that many of the states had developed in the beginning of the century and on several concepts, new for America, which fell under the rubric of "social security." They dated back to the social insurance started by Bismarck in nineteenth-century Germany.

Secretary of Labor Frances Perkins, who headed the Presidential committee to draft the law and who was largely responsible for the shape of the recommendations, said, "As I see it, we shall have to establish in this country substantially all of the social-insurance measures which the western European countries have set up in the last generation."[35] She originated the proposals for old-age and unemployment insurance and for wage-and-hour legislation. The goal was to create a permanent system of social insurance that would make it unnecessary for large numbers of people ever again to be dependent on government largesse for assistance. Those who were to benefit from the program would contribute to its cost, and there would be no means test.

Paternalism v. Thrift

J. Douglas Brown, the chairman of the National Advisory Committee on Social Security, explained, "The task of a democratic government under capitalism is . . . to prevent dependency rather than to feed its growth—to reduce the area of paternalism and broaden the area of cooperative thrift. Paternalism corrodes freedom by the subtle process of dependency, which in turn bogs down the very drives of incentive and enterprise that make capitalism effective. Townsendism, dangerous as it is in its immediate economic consequences, is still more menacing as a primrose path to a paternalistic, stagnant society."

He said social security, under which people contributed payments over the years, was an example of thrift as opposed to dependence. "As an educational force, employee contributions enhance public understanding of the distinction between social insurance and paternalism."[36]

Elizabeth Wickenden was director of the transients program during the relief administration and then worked in the WPA and the National Youth Administration during the Depression years. She has said that in the past, laissez-faire economics and social Darwinism combined "to reassure the prosperous that their private gain is a social good and that the plight of those who fail to reach this happy state lies somewhere in their own inferiorities."[37] Social insurance was based on a different notion—that the loss of income was a result of the nature of the economic system, and that protection against that loss ought to be built into the economy rather than left to individuals or families."

She said the Social Security Act of 1935 was a turning point in American welfare. However, part of the "grand design" was forgotten in the full employment that came with the war. "When Roosevelt said we should get the government out of the business of relief," she said, "he meant that the federal government should get jobs for everyone who could work." The plan called for turning the smaller number of unemployables back to the states for care and for giving joint federal-state aid to mothers and dependent children, the aged, and the blind "who were persons considered to be rightfully outside the labor force."[38]

There was debate at the time over whether there ought to be uniform benefits for everyone in the social security program or benefits dependent upon the peoples' past earnings and contributions. Congress decided on the latter. It altered the original Labor Department draft and excluded domestic and farm workers from coverage. The bill also excluded state and federal government employees and people who worked for nonprofit organizations.

Benefits were scheduled to begin for workers over sixty-five in 1942.

Unemployment Compensation

The other major "insurance" program adopted was unemployment compensation. It was run by the states and financed by a tax on payrolls paid by employers. States could set their own standards for coverage, length and amount of benefits, waiting periods, and eligibility qualifications. Almost every state excluded firms with few workers, domestics, farm workers, and employees of government and, until recently, nonprofit institutions, such as colleges and hospitals. Benefits generally ran to fourteen or sixteen weeks. They averaged $11 a week, from $14 in Michigan to $6 in Mississippi.

Insurance companies and savings banks protested that the government was in competition with them. Senator Lonergan of Connecticut, the major headquarters for most of America's insurance companies, succeeded in striking out a provision which would have allowed the 22 million self-employed to buy old-age pensions from the Social Security Administration.[39]

Both insurance programs came under sharp attack from business leaders and Republicans. The NAM said they would bring "ultimate socialistic control of life and industry."[40] A representative of the Illinois Manufacturers' Association said they would undermine our national life "by destroying initiative, discouraging thrift, and stifling individual responsibility."[41] A representative of the American Bar Association said they would begin a pattern which "sooner or later will bring about the inevitable abandonment of private capitalism." Business leaders testified in Congress against the bill. No one would work or save if the bill was passed, they said.[42]

Republicans in Congress agreed. Representative John Taber of New York declared, "Never in the history of the world has any measure been brought in here so insidiously designed as to prevent business recovery, to enslave workers, and to prevent any possibility of the employers providing work for the people."[43]

Another New Yorker, Representative James Wadsworth warned, "This bill opens the door and invites the entrance into the political field of a power so vast, so powerful as to threaten the integrity of our institutions and to pull the pillars of the temple down upon the heads of our descendants."[44] And Representative Daniel Reed declared, "The lash of the dictator will be felt, and twenty-five million free American citizens will for the first time submit themselves to a finger-print test."[45]

Most of the debate in the House was over the old age rather than the unemployment compensation provisions. The other programs that were part of the social security package — aid to the aged, the blind, and dependent children — were viewed in part as transitional measures which would become less necessary after the insurance programs took effect.

Dispute Over General Relief

The Advisory Committee on Public Employment and Relief, a group of social workers and public welfare officials, had recommended federal grants to states for general relief rather than a program based on categories. This became an important issue. The committee feared the repetition of all the evils of the old poor-law system for those left out of the federal program. However, the government committee on Economic Security, which developed the law, believed that aid to unemployables should be returned to the states, with the federal government helping them give assistance to the aged poor and the blind and to families without bread-winners.

In 1935, thirty-eight states had old-age assistance laws, but most of them were voluntary for local governments and without state appropriations. They generally required people to support their poor relations, and residence requirements were as long as five years. The program adopted by Congress said that the aged poor over sixty-five would be entitled to pensions, with the federal government paying 50 percent, but no more than $15 a month. After the total pension exceeded $30, the state would get no added reimbursement. Payments were to be made in cash.

When the old-age assistance program went into effect in 1936, nearly 13 percent of the population aged 65 and over received aid. The average monthly grant was $18.67, with average benefits ranging from $32.36 in California to $5.65 in Mississippi. (Average *weekly* earnings in the country were $25.)

Aid to the blind, which had existed in some states, was written into the social security law on the same basis as old-age assistance, with 50-50 federal matching grants.

The last program was almost an oversight and was not included in an original draft of the program. It was based on the system of mother's pensions that existed in all but three of the states. These laws were mostly voluntary for local governments; less than half the counties in the country actually gave aid, and the average allowance was little more than $11 a month. There also were long residence requirements; fifteen states specified more than ten years. Only twenty-one states helped children of divorced mothers, and others did not help children whose fathers had deserted.

Mothers and Children

The purpose of the new program, which was called Aid to Dependent Children, was to promote family life and enable mothers to stay at home and care for their children rather than work. Although during the Depression people welcomed the opportunity to keep women at home and give men the jobs, the measure contradicted the work ethic that was such a basic part of American poor-law tradition. It was a contradiction that would cause constant dissatisfaction with the program. Although Congress asserted in law that mothers without husbands should not work, the country in time rejected the spirit of the notion.

Under the ADC program, the federal government agreed to provide $1 for every $2 spent by the states up to $18 for the first child and $12 for each additional child. It provided less aid than the 50-50 matching grants to the aged poor and blind and provided no money at all for the mother.

The law originally was drafted to provide aid for children up to sixteen living in homes "in which there is no adult person, other than the one needed to care for the child or children, who is able to work and provide the family with a reasonable subsistence compatible with decency and health." That meant that aid could go to families where the breadwinners were ill or disabled or unemployed, or even underemployed.

However, the law that passed provided aid only to children in homes deprived of parental support because of the death, absence (through desertion, divorce, or confinement in an institution), or physical or mental incapacity of a parent. In practice, that meant that children were not aided as long as their fathers were living at home.

The law prohibited states from requiring more than one year of residence for eligibility. States varied their aid from an average of $10.76 a month in Arkansas to $62.91 to families in Massachusetts. The average national payment was $31.73 a family, substantially lower per person than payments to the aged or the blind.

"Moral" Requirements

Many states had rigid rules about the "character" and "morality" of women receiving mother's pensions, and they transferred the same attitudes to the new ADC program, although the federal law itself said nothing about the "fitness" of the children's parents. Half the states continued to require that children live in a "suitable family home meeting the standards of care and health, fixed by the laws of this state." Some social workers were in favor of the suitable home rules, because they believed they would assure proper standards of care by parents. (One of the first memoranda of the FERA was that while there had to be investigations to determine eligibility, they would not be a traditional caseworker approach.)

The idea of moral fitness was a standard applied almost exclusively to women. It was generally a requirement for strict adherence to local sexual mores. That is, mothers receiving ADC should not have sex lives. It was made clear to recipients that the money would stop if their personal behavior displeased the community. The children of unwed mothers were often deemed to be living in unsuitable homes. When the program began, 61 percent of the mothers who got aid were widows.

Casework was another factor in ADC. It was never included in the administration of unemployment insurance, another program for people whose basic problem was that they lacked money. In fact, many of the problems that social workers sought to diagnose arose from the low level of assistance to the mothers. Congress was reminded of its failure to include stipends for the mothers in the grants, but for years it did nothing to remedy the fault. Sometimes social workers tried to help the women find work, a goal that contradicted the purported reason for the program.

The architects of the law had designed old-age assistance, aid to the blind, and aid to dependent children as supplementary programs. They were to diminish as more people became eligible for old-age and unemployment insurance — and later for survivors insurance for workers' widows and children. Congress rejected a provision for the assistance programs that states be required to provide "a reasonable subsistence compatible with decency and health." One reason for this was the fear of southern congressmen that Washington would require them to pay more money to blacks.

All the Republicans but one voted to recommit the bill, but it finally passed the House, 371 to 33, and the Senate, 76 to 6.

Two Classes of Recipients

In effect, the social security law created two classes of recipients, one which was said to have earned its benefits, which qualified under clear definitions of eligibility, which was not subject to a means test, and which did not suffer public stigma or government efforts to reduce its benefits, and another which was considered the recipient of public charity, which had to undergo a means test, which was subject to wide administrative discretion in determining eligibility and which was considered a "problem" that cost the taxpayers money.

Roosevelt considered direct federal cash grants to the poor to be a temporary measure. "What I am seeking," he declared, "is the abolition of (federal) relief altogether. I cannot say out loud yet, but I hope to be able to substitute work." He added, "There will, of course, be a certain number of relief cases where work will not furnish the answer but it is my thought that in these cases all of the relief expenditures should once more be borne by the states and localities as they used to be."[46]

Thus, in 1935, he ordered that direct federal relief be ended while the government concentrated on providing jobs for the unemployed. However, people would still benefit from direct assistance when states developed programs to take advantage of the new federal matching grants under the social security law.

General Relief Returned to States

The government made another appropriation for a new Federal Workers Program, continued aid to farmers, and went on distributing food. General relief for those who could not get work relief was left to the states and local communities.

Nearly 3 million people received aid under old-age assistance, aid to the blind, and ADC when the programs took effect in 1936. However, many of those eligible for aid did not receive it. In some cases, state appropriations for the shares were so inadequate that old people had to wait until someone else died to get on the lists.

The inadequate state and local grants caused much suffering in the winter of 1936. Often there was not enough money to give even minimum allowances for food. Even people who got WPA wages often needed supplemental relief to support their families, and at its peak, WPA accounted for only a quarter of the unemployed.[47]

In New Jersey, people were issued licenses to beg instead of relief.[48]

Without the federal aid program, states went back to the old poor-relief system. *Commonweal,* a liberal Catholic magazine, criticized the "pantry snooping" and "pauperizing" of relief recipients that resulted from the notion that one should "avoid doing anything which might be construed as competing with private enterprise."[49]

WPA Cut Back

In 1936, WPA rolls were reduced, and in 1937, it was announced that they would be cut in half. WPA workers were required to accept private jobs if they were offered. Federal funds were cut again in 1937; Roosevelt was trying to balance the budget, and the result was Black Tuesday, a stock market crash in October that led to another recession in 1938. Five million people lost their jobs and relief rolls rose to include 14 percent of the population.

The federal government increased WPA appropriations, then cut them again a year later. Congress required that no one except veterans be in a work-relief program for more than eighteen months at a time. The purpose of that provision was to get people to look for jobs in the private sector. Wages on federal work-relief projects were kept low deliberately to discourage workers from remaining on the government payroll.

One commentator in *Nation's Business* suggested that the government should "make relief unattractive and make it unprofitable." He suggested longer hours for the same pay. "If men bestir themselves to get off charity there will be sound improvement in business. Men seeking jobs make jobs. Some set up small businesses and become employers. Others convince some employer that he should hire another worker at wages he can afford for a man who will work." He admitted that cutting relief benefits "undoubtedly would mean hunger and hardship, but not starvation."[50]

In mid-1938, twenty-three relief offices in Chicago were closed for lack of funds. Some ninety thousand families were affected. Other cities were on the verge of stopping relief or had only enough money for a few more months. *The New Republic* asked "whether the Federal government can continue to leave the entire burden of direct relief—the indispensable complement to the work-relief program—on the shoulders of the cities and states."[51]

That same year Harry Hopkins told a special congressional committee to investigate employment and relief, "On the question of a work program as against direct relief, it is my conviction, and one of the strongest convictions I hold, that the Federal government should never return to a direct relief program. It is degrading to the individual; it destroys morale and self-respect; it results in no increase in the wealth of the community; it tends to destroy the ability of the individual to perform useful work in the future and it tends to establish a permanent body of dependents. We should do away with direct relief for the unemployed in the United States."[52]

State Aid Inadequate

Meanwhile, in 1939, the American Association for Social Workers reported that in one state, "food grants are approximately one-fifth of a minimum standard food budget" and "many states have no state-wide program of general relief." It described the "hobo express" by which some counties transported vagrants to the county lines and dumped them there.[53]

When officials in Cleveland and Toledo, Ohio, asked Republican Governor John Bricker to call a special session of the legislature to provide more relief funds—they had no money for food for the unemployed—he replied that they had been warned in advance of the state's reduction of its share of relief costs. The state also refused the cities permission to raise more money by increasing taxes. In Cleveland, people were put on two-thirds food rations.[54]

Chicago also distributed food grants that allowed two-thirds of the established standards. *The Atlantic Monthly* reported, "The number of children found to be weakened for want of proper food compelled one nationally famous Chicago community center to modify its program substituting quiet activities for games like basketball and baseball."[55]

In New Jersey, a local relief director boasted that he got local funds by proving that it would cost less to give people grocery orders than to bury them.[56] Over half the states gave little or no direct relief to "employables." Generally, if a person was able-bodied, he or she was considered employable and thus ineligible. In at least one state, anyone physically able to get to the relief office was classified as able-bodied and thus the ability to apply for relief made one ineligible.[57]

The Social Workers Association reported, "Harrassed parents have come to the offices of voluntary relief agencies in Chicago seeking to arrange for the adoption of their children, because they could not be cared for properly on relief budgets."[58] Sometimes, instead of sending the children away, fathers left home to make their families eligible for ADC payments.

Another observer wrote, "In Omaha, with the thermometer at 18 below zero, the indifference of the county commissioners about providing fuel has continued. The suffering among the destitute has been almost indescribable. The federal government has seen this tragedy but has done nothing. The state government will do nothing. Children are too hungry to go to school and stay huddled in bed because there are no fires to heat their miserable homes. With rents not paid, these unhappy people live where and as they can."[59]

Nevertheless, nearly twice as much was being spent for relief in 1939 as in the depths of the depression in 1933 and 1934. Twenty-one million people were aided at a cost of $3 billion. Nearly a sixth of the population was dependent on relief. In the years from 1933 to 1939, the federal government had spent almost $13 billion, about $7 billion on direct relief. In 1939, Congress also made widows and children eligible for "survivor's benefits" under social security, and it began an experimental food-stamp program to allow people to buy food at one-third off.

Criticism of Relief

However, during this period there were also efforts by businessmen, Republicans, and conservative Democrats to dismantle the federal work-relief programs and turn the funds over to the states for them to administer as they wished. One proposal was for a system of community relief boards to decide who would get aid. *Collier's* magazine endorsed the proposal and said, "Unless we want relief taxes to keep on digging deeper into our pockets until they scratch bottom, we must bring the politicians and Workers' Alliance and undeserving reliefers under some kind of firm and continuous control."[60]

The plans were proposed as measures to promote economy, states' rights and local initiative, and the elimination of politics from relief administration. *The New Republic* charged, "There is good reason to believe, however, that these plans are really an attempt to destroy the work program entirely and go back to the dole."[61]

The U.S. Conference of Mayors said that the federal government should handle work relief but that states and localities should be responsible for direct relief to unemployables. More than $1\frac{1}{2}$ million people were then getting direct relief. The biggest problem was the employable unemployed.

There was also criticism from the Republicans that the federal relief system was being used as a political tool, that WPA jobs were given to buy votes, that WPA administrators were political bosses. The Roosevelt Administration opposed an amendment to a relief appropriation bill that banned relief and work-relief recipients from engaging in political activity. *Collier's* magazine called opponents of the measure "misguided office-seekers who are trying to use public charity to mobilize the weakest groups of the country into an army of mercenary voters."[62]

Public Attitudes

A *Fortune* poll in 1939 reported that some 18 percent of those interviewed said they would support a bill depriving relief recipients of the right to vote. This would prevent politicians from making capital out of poverty and would end the danger of a dependent class using the vote to keep its friends in power in order to continue to draw public funds.[63] One critic asserted, "America has created something new. For the first time in history beggars are dictating how much benefactors shall give. . . . Once the political power of relief is eliminated it will dry up and disappear."[64]

A Gallup poll that same year reported that some 70 percent of the respondents said they thought the government should take responsibility for the unemployed, and the same number thought people on relief in their communities were getting as much as they should get.[65] (As late as 1934, the constitutions of fourteen states deprived relief recipients of the right to vote and hold office. In four cases, this was limited to inmates of poorhouses.)[66]

The depression ended with the beginning of World War II. The government Defense Plan Corporation built war plants and leased them to private manufacturers to make war supplies on contract. The War Manpower Commission recruited, trained, and assigned skilled labor to the plants. The Office of Price Administration set price ceilings on consumer goods so that rising prices would not cause hardships. When it was possible, war plants were established in areas of particular unemployment and poverty. The government alone bought more goods and services than had been produced in any of the years since the depression.

The war produced full employment, and in 1942, the old-age insurance and unemployment-compensation provisions of social security went into effect. When the war was over in 1945, the country appeared to forget the lessons of the Depression and it revived the old poor-law attitudes about those dependent on public assistance.

The "worthy" poor on old-age or unemployment insurance were not attacked, but those who needed ADC and general relief from the states were fair game. The theme was that people on relief were chiselers who were costing citizens money when they really could go out to work.

Relief "Chiselers"

The *Saturday Evening Post,* a popular mass-circulation magazine, ran numerous articles about relief chiselers. One in 1949 gave lurid examples of welfare recipients spending money on maids, radios, television sets, cars and jewelry, and charged, "One reason given for Detroit's high ratio of relief recipients is that, because the big industrial plants there attract so many workers, a great many come who are unstable, fringe-type workers who are frequently laid off for inefficiency. Relief, which embodies no work, appears more attractive to some of them than working. And the State Senate Committee has described Detroit as a 'soft touch' for welfare chiselers because of the Welfare Department's lenient attitude."[1]

5
POSTWAR RELIEF "CHISELERS"

A year later, the *Post* ran a story by a New York City domestic relations court judge who told tales of men and women who deserted their families and had children out of wedlock to get welfare. The headline declared: "Want $3680 a year, tax free? You are required only to have no self-respect and never get a job. Buy all the liquor you like. Desert your wife to take a mistress—and the Welfare Department may raise your income so you can afford both." The author declared, "No man, to put it bluntly, should get anything unless he works for it."[2]

Defenders of the program wrote articles as well. *Nation's Business,* in 1950, ran a story which pointed out, "A year or so ago there was a great to-do in New York City when it was found that a woman wearing a mink coat had been collecting a relief allowance. Ultimately it transpired that the coat was a relic of long ago better days, good for nothing but warmth and not much good for that. It was so worn and shaggy that it could not have brought $10 in the open market."[3]

The author declared, "Except in a few large cities, a recent rash of exposés of 'scandals' in relief administration in many communities similarly have fizzed out. True, some chiselers have been kicked off the rolls; some instances of mismanagement have been uncovered. But altogether the smoke of surveys and investigations in most places has revealed little fire, and citizens and the press have settled down into quiet acceptance of the fact that the majority of recipients of relief payments are in real need of what they get."

That last judgment was not to be fulfilled. "Relief chiselers" remained a popular topic for editors, public officials, and businessmen throughout the 1950's and after.

General assistance, which was paid by many of the states to people not eligible for the federal categorical programs, was always lower than aid to the aged, blind, or dependent children. It was assumed that recipients of general assistance were employable.

Truman Calls for Federal General Relief

In 1949, during a period of increasing unemployment, President Harry Truman called for federal aid for general relief. The government would pay $50 a month for the first two persons and up to $20 a month for each additional individual, $140 for a family of four. However, Congress was opposed to federal relief for the unemployed, and the proposal was rejected.

In 1950, about one person in thirty was dependent on public assistance at a cost of more than $2 billion a year, about 1 percent of the national personal income.

U.S. News and World Report, sought to explain in the midfifties "Why 5,500,000 Americans Get Relief Money." It said that sons and daughters no longer cared for their parents, that relatives did not care for children whose fathers had left or died, and that people were not "embarrassed" or "disgraced" by taking welfare aid; in fact, old people viewed pensions as their "right."[4]

Although most of the criticism about relief chiselers appeared to focus on people who could work but did not want to, in fact, the number of employables on the relief rolls was negligible. The greatest increase in relief occurred in the category that had been included in the social security law as an afterthought: aid to dependent children.

Economic Dislocation

The end of the war brought economic dislocation. War plants were shut down, large numbers of soldiers returned to look for work, the day-care centers that had been set up by the government were shut down and women were forced to leave their jobs. As soldiers returned, there was an increase in marriages and births and also a rise in divorces. Then in 1950 came a recession. The ADC caseload shot up. As more widows and their children became eligible for social-security survivors insurance, ADC became a refuge for those who were unwed, divorced, or deserted. Though still a minority, increasing numbers were black.

Suitable Home Rules

More than half the states responded by using "suitable home" rules to deny aid to black and unwed mothers and to women whose behavior did not coincide with community mores. A mother, for example, might have to sign an affidavit that said, "I do hereby promise and agree that until such time as the following agreement is rescinded, I will not have any male callers coming to my home nor meeting me elsewhere under improper conditions. I also agree to raise my children to the best of my ability and will not knowingly contribute or be a contributing factor to their being shamed by my conduct. I understand that should I violate this agreement, the children will be taken from me."[5]

Children in such "unsuitable homes" were rarely removed and sent to institutions or foster homes as might happen in cases where actual neglect existed under the meaning of the law that applied to people not on welfare. It was more common that the family would be given the lower state general-assistance grant or cut off from aid entirely.

In the decade of the 1950's, twenty-three states adopted suitable home rules. The Michigan law declared, "When the Bureau makes a positive determination that an ADC recipient is cohabiting with a person to whom he or she is not legally married, the home must be considered unsuitable."[6]

The Mississippi statute of 1958 said, "If promiscuity or the existence of a casual relationship is known to the county department at any time, the home shall be considered unsuitable, and the grant cancelled."[7]

The Florida law of 1959 provided that the home was unsuitable if there was "failure of the parent or relative to provide a stable moral environment for the child by engaging in promiscuous conduct either in or outside the home, by having an illegitimate child after receiving an assistance payment from the department or by otherwise failing to demonstrate the intent to establish a stable home."[8]

In some cases, the ruling was used against people who could not afford divorce and simply lived together in common-law marriages. One case involved a couple taking care of their grandchildren. They had lived together for many years, but could not afford the legal fees needed to end their previous marriages.

In the first year of its law, Florida officials declared some seven thousand homes with over thirty thousand children unsuitable. About three thousand mothers were asked to give their children up to relatives.

The law provided that applicants for aid would be informed that if their homes failed to meet the new suitable-home standards, the department would seek to have their children removed—as long as the ADC application was pending. Some two thousand reacted by withdrawing from the ADC program. One mother declared, "People give away puppies and kittens, but they don't give away their children."

A national study in 1961 showed that blacks were nearly twice as likely as whites to lose their grants because of "unsuitable home" charges.[9]

Unwed Mothers Denied Aid

Some states also chose to deny aid to families of unwed mothers. A study in Mississippi showed that births out of wedlock *rose* after the measure was instituted.[10] Criticis of the law pointed out that, without aid from the government, the recipients were forced to depend on others, including boyfriends, for their support. A woman might be forced to sleep with a man in order to get food for her children.

The federal government took no action during the 1950's to prevent these state actions although the social security law required aid for all those in need and said nothing about the children's birth status or their mothers' sex lives.

Then, in the summer of 1960, Louisiana enacted a suitable-home law and cut nearly thirty thousand people off the welfare rolls on the grounds that the mothers had given birth to out-of-wedlock children after going on relief. The state said they could receive aid again if the mothers could prove that they had ceased their "illicit relationships." The law was made retroactive and included women who had had their babies years ago.

It was an election year, in the last months of the Eisenhower Administration, and federal officials did not want to anger the South. The government delayed hearings until November, after the election. The Social Security Commissioner ruled finally that Louisiana's action was permissible since there was no rule against suitable-home requirements. However, a few days before the new Democratic Administration was to take over, Secretary of Health, Education and Welfare (HEW) Arthur Flemming announced that states could not deny aid on the basis of unsuitable homes while the children were still living there. They would have to make other arrangements to meet the children's needs.[11]

The ruling, however, did not solve the problem. States proceeded to discourage applications from unwed mothers by threatening to bring neglect proceedings against them and take away their children. In 1962, the Chicago Public Aid Commission voted to report cases of children born to unwed ADC mothers to the state's attorneys for possible prosecution under adultery or fornication laws and to take the children away from those "unsuitable" homes. HEW informed the commission that this would violate the federal law, and the order was not put into effect.[12] Nevertheless, in 1966, officials of Monmouth County, New Jersey, announced that, "unmarried persons who seek welfare assistance will face possible prosecution on adultery or fornication charges." A case later went to court on these charges, and the law was ruled unconstitutional.[13]

In 1967, the state attorney for Prince Georges County, Maryland, decided to make an example of some unwed ADC mothers. When three women came to get his signature on a routine form showing that they had attempted to locate the fathers of their children, he charged them with neglect.

The court ruled that they could not be charged with neglect until it was demonstrated that their children actually were neglected. The state attorney then dropped those charges and began proceedings to prove that the children were neglected under a Maryland statute which says that a child "living in a home which fails to prove a stable moral environment" is neglected. The judge in that case ruled the children neglected, declaring that having babies out of wedlock reflected weakness in the women's character. However, he did not order the children taken away.[14]

Rules Against Providing Birth Control

Welfare departments seemed a lot more interested in punishing women for bearing children out of wedlock than in providing them with information and materials for contraception. The caseworkers assigned to help people with their problems did not seem to think birth control a fit subject to bring up, and even if a poor and uneducated woman knew about contraception, the rules about suitable homes might prevent her from admitting that she had a sex life. Many states specifically prohibited caseworkers from providing contraceptive information.

The New York City Welfare Department in 1958 issued a

memorandum which said, "The dissemination of birth control information or therapy for non-medical reasons by staff of the Department or panel physicians is not a function of the Department of Welfare and is prohibited."[15]

That same year the Detroit Public Welfare Commission said that caseworkers could not suggest contraception, although "when a recipient raises the question first," they could be referred to a clergyman or private physician. "No Department of Public Welfare employee may give information about, or refer a welfare family to, any health clinic administered by the Detroit League for Planned Parenthood, Inc."[16] Thus, women on welfare were advised to go to private doctors, which they could not afford, and were expressly denied information about the free Planned Parenthood clinics.

In 1962, when the welfare rolls began to climb sharply, only half a dozen states provided payments for birth control, and a few more offered some birth control services themselves.

The Sacramento, California, Welfare Department issued an order to caseworkers that year which said; "If a client asks for birth control information, such a client is referred to a doctor or religious counselor. If the doctor sends Welfare his bill, Welfare does not pay it. We never refer to the subject unless the client mentions it specifically."[17]

A Buffalo caseworker told his supervisor that one of his clients was a woman with eight children who might like to know about birth control. He was told, "That's not part of your job."[18]

When Arnold H. Maremont, chairman of the Illinois Public Aid Commission, decided in 1962 to provide birth control devices for ADC mothers, he was attacked by the Vicar-General of the Roman Catholic Archdiocese who said that he was interfering with the rights of individuals and would "foster irresponsibility and a breakdown of public morals."[19]

Maremont believed, "The most important element in public aid is to help these people control the births of children they don't want." The Protestant Illinois Council of Churches supported his policy.

However, Chicago is the country's largest Roman Catholic Archdiocese. Mayor Richard Daley, also a Catholic, announced his opposition to the program. The Republican candidate for mayor filed suit for an injunction to stop the plan, saying it "subsidized immorality with the taxpayer's money." The Democratic attorney general of the state, whose office was supposed to defend Maremont, filed a brief in support of the suit. He said the birth control program would make the state "an accessory to sexual promiscuity and prostitution," and ordered the state treasurer and auditor not to pay any bills to doctors or druggists who provided services for the program.

Maremont aroused more opposition by declaring that he would seek authority to pay for divorces for relief recipients. The members of the Public Aid Commission denounced the proposal. The proposal's supporters wondered how women whose husbands had left them were ever supposed to be able to remarry and have "legitimate" children under "moral" conditions if they could not get divorced.

Democrats in the state legislature proposed a bill to prohibit spending public funds for birth control devices. A judge issued an injunction against the program. Finally, a compromise was reached that restricted birth control to married women living with their husbands, thereby excluding 80 percent of the women on ADC. The legislature also voted to reduce welfare payments. Some large families had allowances cut almost in half. And Maremont was removed from office.

Substitute Father Rules

Another restriction on recipients' personal lives came in the form of the "substitute father" or "man in the house" rules. In some states, if a woman had a boyfriend, a lover, or even a male acquaintance she saw outside the home, the welfare agency ruled that her child was not "deprived of parental support," and aid was cut off.

In 1950, South Carolina established a policy that said children would not be considered "deprived" if there was "any man with whom the mother had a common law relationship." It added, "Though not staying in the home regularly," if he "visits frequently for the purpose of living with the applicant, the two shall be considered as living in common law relationship. Where there is a pattern of the mother having a series of relationships, resulting in children or not, this is considered the same as if she has a continuous common law relationship with the same man."[20]

It was up to the mother to prove that a sexual relationship did not exist. Although this definition of common law marriage was not the same one that applied to people not receiving welfare benefits, the federal government did not rule the measure illegal. There was no general assistance in the state for families cut off ADC.

Two years later, Georgia adopted a similar regulation that referred to substitute fathers "in or around the home." The federal government did not object. There was no general-assistance program in the state.

Michigan had a like ruling. It called the substitute father the "male boarder." One study of the operation of the rule found that such little evidence was required to prove the man's existence that it referred to him as the "phantom father."[21] This was not the first time Michigan had enforced such "man in the house" rules for women receiving public aid. At the time of the mothers' pensions, Michigan and Massachusetts said that no male boarder, other than the woman's brother or father, could live in the house.[22]

In Alabama, which also passed a substitute-father rule, one woman with four children was cut off ADC with an explanation from the welfare department that they had learned she was "going with" a man.[23]

Welfare-rights attorney Edward Sparer noted, "The Georgia manual tells the mother how to prove the man is not a substitute father. Prove it by collecting affidavits from people who should know. The clergyman, the clergyman should know; get an affidavit from him. Get an affidavit from your neighbors. Get an affidavit from your relatives. They include among the list the groceryman, he should know."[24]

Rules on Dating

Sparer added, "Louisiana has a little section on dating. When is dating allowed by a mother on ADC? When is it not allowed? Dating is allowed by a mother on ADC when:

"a) There is no intimate relationship between her and the man, otherwise he is a substitute father,

"b) There is no legal impediment to a marriage, that is,

there's no existing marriage on her part; there is no existing marriage on his part; thus the relationship can flower into a marriage. Then she'll be off ADC. Since she's got a husband."

In Washington, D.C., the welfare agency looked to see if the man had a fatherly interest in the children. "Does he take the children to the movies?" "Has he been interested in their education? Has he helped the mother pick up her surplus food from the depot?" Children on welfare were to have limited contact with adult males.

Surprise Visits

The "man in the house" rules were enforced through surprise investigations often conducted late at night or early in the morning. One report tells of a complaint by a woman against a Chicago investigator who arrived while she was tak- a bath. "He pushed past her nine year old daughter who answered the door, looked in the bedroom and the bathroom searching for a man or evidence of male company. He had no warrant. He did find a suit in a closet belonging to the mother's boyfriend, who visited on weekends, and about whom the department had been fully informed. Nevertheless, assistance was discontinued on the assumption a man was living full time with the family and that they could look to him for support — support which the part-time boyfriend could not provide."[25]

The report said the mother and daughter appeared "destitute and malnourished" and frightened when they were interviewed.

In another case, an investigator climbed into a tree at two o'clock in the morning to look into the window of a welfare family's apartment to see if a man was there.[26]

In a third, a family was cut off because a man was seen entering a building with three apartments, one of which was inhabited by the family on welfare, although the investigator had no way of knowing whom the man was visiting.[27]

In another instance, assistance was ended when investigators said that a shirt they had found did not belong to the woman's teen-age son as she and the boy asserted.[28]

In another case, the family of a mother and nine children were in danger of being cut off welfare because the divorced father was discovered visiting "too frequently." The Washington, D.C. welfare code says that for a family to maintain eligibility, one parent "must be continually absent from the home and must have dissociated himself from all normal family relationship." The children of the divorce are thus prevented from seeing their father "too often."[29]

In California, Sparer said a program of midnight raids was carried out against recipients "who were selected en masse without regard of any implication of guilt in terms of association with a man, to see whether or not they would find at 6 o'clock Sunday morning, a man in the home."

The instructions were "to look in the bedroom, look in the closets, look behind the shower curtain, look in the drawers for articles of clothing, he was even to lift the blankets off the children and count kids, make sure all the kids who were reported to be on the ADC grant were really there."[30]

The welfare agency countered that the caseworkers had to first request permission to enter the homes and that the recipients could refuse to admit them. However, if a woman refused to let investigators enter and search her apartment, aid could be cut off for "refusal to cooperate."

Critics charged that women could hardly develop the kinds of relationships that lead to marriage when even dating a man resulted in the end of welfare payments.

In some cases, investigations were held when the welfare agency suspected that a jobless or low-paid father had deserted his family in order to allow them to be eligible for welfare and that he secretly visited at night. Fathers admitted that this was the only way to keep their families from destitution. Many welfare departments required women to file criminal charges of desertion and nonsupport against their husbands before they could receive aid.

Cheap Labor

Although the ADC program was instituted with the idea that women ought to have the option to stay home to take care of their children, states quickly eliminated that notion when it came to certain groups, especially blacks and other minorities. Often, they were cut off welfare during the months that farmers wanted them to work in the fields.

In the late 1930's, a welfare supervisor in the South reported, "The number of Negro cases is few due to the unanimous feeling on the part of the staff and board that there are more work opportunities for Negro women and to their intense desire not to interfere with local labor conditions." She said most whites believed that black women should work in the fields or as domestics rather than get welfare.[31]

In 1943, Louisiana adopted an "employable mother" rule denying aid to all women with children over six if the women were needed in the cotton fields. Still, a Louisiana civic organization in 1954 complained that, "public assistance results in reducing the unskilled labor supply in employment where women and children form a principal part of the labor supply."[32]

A Georgia ruling in 1952 refused aid to mothers with children under twelve if work was available in the area. The women could not get supplemental grants even if their wages turned out to be less than their welfare aid. Arkansas adopted a similar requirement a year later.[33]

New Jersey applicants sometimes were refused aid if caseworkers believed that they should get jobs. A hearing in Illinois by the U.S. Civil Rights Commission in 1966 revealed that people on relief were required to do farm work at 50 cents an hour. In May, the welfare department would send letters to recipients telling them their grants would be cut because seasonal work was available.[34]

One of the results of the employable-mother policies was to guarantee a cheap labor supply for the community. In some cases, even applicants for federal surplus foods were required to show notes from their employers attesting to the fact that they had jobs.

Discrimination

Sometimes, discrimination against blacks was more direct. Georgia, in the late 1930's, had a quota system that set a fixed ratio of black and white recipients. The quotas were stopped as a result of federal disapproval, but blacks still continued to be underrepresented on relief rolls there and elsewhere.

Nation's Business in 1950 cited one comment:

"The right of Negro ex-sharecroppers to the relief is unquestioned, but old-age grants plus an additional average of $58 a month where a household has children whose father is absent or disabled have so raised incomes that they are flocking to the towns. Recently the Avoyelles

Parish (Louisiana) police jury formally demanded that state authorities halt the movement."[35]

In some big cities, such as Chicago, people got on and off welfare according to whether they supported local political bosses. Sometimes "helpers" went into the voting booths with them to make sure they voted correctly. During voter registration drives in Mississippi in the early 1960's, the state cut blacks off welfare in reprisal for attempting to vote at all.

Sometimes, blacks and whites on relief got different payments, especially in small cities and rural areas. A study in 1961 showed that towns of under half a million, the median ADC payment to blacks was $24.40 a month compared to $30.40 for whites. In farm areas, the payments were $11.70 and $21.90. Sometimes, states gave blacks less money on the ground they could not handle cash wisely.[36]

The Newburgh Case

Shortly after Louisiana cut thousands off the relief rolls for illegitimacy, there was another cause célèbre, this one in the North. The city of Newburgh, a town of some thirty-one thousand on the Hudson River, sixty miles north of New York City, established a "reform" program based on the notion that people on welfare were either chiselers who could get jobs if they wanted to or newcomers who had moved to the city to go on relief. Neither charge turned out to be true.

In 1961, Newburgh was in economic trouble. Much of its employment was dependent on low-wage industries like the needle trades and seasonal farm work. Twice as many people were collecting unemployment insurance as were on welfare. In ten years, the white population had gone down, and the black population had increased.

City Manager Joseph Mitchell's first attempt, backed by the City Council, to reform welfare was to cut ADC checks and general relief to pay for snow removal in the winter. The State Department of Social Welfare told him he could not do this. Later, Mitchell told a civic club that welfare was attracting "the dregs of humanity into this city" in a "never ending pilgrimage from North Carolina."[37]

In the spring, letters went out to welfare recipients, including the aged, the blind, and the disabled, informing them that their next checks could be picked up at the police station.

When the claimants arrived, they were questioned in a small back room. If there were any "chiselers" among them, none was discovered.

The next move was the announcement of a program which included:

- vouchers instead of cash for food, clothing, and rent;
- assignment of able-bodied males to the chief of building for forty-hour work assignments;
- denial of relief to able-bodied recipients who refused any kind of private job;
- denial of relief to unwed mothers who had additional children;
- no family grants higher than the take-home pay of the lowest-paid city employee with the same-size family;
- requirement of proof by newcomers that they had concrete job offers before coming to the city; newcomers with proof would get two weeks of relief, others would get one;
- limit of aid to three months a year except for the aged, blind, and disabled;
- placement of children in foster care if home environment of AFDC* cases was not satisfactory.[38]

The reaction around the country was largely favorable. The Gallup Poll found that the action was supported by a majority of the population.[39] *Life* magazine ran an editorial saying, "Newburgh has shown real guts in flatly announcing that if Federal reimbursements are withheld as 'reprisal,' it will pay its own bills and go it alone."[40]

The *Saturday Evening Post* declared, "Surely a community should have some defense against Bankruptcy by Bastardy."[41] Conservative leader Barry Goldwater sent Mitchell a letter commending his actions.

However, a state supreme court judge granted the injunction against implementing the plan sought by the state attorney general, and state welfare officials began an investigation into conditions in Newburgh.

They discovered that the majority of relief recipients were white, not black; that in the past two years, the city had spent some $1,400 out of a budget of over $600,000 on newcomers; and that less than a fifth of the spending went for AFDC and home relief.

*In 1950 legislation, ADC became AFDC—Aid to Families with Dependent Children.

When the time came to put the "able-bodied chiselers" to work, there was another surprise. Television cameras and newspaper reporters stationed at City Hall informed the nation that one "able-bodied" man had been found, a one-eyed apprentice steelworker who had been laid off months before, who was later a patient in a mental hospital and who then had lost an opportunity for a job, because he had to care for his five children when his wife went to the hospital with pneumonia. The man was white and had been born and raised in Newburgh.[42]

In addition, New York's social welfare law already required employable persons to register with the local state employment service and to accept reasonable job offers, and it also already permitted local welfare districts to set up municipal work-relief projects and require home-relief recipients to participate in them.

Mitchell backed down on his plan after the state injunction, but he continued to defend it in speeches around the country. He told the Economic Club of Detroit, "We challenged the right of social parasites to breed illegitimate children at the taxpayer's expense. We challenged the right of moral chiselers and loafers to squat on the relief rolls forever. We challenged the right of cheaters to make more on relief than when working."[43]

After Mitchell left his job as city manager of Newburgh, he went to work for the segregationist Citizens Councils of America.

In 1961, the year of the Newburgh "reforms," New York State passed the Welfare Abuses Act which said no aid could be given to those who came to the state for the purpose of claiming welfare. The assumption was that anyone who came without an adequate plan of support came for the purpose of getting public assistance. Emergency aid would be given only to those who agreed to leave the state. Thousands of families were subsequently denied aid and given bus tickets back home.

Attacks on Recipients

Attacks on the "unworthy" continued, and cities and states launched investigations and cut relief allowances. Newspapers and magazines ran stories about people on relief who were drug addicts, had illegitimate children or had secret jobs. A Gallup poll showed that over 75 percent of Americans favored stricter relief rules. The cost of welfare had gone from $6 billion in 1940 to over $33 billion in 1961.

Look magazine ran an article entitled, "Welfare: Has it Become a National Scandal?" and reported, "In Denver, in one two-month period, 26 percent of relief checks were cashed in bars," and, "In North Dakota, one sixteen-member Indian family cost the Government $11,684 in welfare payments in a single year."[44]

The *U.S. News and World Report* wrote, "Women, and sometimes men, are said to have refused to accept jobs because they said they could make more money on relief."[45] Another story was headlined, "Where relief grows and jobs go begging." It said that California welfare agencies were trying to get men off relief and into jobs as farm workers where there was a labor shortage as a result of the end of the *bracero* program that had allowed Mexicans into the country during planting and harvesting seasons.[46]

It reported that Los Angeles had put a "no work, no dole" plan into effect with the aim of filling some of the seven thousand jobs that had been done by the low-paid *braceros* in the past. Wages would be raised to $1.25 an hour. Some 680 recipients were referred to state agencies for farm jobs. Of these, 222 were accepted for job referral, and 34 were hired by farmers.

Nation's Business ran a story called, "Welfare Frauds Exposed," about a town in New Mexico. The local newspaper had started printing the names of the county's welfare recipients, and the story said some people had discovered that their domestics and yard workers were getting aid. A local judge was quoted as saying, "Many people on welfare could be earning a good living but won't."[47]

A bank president in the town declared, "Unless a person is incapacitated physically or mentally, there are jobs for them in this county. Farmers are looking for laborers and having trouble finding them. There's a shortage of people who'll do yard work." Another banker asserted, "It's difficult to get ranch and farm workers because of the welfare program. We can pay 80 cents to $1.25 an hour, but some people on welfare are getting what amounts to more than a dollar an hour for just sitting."

The *Reader's Digest* ran a story that charged that "the Federally subsidized ADC relief rolls are contributing to debauchery and fostering a demoralizing dependency on government handouts."[48]

A *Life* story called, "The Deceit, Corruption and Scars of Relief," reported, "One woman, whose jobless husband was unable to support their children, told a lawyer in Hazard that she wanted a divorce 'so the children we have from now on will get relief. That's about the only way poor folks can afford to have younguns.' "[49]

It cited political corruption as well: "An unemployed worker with the right connections and proper voting record can become 'disabled' enough to qualify for monthly checks. An erring voter, on the other hand, may find himself suddenly pronounced physically fit again and dropped from the rolls."

Efforts to Find Ineligibles

In 1962, Senator Robert Byrd of West Virginia headed an investigation of welfare fraud in the District of Columbia and then charged that 60 percent of the ADC cases in the study were ineligible. However, of the 133 ineligibles he found, all but 13 were either women who had been listed as "employable" and expected to make their own child-care arrangements so they could look for work; women who had relationships with men; women who had refused to submit to midnight visits and the like.[50]

The states and the federal government conducted their own investigations. In 1959, the California Department of Social Welfare reported that a study of the caseload revealed a $1\frac{1}{2}$ percent rate of ineligibility.[51]

A study in Chicago in 1960 turned up the fact that 90 percent of the ADC recipients had lived in the state for five years or more. Those from out of state had come to take jobs, join their husbands, or be with relatives. Racial discrimination in employment was found to be one of the most serious causes of their need for welfare aid. Ineligibility or the suspicion of ineligibility was discovered in under 2 percent of the cases.[52]

A national survey by the Department of Health, Education and Welfare showed in 1963 that 5.4 percent of the ADC families were not eligible; the number included families that had gotten overpayments because of administrative errors.[53]

Sometimes, studies found irregularities on the part of the welfare administration. In Chicago, investigators found that people who were eligible for relief had been denied aid and that the level of aid was far below the reasonable-subsistence standard required by state law.[54] A state legislative commission in New York reported in 1962 "some evidence that closings are arbitrary."[55] Payments were not very high anywhere. Average *monthly* grants were $21.13 per person in 1950 and $30.06 in 1960. The average earnings of the "working class" in those years (blue collar and nonsupervisory sales and office workers) were $53 and $81 *a week.*

During this period, there were numerous changes made in the federal social security law.

Changes in the Law

In 1950, coverage for social security was extended to many self-employed persons and to some regularly employed domestics and farm workers, so that 80 percent of the jobs in paid employment were covered. Benefits and tax rates were increased, and the law added a category of Aid to the Permanently and Totally Disabled.

It also enacted what was called NOLEO: Notice to Law Enforcement Officials. That required notice to local law enforcement agencies when an applicant sought aid because of the desertion of a child's parent. The object was to prosecute the fathers and require them to make support payments.

Finally, the law extended aid to the "caretaker" of the children getting ADC. Prior to this, budgets did not include the cost of supporting the mother. The program now was called AFDC—Aid to Families with Dependent Children.

In 1951, Congress passed an amendment that would allow disclosure of the names of people on welfare if the lists were not used for political or commercial purposes. About half the states passed laws opening the rolls to public inspection.

In 1954, social security benefits were extended to cover 90 percent of workers, including part-time domestic and farm workers and groups of state and local government employees.

In 1956, an amendment required state welfare agencies to provide social services to AFDC families.

In 1961, Congress passed a law making AFDC funds available to families with unemployed fathers. The new program was called AFDC-UP: Aid to Families with Dependent Children — Unemployed Parent. (Later the acronym was changed to AFDC-UF.) However, the program was optional, and only about half the states ever put it into effect.

In 1962, Congress agreed to pay 75 percent of the cost of social service programs. The argument was that the rolls would go down as "rehabilitation" helped families become self-supporting.

Work Incentives

The law also allowed old-age assistance recipients to keep part of their earnings: $10 a month plus half the rest up to $50. The blind were allowed to keep $85 a month plus half the rest. Recipients of AFDC could deduct working expenses and certain amounts put aside for their children's future specific needs. (The latter never amounted to very much.) Aside from that, any money earned was deducted from the welfare check, a virtual 100 percent tax that discouraged many people from seeking the part-time or low-paid employment they might be able to find.

In 1964, the Food Stamp Act allowed local welfare departments to choose between selling food stamps, which were generally worth about a third more in the stores than the purchase price, or to continue to distribute federal surplus commodities.

In 1965, states were allowed to exempt up to $150 a month earned by dependent children under eighteen, with a $50 limit per month per child. Allowable earnings for the aged and the permanently and totally disabled were set at $20 a month, plus half the next $60.

Congress also established the Medicaid program which provided government payments for doctor and hospital care and was financed by a .6 percent tax added to social security payments. Many states set eligibility levels substantially above the welfare level on the assumption that even people with higher incomes could be "medically poor."

By 1972, more than 15 million people were on the public assistance rolls, almost twice the 8 million who were on relief in the depths of the Depression. And unlike 1940, when aid was largely for the workers and their families who were victims of the sudden massive unemployment, about 10 million of the recipients in 1972 were mothers and children with no adequate source of support. A million were unemployed or disabled fathers and their families.

Another 2 million were people on old-age assistance (many of them people with inadequate social security payments), over a million got aid to the permanently and totally disabled and some eighty thousand received aid to the blind. An added million, mostly families with unemployed or low-paid fathers, were aided by some state and local general-assistance programs.

Over 7 percent of the population was on relief—one out of every fourteen people.

Why the increase? And who are the new relief recipients?

The figures are distorted to begin with, for they do not count the 28 million people who receive social security retirement and survivors benefits—one out of every eight people in the country. And they do not count the more than 6 million who at one time or another in the year collect unemployment insurance benefits. These programs are related to work, although employers, not workers, are taxed for the unemployment compensation program, and they do not count as "relief" in the mind of the public.

6

RISING ROLLS
AND REACTION

Why the Increase?

But still, why the increase in public assistance, the program that was supposed to "wither away" as the work-related programs took hold?

One attempt to explain it was to point to the migration of blacks from the South, some 4 million since the war, who had come North seeking better jobs. They had been pushed out of the South by the mechanization of agriculture and by the discrimination and lack of opportunity they found in southern cities. However, northern cities did not prove very different, and thousands of families ended up on welfare, often after fathers deserted in despair, sometimes leaving deliberately in order to make their families eligible for AFDC.

Although critics later charged that blacks had come north only to go on welfare, the statistics showed that most of them lived in the north for several years before they sought aid.[1] The New York City welfare commissioner said that little more than 2 percent of the recipients there had been in the city less than a year.[2]

However, being in the North did make a difference. Policies generally were more liberal, and a higher percentage of applications were accepted. In 1968, in Cleveland, 80 percent of those who applied were put on the rolls compared to 30 percent in Houston. At that time, only a third of the 27 million poor were getting any public assistance, some because of restrictions of the law that denied aid to families with able-bodied fathers, but others because of discriminatory state policies. And even that was an increase from 1960 when only a fifth of the poor got any government aid.

Federal programs were another cause of increased welfare rolls. When urban renewal pushed poor people out of apartments they could afford, they were forced to turn to welfare to supplement their meager incomes so they could pay the higher rents. Sometimes, people who were contacted by social workers when they were ordered to move, learned for the first time that they were, even then, eligible for welfare aid.

In the same way, when medicaid went into effect in 1966, hospitals referred poor patients to welfare so that they would be assured of collecting their bills from the government.

The surge of civil rights activity in the beginning of the 1960's and the antipoverty programs that began in 1965 were another cause of the rising welfare rolls. People began to demand their entitlements, and antipoverty organizers helped people who had been arbitrarily turned down by welfare agencies or who had not been given their proper grants.

Sometimes welfare recipients received federal antipoverty funds to set up day-care centers or adult education programs or to help other recipients with their problems. As recipients got organized, they increased their demands on welfare agencies, and they informed people in their communities about their right to public assistance. New York Governor Nelson Rockefeller said in 1969 that the reason was that "the state never believed that all the people who are eligible for programs would learn about their eligibility and take advantage of it. In short, the original cost estimates," he said, "were shattered by many grass-roots public information efforts, including that of the anti-poverty program."[3]

To Maintain Social Order

Another theory, expounded by social-work professors Frances Fox Piven and Richard Cloward in a book called *Regulating the Poor,* points to historical evidence that relief has been increased in periods of civil disorder produced by mass unemployment and that it has been cut when political stability is restored. The purpose of relief, they said, has been to maintain order; when order is assured, restrictive policies are put into effect to force people back to work at low wages. They wrote that "for the poor man, the specter of ending up on 'the welfare' or in 'the poorhouse' makes any job at any wage a preferable alternative."[4]

Piven and Cloward noted that the great migration of the poor to the North had occurred in the 1950's, a period of urban unemployment, breakup of families, and rising living costs, but that relief rolls did not begin to rise sharply until the 1960's, a time of racial turmoil and protest, when increasing numbers of blacks registered to vote, and a time of "governmental programs designed to moderate widespread political unrest among the black poor."

They said too that "relief practices are always determined by the conditions of work among the lower classes. Relief payments are not likely to rise above the lowest wages, and will almost invariably be much lower. Nor are relief recipients likely to be treated well as long as there are workers who are so poorly paid that they must be coerced into staying at their jobs by the spectacle of degraded paupers."[5]

They said that they opposed "work-enforcing reforms," asserting that such reforms in the past have led to the eventual expulsion of large numbers from the welfare rolls, "leaving them to fend for themselves in a labor market where there was too little work and thus subjecting them once again to severe economic exploitation." For example, they pointed out that, "as the Depression wore on, direct relief was replaced by work relief, then work relief was abolished, and millions of the poor were rapidly shunted into a labor market where there was insufficient work."[6]

Those who were allowed to stay on the rolls, the aged, blind, and dependent children eligible under the "categorical" programs, "were once again subject to the punitive and degrading treatment which has been used to buttress the work ethos since the inception of relief several centuries ago."[7]

In spite of the sharp increase in AFDC rolls, critics charged that even in the 1960's, only half the people eligible for collecting public assistance were actually receiving it.

Economic conditions had increased the roster of eligibles. The wages of unskilled workers did not keep pace with the rising living costs that resulted from inflation. Automation caused many unskilled jobs to disappear altogether. With economic recession, the untrained, the minorities, and women were the first to be fired. And, though the states were slow to recognize the effects of inflation, they did periodically raise the amount of money designated as the "need standard" and thus made increased numbers of people earning below that level eligible for aid.

The "Poverty Line"

The "poverty line" on which this need standard was generally based was a figure devised by the U.S. Labor Department. It is related to the cost of a temporary, low-cost food budget defined as the absolute minimum a family needs in a financial emergency. The food budget is multiplied by three on the assumption that food is one-third of the expense of a low-income family.

In 1972, a budget based on those standards was about $4,200 for a family of four. It meant eating beans, potatoes, flour, and cereal and rarely having meat, eggs, fruits, and vegetables. The Labor Department reported that only one in four of the people on such a budget had nutritional diets.

The establishment of a "poverty line" underlined the fact that not only the jobless were poor. In fact, a worker who earned even the federal minimum wage of $1.60 an hour ($1.30 for farm workers) received only $3,200 a year. There are some 25 million poor today, but 7 million (70 percent of them white) live in families where the fathers work full-time without earning enough to escape from poverty.[8] A third of New York City's jobs pay above the $1.60 minimum wage but less than $4,600, only slightly above the poverty line for a family of four.[9] In 1968, the average payment for an AFDC family of four in New York ($277 to $287) was more than the total cash earnings of a person who worked full-time at the minimum wage.[10] In that same year, there were 10 million jobs in the United States which paid *less* than the minimum wage.[11]

New York City has a supplemental assistance program. Workers earning below welfare levels can be brought up to what they would get on welfare. However, less than half the states use general assistance to supplement working households.[12] In the states without such programs and in the twenty-four states without AFDC-UF—the federal program for families with unemployed fathers—families can get welfare assistance only if the man in the house is absent or unemployable.

Why Men Desert

Some men leave for the same reason other men get divorced. Divorce costs money; desertion is the poor man's divorce. Others go because they have no sense of responsibility for their wives or children, a condition which is equally evident in other economic classes. Still others walk out because they cannot support their families and they know that while they remain, their wives and children cannot get welfare assistance.

Whatever the reasons, today the nature of the AFDC caseload has changed dramatically from the 1930's, when the majority were widows and almost all were white, to a situation where only 5 percent of the cases are the result of a husband's death and where while the largest number of recipients still is white, increasing numbers, some 46 percent, are black. In the central cities, the majority are blacks and other minorities: 80 percent in Detroit and 90 percent in New York.

During the Depression, the ADC caseload was less than half a million. It began to climb after World War II and by 1956 was more than 2 million. It had nearly doubled seven years later, went to 5 million in 1967, 6½ million in 1968 and 8½ million by the end of 1970. By 1972, it had reached nearly 11 million, a 75 percent increase over five years before.

Almost 10 percent of the nation's children were supported by welfare in 1972. In Boston, one of five persons received some kind of public assistance in 1971. In New York and San Francisco, the figures were one in seven; in Los Angeles, one in eight.

More than two out of five cases are the result of divorce, separation, or desertion of the husband. In more than one in four, the father was not married to the mother of the children. In over a tenth of the cases, the father is ill or disabled. Only 5 percent of the cases, with aid provided only in half the states, include a father who is unemployed or not working full-time.

The Average AFDC Family

The average AFDC family consists of a mother and three children. The average time on the rolls is less than two years. About 14 percent of the mothers work full-time but do not earn enough to support their families. Those who want to work are handicapped by their education (less than three out of five have gone past the eighth grade), by the lack of child-care facilities (about 60 percent have children under six), and by job discrimination and the lower wages they earn as women and as blacks or other minorities.

The amount of money that recipients of public welfare receive is hardly calculated to raise them out of poverty. The average payments for a family of four in July, 1972 ranged from $54 in Mississippi to $297 in New York. In all but four states, the payments were below the poverty level. The average payment was $189. (Blue-collar and nonsupervisory white-collar workers earn an average of $137 *a week*.)

The states make payments according to a "standard of need" which they establish based on budgets for food, clothing, rent, and other essentials. However, thirty-eight states pay less than their own standards. Most pay only a fixed percentage of "need," from 35 percent in Alabama to 90 percent in New York, or else they set a maximum grant regardless of family size.

The "needs" of AFDC recipients are generally figured out to be less than the needs in the "adult" categories. For example, one state's food budget allowed $25.50 a month for AFDC mothers but $39 a month for the aged. Grants also vary with categories. The aged, the blind, and the disabled get more than mothers and children. Unemployed fathers and their families on state and local general assistance get less.

The Elderly Poor

The Senate Committee on Aging reported in 1971 that over a quarter of the people over sixty-five live in poverty — nearly 5 million. They were the victims of economic conditions over which they had no control. They could not earn a living by working, since retirement at age sixty-five generally is mandatory in industry and government, and companies show a disinclination to hire older workers even at forty and forty-five. Inflation had destroyed the value of their savings or pensions, if they had any. The work ethic had little to do with their ability to avoid poverty in their old age.

Although social security was established to solve the problem of the needy aged, minimum monthly payments are $84.50 a month, with averages of $161 for individuals and $270 for couples. Until the recent increases, some 40 percent of those who received social security retirement or survivors benefits lived in poverty. (The 1972 poverty line was $158 a month for a single person and $200 for a couple.)

The social security program is based on a payroll tax of 5.85 percent each paid by the worker and the employer. Self-employed people pay 8 percent. A worker is eligible after paying into the fund for ten years when he or she reaches sixty-two. Wives, children, and dependent husbands also are eligible when the worker retires or dies.

In addition, workers under seventy-two get reduced payments if they earn over $2,100; $1 in benefits is deducted for each $2 earned above that. However, this applies to wages, not to incomes from pensions, interest on bank accounts, or dividends from stocks and bonds.

Social security now covers about 90 percent of the workers in the country. It excludes federal and railroad workers who have their own system.

One in ten of the 20 million people sixty-five and over get old-age welfare assistance. Forty percent of those on welfare do not get social security.

Legislation signed by President Nixon a week before the Presidential election in 1972 abolished the federal-state matching program for aid to the aged, the blind, and the disabled as of January 1, 1974, and replaced it with a minimum federal guarantee of $130 a month for an individual and $195 for a couple. States could continue to supplement payments.

Before that, a needy woman in 1972 got $167 a month in New Hampshire and $49 a month in South Carolina. The average payment was $78 a month. Payments however were substantially above the amounts given to mothers and dependent children. Three out of four old-age recipients are white.

Nearly half the states set maximums or percentages to reduce the payments to amounts less than their own established standards of need. Most states cut payments when social security benefits were increased.

The Disabled and the Blind

Recipients of Aid to the Disabled in 1972 received payments averaging from $56 per person in Louisiana to $119 in Alaska, with a national average of $102. The disability had to be so severe that a person could not do any kind of work that existed in the national economy, regardless of whether such work existed in the immediate area, whether a specific job vacancy existed for the person or whether he or she would be hired if an application for the job were made.

In this program too, most states used percentage formulas and maximum standards to reduce their payments below their own need standards. Nearly a million people get aid to the disabled, most of them elderly; only one in four is under forty-five. Only a small proportion have ever finished high school.

Over eighty thousand people got aid to the blind payments that averaged $107 a month in 1972, ranging from $67 in South Carolina to $172 in Alaska. All but a handful of the recipients are over fifty. There again, over half the states limited payment to less than the standard of need.

Unemployment Insurance

The category that provides the most limited aid to the poor is the one established for unemployed men and their families. Under the original design of the social security law, able-bodied male workers were not supposed to get public assistance at all. It was assumed that they would enroll in government work programs. Aside from local general-assistance for emergencies and special cases, the means of providing for jobless male workers since the demise of the WPA has been unemployment insurance. When it was instituted in 1935, it covered 60 percent of the country's work force. Amendments during the following years extended coverage so that today only farm workers, domestics, the self-employed, and state and local government workers are not included by federal mandate.

The program is paid for by a payroll tax paid by employers on workers' earnings up to $4,200. In order to qualify for benefits, one must work a certain amount of time in covered employment, generally twenty-six weeks. Benefits reflect the amount of wages a worker has earned and are also related to the average weekly wage of the state. In most cases, workers get about a third of their salaries, from $49 a week in Mississippi to $90 in Hawaii in 1972. A few states give extra money for dependents. There also is a limitation on the time benefits will be paid out. Most states set a maximum of twenty-six weeks.

As a result of the restrictions, large numbers of the jobless do not collect unemployment insurance, or their benefits run out while they are still looking for work. In 1968, which was a comparatively good year for employment, there were nearly 3 million jobless people every month, and only a million of them got unemployment benefits. During the course of the whole year, some 11 million people were out of work.

During the recessions of 1958 and 1961, the federal government extended unemployment compensation benefits for an extra thirteen weeks. In 1970, Congress voted to extend benefits automatically whenever unemployment went above 4½ percent for at least three months. In 1972 it was agreed to provide up to thirteen weeks of additional unemployment compensation for workers who had used up their benefits in states with high unemployment rates.

General State Assistance

Some twenty states also give general assistance, or home relief, paid for by state and local funds, to people who do not qualify for any of the federal programs. Twelve states give only emergency or short-term assistance. Average payments in 1970 were $58 a month per person, from $5 in Arkansas to $119 in New Jersey. (Blue-collar and nonsupervisory sales and office workers were averaging about $120 a week in wages.) Only about half the states gave all their aid in cash. The rest gave surplus food and vouchers for rent and utilities.

Aid may be dependent on the availability of seasonal employment, no matter what the wage scale. In California, for example, there is no home relief during the fruit and vegetable picking season.[13]

Some states supplement low wages earned by working fathers. In New York City, one in four of the general relief and AFDC-UF cases involve families in which workers have jobs but do not earn enough to live.

In 1971, the cost of public welfare reached $15 billion, with half paid by the federal government. It was more than the government had spent in the most costly year of the Depression. The figure did not include payments under social security or unemployment insurance.

The federal share has risen since the law was passed. The present formula for AFDC—beginning in 1974 the only shared program—is based on the state's average monthly payment and on its per capita income.

However, in spite of the increased federal share, state and local officials have chafed at the rising costs. They say their budgets are being stretched impossibly by the growing welfare rolls and that they have had to look for ways to reduce the costs.

Several methods have been popular: increased efforts to eliminate ineligibles, cutbacks in the amounts of grants given, and programs to require recipients to work.

The social security law forbids states from requiring applicants to qualify for aid on any other basis than need. One could not demand that recipients work for their grants. The federal program, in fact, had been established precisely for those groups who could not work. However, in 1967, Congress heeded the growing discontent with the rising cost of welfare aid to mothers and children and passed amendments aimed at getting "employables" off the rolls.

The House and Senate committee report on the bill said, "We are very concerned that such a large number of families have not achieved and maintained independence and self-support, and are very greatly concerned over the rapidly increasing costs to the taxpayer."[14]

New Work Rules

The new law was aimed at putting welfare recipients to work. The states would determine which adults and out of school youths over sixteen were eligible, and they would refer them to jobs or training. In training, they would get $30 a month in addition to their regular grants. At work, they could keep the first $30 a month of earnings, plus a third of the rest until the money that was deducted equaled their welfare grant. Students who worked could keep up to $150 a month.

People who were not good prospects for private employment or for training could be put into jobs at public and private nonprofit agencies. The welfare department would continue to pay enough to ensure that recipients received 20 percent above the amount of their grants.

State welfare departments were authorized to determine who was "employable" and what jobs were "suitable." They were also required to provide adequate day care for the children of mothers in jobs or training. Some states exempted mothers with small children from the work provisions. Those who were exempt could volunteer for work or training.

If a recipient refused to participate in the program, his or her "need" would be excluded in figuring the family grant. The program was called WIP, or Work Incentive Program; later, the acronym was changed to WIN.

Another goal of the 1967 amendments was to cut down on illegitimate births. Congress required states to supply family-planning services to welfare recipients. It also voted to freeze all AFDC grants to the percentage of children, in relation to each state's child population, that was on the rolls as of January 1, 1968. The freeze applied only to children receiving AFDC as a result of the absence of their father, not to those getting aid because of the death, disability, or unemployment of their father. Children were then receiving about $1 a day for all their needs, 45 percent below the government poverty level.

Congress that year also voted to increase social security payments by 15 percent, raising the minimum form $44 to $55 a month.

The federal freeze never went into effect. It was postponed and then repealed.

The 1967 amendments included another provision that was worked out with little benefit to the recipients: the requirement that welfare departments reflect rises in the cost of living when they set their need standards.

A few states raised payments. Hawaii granted a 3 percent cost of living increase, Oklahoma raised AFDC payments $1 per month, Mississippi grants went from $12.07 to $13.97 a month, and Washington began to pay 85 percent instead of 75 percent of need.

Cuts in Grants

However, most of the changes were in the opposite direction. Arizona passed a closed-end appropriation, which would cause reductions if the program grew bigger than the budget. Connecticut instituted a flat-grant system that eliminated payments for special needs. Kansas cut AFDC benefits 20 percent across the board. Maine eliminated AFDC for unemployed fathers. Nebraska cut payments 10 percent. New Jersey ended aid for unemployed fathers, replacing that with a program for assistance to the working poor that paid two-thirds of the AFDC standard. Texas cut maximum payments for a family from $135 to $125 a month.

Community and civic groups and organizations concerned with social welfare held "hearings" in New York in 1969 to see how the cuts had affected welfare recipients. They discovered that blind people had lost the funds they had been given to feed their seeing-eye dogs. Diabetics and heart patients had lost the money they had been given for special diets. In one case, the Welfare Department had cut out the carfare that had made it possible for a blind boy to attend a special school. A disabled woman was denied the wheelchair she needed to get out of the house.[15]

However, the chief "new" strategy for reducing the rolls was the work program. The goal was not the same as during the Depression when work programs sought to keep up the morale of the jobless or to "prime the pump" of industry. People were going to be helped toward independence, and "chiselers" would be discouraged from applying for aid if they knew they would have to work.

States had already set work requirements for general relief, often using recipients in public jobs as watchmen, parks and maintenance workers, or food servers in state institutions. At the beginning of the 1960's, some four hundred localities were using over thirty thousand people in relief work. And after Newburgh, the law was changed so that employable men (mothers were exempt) on AFDC could be required to work off the state and local share of their grants.

Work Incentive Program

The Work Incentive Program got off to a slow start. The federal government noted "the hesitation of some State legislators to appropriate the full sums requested for what they regard as another aspect of the welfare program." There was also a lack of child-care facilities. The bill had provided no funds to construct them, only money to pay for child care in existing facilities—which for the most part did not exist.

In some cases, the reaction to the program surprised officials. The government reported that "so many welfare recipients have volunteered for training that, in many instances, this source alone filled nearly the full quota of training slots." In California, eighty thousand people applied for sixteen thousand openings.[16]

In many states, women with children under six were not required to sign up for work or training. Elsewhere, they were deemed "employable." In Indiana, a nineteen-year-old woman with a two-year-old daughter applied for welfare and was given a list of jobs that included zookeeper and go-go dancer. She was ordered to apply for the jobs and turn in the results in writing before her application for aid would be accepted. The caseworker ignored her plea that she lacked bus fare to visit all the addresses, and when the woman finally began to make the rounds, she was told repeatedly that there was no job available.[17]

The government never appropriated enough money to provide training for those who wanted it, and economic conditions made it difficult to find jobs that would pay enough to make the families independent and get them off welfare. A Denver official declared, "In your core city, the jobs that are available will not pay a sustaining wage. They run from 80 cents per hour probably up to $1.30. A person who has a family to support cannot do it on this wage scale."[18]

He added that "jobs that do pay a sustaining wage are located in your suburban areas. There is no way of getting transportation to get to them. Transportation in Denver is inadequate. They don't run adequate buses to job sites. Most of the people [on welfare] don't have cars."

Cutbacks in the original WIN appropriations forced states to stop training people for skilled jobs and instead to train them for clerical and service work.

By late 1972, more than 425,000 people registered in the WIN program. Over 77,000 had gone into jobs that they had held for at least three to six months.[19]

One in four recipients was not referred at all because of the age or number of his or her children; one in seven were excluded because of illness, disability, or advanced age; and others were eliminated because of the lack of child-care arrangements or because they were attending school full-time or for other reasons.[20]

In its brief against forced work rules, the Center on Social Welfare Policy and Law pointed out that a 1971 New York State report found that less than 3 percent of the people receiving assistance were employable, and that included many who lacked education and training.

It noted that over 100,000 people had been referred to the state employment service twice a month, but that only 15,755 found jobs between July and December 1971, some of them only short-term jobs.

The state itself attributed the small number of people in jobs to "lack of employment opportunities caused by the general business slowdown during the past year and by a shortage of day care facilities."

The first welfare rights group was organized in Los Angeles, California in 1963. Johnnie Tillmon had been working, but she was forced for medical reasons to quit her job and go on welfare. Five months later, she and a half dozen other women started the Aid to Needy Children Mothers' Organization.

Their complaints were about midnight raids aimed at finding men in the house, checks that were delayed or stopped for no reason, the practice of social workers making visits without notice, and the difficulty of finding employment.

Ms. Tillmon had not had any of those problems, she said, "But evidently something was wrong when the others kept complaining about those things."

The women's first project was to interview 500 other welfare recipients in three housing projects to find out what their problems were. Then they began to help people: people who reported stopped checks; people who were threatened with eviction because their checks had not arrived. ANC Mothers opened an office. Ten years later, it was still in operation.[1]

It was the beginning of the welfare rights movement. And Johnnie Tillmon was to emerge as a national welfare rights leader.

A few months after the beginning of ANC Mothers, another group was born. A fire had destroyed the roof of the house of a thirty-eight-year-old woman with children living on AFDC. The caseworker held up her next check because she was "living in unfit housing." The woman said that she needed money to move, that she had no food, and that the

7
WELFARE RIGHTS

beds and clothing had been burned up in the fire. A college social-work student discovered what had happened and helped her get the check. Then the two women sought out other welfare recipients and organized the Alameda County Welfare Rights Group.

In Detroit, the city ended the payments it had been making to six thousand families to supplement their inadequate state welfare grants. The Federation for Aid to Dependent Children was established, and with support from other community groups, it got the mayor to agree to rescind the cut.[2]

In Chicago two years later, a welfare union was started when the city refused to pay the hospital bills of a young girl with chronic leukemia after officials found that she was pregnant.[3]

Antipoverty Projects

Also in 1964, Congress passed the Economic Opportunity Act, which provided federal funds for local community-action programs to be run with the "maximum feasible participation" of the poor. Many of the antipoverty projects included "neighborhood service centers," and it was soon evident that the chief problem for large numbers of poor people was the welfare department. People came to neighborhood service centers when they had trouble getting their applications accepted, when they were cut off without cause, when they did not get adequate grants, and when they did not get budgets adjusted for new needs.

Soon groups of welfare recipients themselves were setting up antipoverty projects and getting money from the government to run them. One of the first things they usually did was to knock on doors throughout the neighborhood to find people who were entitled to aid but who were not getting it.

In New York City, the Committee on Welfare Families in 1965 held the first recipients meeting with a city welfare official since the Workers' Alliance of the Depression. It won an agreement for winter clothing and formal grievance procedures.[4]

When people were turned down or given less than their due, antipoverty-program lawyers accompanied them to the welfare offices, demanded hearings, and filed appeals. Most of the cases never even got to court. The departments usually acceded to the attorneys' demands.

The first major welfare-rights action to get national attention was a march on the state capital of Ohio in June, 1966. AFDC payments in Ohio provided about 70 percent of the minimum standards the state had set seven years before, about 73 cents a day for food, clothing, and everything else but rent for a family of four. On June 20, about forty people started out from Cleveland on a 155-mile, ten-day march to present their grievances to the governor. They were joined by sympathizers and sang songs as they marched:

> We feed our children bread and beans
> While rich folks ride in limousines.
> After all we're human beings
> Marching down "Columbus Road."[5]

Some two thousand joined them for the demonstration in Columbus. (Now that date is celebrated as the movement's "birthday.")

That same day, in New York, another two thousand marched outside City Hall, and twenty-five hundred more, in fifteen cities from Boston to Los Angeles, held demonstrations against the inequities of the welfare system.

The coordinated action had been organized by the Poverty-Rights Action Center in Washington, a group headed by former CORE (Congress of Racial Equality) official George Wiley, who had learned of the Ohio protest and thought it would be useful to stage demonstrations around the country on the same day.

The June action led to a number of events. To begin with, welfare-rights leaders in New York met with city officials the next day and won an agreement to increase special grants for school clothing by 10 percent. The welfare commissioner agreed that most of the grievances of the Citywide Coordinating Committee of Welfare groups were valid.

Welfare Recipients Hold Conference

The center called an August meeting in Chicago for welfare-rights groups from all over the country. Some 135 delegates representing about seventy-five groups in twenty-four cities attended. They voted to begin a nationwide organizing campaign focusing on legal and administrative violations by welfare departments and on a demand for recognition of recipients' rights.[6]

They planned to demand the full benefits to which people were entitled based on the current cost of living; establishment of a system of application by affidavit; an end to residency requirements and to illegal coercion and invasion of privacy such as the midnight raid; and restriction of relative-responsibility laws to parental responsibility for children.

They sought an end to "man in the house" and "suitable-home" regulations; an end to discrimination against families of unwed mothers; grants in cash instead of vouchers or food stamps; jobs and training for recipients who wished to work; clerical and subprofessional jobs in welfare departments for recipients; and rights for such workers to keep their earnings above welfare payments until their incomes exceeded the poverty level.

They agreed to demand fair hearings for clients who sought to challenge department decisions; the right to represent welfare recipients at interviews and hearings; the right to be present at welfare centers to aid applicants and recipients; and the right to represent recipients in negotiating agreements with welfare officials.

The conference also set some long-range goals: a national federal grant for all in need, including the employed, which was not dependent on categories; and the division of public welfare administration in two, one agency to distribute money and another to provide social services. Finally, they voted to form a National Coordinating Committee of Welfare Rights Groups.

On a local level, groups continued the projects they had begun, and new unions of welfare recipients were established. When the school year began in New York City, nearly a thousand recipients picketed the welfare department demanding money for clothing for their children. Mothers staged a three-day sit-in at the welfare offices. In Cleveland, some two hundred people conducted a "buy-in" at a local department store. They chose clothing for their children and told the store manager to bill the welfare department.

In California, they protested the state policy that required men to work off welfare aid by cutting brush in city and county drainage and irrigation ditches. They demanded decent jobs at regular wages.

A group in Baltimore served the mayor a meal of Spam, rice, corn, and dried raisins, all surplus foods. He declined to eat it. Another group organized a "banquet" for California state officials. The menu listed varieties of beans.

AFDC mothers in Georgia in 1966 filed suit against the state's employment rules. Officials in the welfare agency classified field labor and domestic work as "suitable" for blacks but not for whites. Blacks had their grants cut off whenever field or domestic work was available; whites kept receiving checks until "more suitable" jobs were found.[7]

The situation had been common in the South from the beginning of the welfare program. In the 1930's, a welfare field supervisor explained that one Southern county had accepted 250 Negro families into the program, and there was "grave doubt about the wisdom of this decision, but otherwise they would have starved."[8]

In February, 1967, there was another national meeting, this time of some 350 people representing over two hundred welfare-rights groups in seventy cities. A structure was established, officers were elected, and the Poverty-Rights Action Center in Washington became the new headquarters of the National Welfare Rights Organization.

The national office served as a center of communications for the movement and as a source of information about the kinds of projects local groups might undertake. The national officers represented the welfare rights movement in meetings with federal welfare officials and in hearings before congressional committees.

Bill of Rights

The NWRO national office distributed a welfare "bill of rights" that told recipients that they had the right "to have the welfare department make a decision promptly after application for aid," "to be told in writing the specific reasons for any denial," "to a hearing before your check can be reduced or cut off," and "to receive welfare aid without having the welfare department ask you questions about who your social friends are (such as who you are going out with)."

Local groups helped individuals who had problems with late checks, wrong amounts, or no checks. They aided recipients who suffered abuse or harrassment or intimidation by caseworkers. They sought to get needed school supplies, winter clothing, furniture, and medical aid.

In 1967, the NWRO organized delegations to visit U.S. senators to lobby against the restrictive provisions of the welfare bill passed that year. Newspapers reported that nearly a thousand members demonstrated in front of the Capitol.

Meanwhile, throughout the country local groups of welfare recipients organized to fight abuses and seek improved conditions. They used a variety of methods, from meetings with welfare officials and delegations to state legislators and governors to demonstrations, law suits, and proposals for new legislation. Often, they got church groups and other community and civic organizations to back their demands.

"Special Needs" Campaigns

In Boston, in 1968, recipients began a campaign that was to spread throughout the country. They sought to make sure that people got the "special needs" grants provided for by state law. The group drew up a list of the personal and household items to which people were entitled and went knocking on doors to see if recipients had what they ought to have. Thousands of special needs requests were filed as a result. When the requests were denied, the recipients filed for fair hearings. Groups of thirty or more went into the centers to demand their rights. Sometimes, they held sit-ins and shut down the centers completely.

There were not enough lawyers to represent the recipients at the hearings, so members of the group were trained to handle cases themselves. One of the results of the action was an agreement that the group could have a desk and a phone in welfare centers to help people that requested their aid. On one occasion, thirty-five members were arrested after a sit-in outside the governor's office. The final result of the campaign was a special needs grant of $10 to $15.[9]

In New York City, recipients followed the same strategy. They discovered that special grants were supposed to insure that each child had a separate bed and that there were enough chairs so that everyone in the family could sit down to eat together. As demands were filed, the cost of the special grants increased until the city was paying $90 million in 1968 compared to $20 million three years earlier. City welfare officials responded by doing away with most special grants and giving everyone a hundred dollars a year for special needs.

In Youngstown, Ohio, sixty welfare-rights demonstrators held a sit-in at the county welfare office to win $100 in winter clothing grants for their children. Officials agreed to give $25 per child. The group also succeeded in reducing school lunch prices for AFDC children from 25 cents to 5 cents.

In Ann Arbor, Michigan, about thirty AFDC mothers sat in at the county courthouse after they were refused a hearing with the Board of Supervisors. They had said their grants were too low to pay for new clothing. After a week of demonstrations, which included students from the University of Michigan, and following over two hundred arrests, funds were made available so that children could get up to $60 for clothing.

The Little Shell Band of the Ojibwa Indians organized a clothing campaign for over two hundred welfare recipients in a town in North Dakota. They said that with temperatures often as low as 30 or 40 below zero in the winter, the welfare allowance of $8 a child could not buy adequate warm clothing.

In Cleveland, Ohio, four hundred mothers and children stormed the welfare department to get more money for school clothing. Ninety-two were arrested, but the department granted $24 a child.

However, actions were not always successful. In Toledo, Ohio, members of the League to Improve Family Emphasis sat in at the local welfare office to demand basic needs and winter clothing grants. Twelve were arrested. Demonstrations continued, and a few days later, twenty-eight people were arrested. The welfare department announced that no additional funds were available, and the president of the county commissioners requested an FBI investigation of the demonstration.

In Washington, D.C., about one thousand recipients filed forms requesting emergency grants for furniture and household needs and told officials they would be back in two weeks to pick up their checks. When some six thousand people appeared at the welfare offices, the doors were locked and the building surrounded by police armed with shotguns and mace. Women and children were maced, clubbed, and gassed when they tried to enter the building. The police later charged that the women and children had attacked them. Forty-four people were arrested.

Members of the NWRO met with the mayor's representative who said that the city did not have enough money for their demands. At a second meeting, there was a promise to seek funds from Congress. However, the NWRO newspaper reported that "the furniture request forms were never processed and there is no evidence that Congress was ever requested to appropriate money for furniture."

When welfare recipients returned to the welfare department two weeks after the meeting, they were arrested.

Protest Cuts; Seek Higher Grants

Many groups protested inadequate grants and cuts in grants. In New Orleans, twenty-two mothers and sixty children were arrested during a protest against a 10 percent cut in welfare. In Ann Arbor, recipients prevented a 10 percent cut that legislators had proposed to avoid increasing appropriations for welfare. The recipients went to the state capital and got the governor to agree to keep payments at the current level, which was $2,122 a year for a family of four, $1,000 below the 1968 poverty level.

Pennsylvania welfare recipients picketed a $250 a plate Republican party dinner attended by their governor. They were protesting the fact that people got only 71 percent of what the state had set as the minimum standard of living more than ten years before.

Women in Kentucky asked the state legislature to pay 100 percent of the living needs of families rather than 87 percent, to set up an emergency assistance program for which federal funds were available, and to make the state responsible for collecting child-support payments from fathers rather than deducting court-ordered payments from welfare checks whether or not they were actually received.

In Atlanta, welfare mothers protested a cut the state made to balance an increase in social security. They secured a court order forbidding Georgia to cut checks until it held fair hearings. However, the state successfully ignored the order.

Major Action in Nevada

A major action was held in Nevada where, in the fall of 1970, the state welfare commission instituted a new method of determining eligibility which was designed to eliminate about three thousand recipients, over a fifth of the caseload, and to cut benefits for more than four thousand. The NWRO national board was about to meet in New Jersey, but it quickly moved to Las Vegas.

NWRO members went door-to-door to inform recipients of their right to demand a fair hearing before any cuts went into effect, and they went with them to file for the hearings. Some caseworkers had suggested that welfare mothers could earn money by prostitution, which is legal in Nevada. The group discovered that the welfare department had failed to notify people in advance of the reductions and to tell them that they could file for fair hearings.

The NWRO organized demonstrations of as many as several thousand people at the gambling casinos of Reno and Las Vegas. The protests and the publicity threatened the tourist trade which is Nevada's main industry, and the casino owners put pressure on state officials to end the crisis. In March, a federal judge ruled that the state had illegally ignored a local court order requiring it to give recipients notice that they were being cut off the rolls and information about their right to hearings. He said the state "ran roughshod over the constitutional rights" of the recipients by its actions. Although the court required compliance with procedural requirements (notice, hearings, etc.) the governor finally signed an order rescinding the welfare department's actions and providing for back payments to those whose grants had been cut off or reduced. The NWRO won that victory in the streets, not in the courts.[10]

In Alabama, recipients picketed the state capitol building and filed for fair hearings when over eleven thousand people had grants reduced or were cut off the rolls. The state had used a method that became increasingly popular in the early 1970's. In the past, it had figured a standard of need, subtracted outside income, and paid a third of the remainder.

For example, if the standard was $100 and a family had $40 a month in social security, the need was $60 and the state paid $20.

Under the new system, the payment was figured as one-third of $100 which was $33, and since the social security was $40, the state subtracted that and did not pay anything. The Alabama Welfare Rights Organization filed a law suit against the state welfare department. The Supreme Court later ruled in a Texas case, Jefferson v. Hackney, that this procedure was permissable.

The welfare-rights groups also sought to make other legislation work for the poor. One major activity focused on the funds made available by Title I of the Elementary and Secondary Education Act of 1965. This money was supposed to be used to improve education for poor children, and welfare mothers argued that their children could not benefit from schooling if they lacked even the clothing needed to attend.

School Clothing Campaigns

An NWRO member told officials in Springfield, Ohio, that inadequate clothing was a learning disability, especially in junior high schools, where students pretended they were ill or roamed the streets instead of attending classes because they were ashamed to face the other students looking "raggedy."

NWRO groups also protested the fact that Title I money was being used for children who were not poor. In Indianapolis, Indiana, for example, it was used to buy data-processing equipment for the school system's central offices. In Georgia, it went to pay for a mobile curriculum-center used by schools not entitled to the money. (By 1972, the U.S. Office of Education had ordered that fourteen states repay nearly $20 million in Title I funds spent improperly for programs not aimed at helping the poor.)[11]

The first welfare-rights Title I project was in Providence, Rhode Island, where school officials agreed to give $32 a child to each AFDC family to buy school clothing. In Milwaukee, Wisconsin, and Indianapolis, they got $50 a child; in Evansville, Indiana, they also got funds for books and breakfast.

However, pressure from school officials around the country led to a ruling in 1970 by the Department of Health, Education and Welfare that Title I money could not be used for school clothing. A few weeks later, pressure from NWRO led to another change. HEW said that communities which already had given out school clothing under Title I could do so again.

School Lunches

Another campaign focused on school lunches. Federal law required that all schools provide free or reduced price lunches to needy children, but many districts ignored the law. In Detroit, NWRO discovered that there were lunch programs for middle-class children, but none for the poor. The reason given was that there were no cafeterias or other suitable facilities in the old schools in poor neighborhoods. A suit was filed against the school board, and the result was lunch programs for all children.

In Kansas City, Missouri, recipients filed a lawsuit against the board of education to get lunch programs. In Little Rock, Arkansas, demonstrations and a lawsuit resulted in a school-board decision to override the superintendent's rejection of school lunches for poor children.

In some communities, the NWRO succeeded in raising eligibility standards for school lunches to include families not on welfare. In Rochester, New York, the cutoff point was set at $5,500 for a family of four, in New Jersey $4,800.[12] The NWRO also won a regulation to ban discrimination against children who got free lunches. Many schools had required them to stand on different lines, sometimes waiting until paying children had gone through, or to have different colored lunch cards.[13]

NWRO participated in efforts to extend food-stamp benefits to states that did not have programs, and it was one of the plaintiffs in a suit against the U.S. Department of Agriculture in 1971 when the government announced stricter eligibility requirements and smaller benefits for over 2 million people who used the stamps. As a result of the suit, the Nixon Administration changed its policy and rescinded the cutback.

In an effort to dramatize the inadequacy of welfare food budgets, NWRO asked legislators and prominent political and civic leaders to go on welfare diets for a week. Eight congressmen's families tried it in 1969, with meals costing

18 cents a day per person. Congressman Abner Mikva of Illinois told news reporters, "I'm hungry," and said he was now aware that people on welfare budgets could not possibly get enough to eat. The family of Senator Walter Mondale of Minnesota lived largely on creamed tuna fish, spaghetti, hot dogs, and peanut butter and jelly sandwiches. Senator Frank Church of Idaho took a peanut butter and jelly sandwich and a carrot to work every day and ate them in the elegant Senate dining room.[14]

Housing Actions

In Rhode Island, welfare recipients fought to get the welfare department to agree not to reduce grants if public housing rents were cut in accord with the Brooke amendment to the Housing and Urban Development Act of 1969. This provided that families in low-income public housing could not be charged more than 25 percent of their incomes.

The recipients held demonstrations, lobbied with the governor and members of the state legislature's finance committee, and finally organized a successful rent strike. After a nine-month campaign, tenants were granted reductions that averaged $20 a family and got retroactive payments of about $300 to cover the months the law had not been put into effect. Later Congress passed an amendment making it mandatory to give welfare recipients the benefits of the Brooke amendment.

Other recipients faced the problem of rent allotments that were unrealistic, especially in view of the discrimination they faced as welfare recipients and, often, as members of minority groups. The Chicago Welfare Rights Organization sought legislation to abolish the maximum $90-a-month rent ceiling in grants.

Groups also fought the ceilings on gas and electric payments that often did not meet the actual costs of utilities, especially in apartments where inefficient space heaters were used to make up for the fact that landlords failed to supply adequate heat in winter. There also were efforts to eliminate high deposits for utilities, deposits that were not provided for in the welfare grant. A series of demonstrations by recipients convinced the Boston Gas and Electric Company to abolish deposits except for very poor credit risks, and after welfare demonstrators closed down their offices, the Detroit utility company did the same.

One welfare-rights action started out to be a protest over inadequate clothing allowances, but turned out to be a dramatic demonstration of inadequate food budgets. Twenty-seven Philadelphia women tried to sell their blood to earn money for clothing for their children, but all but two were rejected because improper diet made their blood deficient in iron. A technician at the blood center told them to "eat plenty of red meats and liver and green vegetables and fruits." The women regarded him with disbelief. "When you don't have money, you eat hotcakes and gravy and fried potatoes and stewed potatoes," said one. "Some people say this was a morbid thing to do," declared another, "but I think it's morbid the way our kids have to go around in rags."

NWRO also sought to inform the working poor about their rights to food stamps, medicaid and income supplements. Some twenty states have supplemental relief for indigent workers. They spoke at union meetings or set up tables outside unemployment insurance offices.

Often, welfare-rights groups concerned themselves with the individual problems of recipients. For example, in Providence, a twenty-seven-year-old woman whose infant child had bronchitis was living in an apartment without heat and with practically no furniture. Her caseworker said the department would not supply the furniture, but he gave her a voucher to buy fuel. However, she could not find an oil company that would accept the voucher.

The Fair Welfare Organization stepped in and got the welfare agency to buy her oil, a stove, a refrigerator, a washing machine, linoleum for the floors, a living-room sofa, and new clothing. The child also got orthopedic shoes needed to treat a bone defect.

Groups protested abusive treatment by caseworkers and welfare department officials. Albany, New York, recipients sued the county welfare agency, charging that they were being intimidated and prevented from speaking and disseminating information at the welfare offices.

Members sought representation on the bodies that made welfare policy. In Delaware, fifty recipients met with the governor to demand representation on the welfare board. In Denver, recipients demanded at least one of the board's nine seats. The Delaware group won its demand, but in 1973 Denver welfare recipients were still seeking representation.

Charge State Violations of Law

In the midst of all the charges about welfare fraud, the NWRO got involved in a major campaign against the states' disregard of federal welfare regulations. It charged numerous violations, including the failure to put into effect the cost-of-living increases required by the 1967 social security amendments.

NWRO representatives met with HEW Secretary Robert Finch before the increase was scheduled to take place, which was eighteen months after the legislation was passed. They wanted to insure enforcement of the law. However, three months after the deadline, nothing had been done, and the NWRO filed a suit against the U.S. government to force it to act in twenty-three states. When the federal agency made its own investigation, it found a total of thirty-nine states out of compliance with the law. It ordered hearings in seven states.

In Arizona, a federal court turned down the state's appeal against a cutoff of federal funds that was ordered after the HEW hearing proved that state out of conformity with federal welfare regulations. Arizona was ordered (1) to stop cutting from the rolls those who left the state for ninety days with intentions of returning, (2) to allow persons without legal custody (such as grandparents) to receive aid for children they were raising, and (3) to add recipients to welfare advisory boards.

In Connecticut, HEW found the state out of conformity on all the thirteen issues raised, including an illegal ceiling on exempted earnings, an illegal method of deducting work-related expenses, violation of the confidentiality of case records, and faulty determination of the medically needy.

In Nebraska, the legislature complied with HEW orders by increasing the state standard of need by 10 percent to coincide with the cost of living. In Sutter County, California, the government found that people were deliberately discouraged from applying for welfare. Often they were given only a one-time $10 or $15 grocery order or a package of surplus commodities. If they were persistent, they were told that they had to live in the state for from three to five years to be eligible.

In St. Louis, Missouri, officials illegally kept three thousand people on a "waiting list" until money was available under current appropriations to add them to the rolls.

The NWRO filed a suit against the federal government and the State of California, charging that Governor Ronald Reagan had gotten a White House agreement to delay a cutoff of federal funds ordered as a result of a hearing that found the state out of conformity with federal rules. California complied with the hearing decision.

Ultimately, the states got around the cost-of-living-increase requirement by raising their need standards but then paying a smaller percentage of that need than before. HEW ruled that as long as the standard reflected the cost-of-living increase, the states were in conformity no matter what they actually paid out. This decision was upheld by the Supreme Court in 1970.

The movement won some major victories through the courts which proved to be substantially greater protectors of recipients' civil rights than state or federal legislatures or government administrators. (NWRO has regular meetings with HEW. It has repeatedly asked why the government does not undertake publicity campaigns to inform people about their rights to public assistance as it does for social security.)

An early Supreme Court decision in 1941 had struck down a California law prohibiting any person from bringing a poor person into the state. It said the law limited peoples' rights to travel freely between the states. Some twenty years later, antipoverty-program lawyers won a case on similar grounds for a woman who had been denied aid under New York State's Welfare Abuses Act. She was a common-law wife with six children who had come from Puerto Rico to find her husband. The welfare department had said that since she arrived without any visible means of support, she had come for the purpose of receiving welfare.[15]

The American Civil Liberties Union won a case it argued on the basis of the Thirteenth Amendment, which prohibits slavery. In the winter of 1962, five men getting general-assistance payments of about $50 a week in Canton, New York, were assigned to public works. On one 12-degree day, they were ordered to cut brush, much of it deep beneath the snow, on a deserted country road. They refused and were put in jail without a trial.

The local judge ruled in favor of the local welfare department saying that the Thirteenth Amendment did not apply to the government, only to individuals. However, the five were freed by the state court of appeals. They had spent between four and eight months in prison for what local officials called "a willful action designed to interfere with the proper administration of public assistance and care."[16]

"Man in the House" Rule Ended

In 1968, the U.S. Supreme Court struck down Alabama's "man in the house" rule in a unanimous decision that affected similar rules in eighteen other states and the District of Columbia. The case, King v. Smith, involved a widow with four children who had a boyfriend with a family of his own. When the welfare department discovered the relationship, it ended AFDC payments, saying that the man was the "substitute father" of the Smith children.

The court said that "parent" as used in the statute could be applied only to those with a legal duty to support. It added that states could not discourage "immorality" or "illegitimacy" by punishing needy children.

Two years later, the Supreme Court strengthened the ruling in a decision against the California MARS (Man Assuming the Role of Spouse) statute with a decision that no state can assume income from anyone other than a natural, adoptive or stepparent with a legal duty to support the child, and it cannot impose such a duty on a man not married to the mother even though he is living with her.

Residency Requirements Outlawed

In 1969, the Supreme Court outlawed residency requirements for welfare. A federal court in Connecticut had ruled against the state's residency restrictions in 1967, and suits had been brought in other states. The court based its decision on the constitutional right to travel. It had to deal with the same issue again several years later when New York and Connecticut passed "emergency" one-year residency laws.

The 1969 decision had said that restrictions on interstate travel could not be justified unless for "compelling governmental interest." New York and Connecticut said the new laws were necessary to avoid financial catastrophe caused by the increasing rolls. Colorado, Rhode Island, Utah, and West Virginia then passed similar statutes.

The ACLU, which filed the suit that overturned those laws, pointed out that less than 1 percent of the people who received benefits were new recipients who had been in New York less than a year.

Due Process Required

In 1970, the Supreme Court ruled that under the Fourteenth Amendment, welfare recipients were entitled to due-process hearings before checks could be cut off. It required adequate notice detailing the reasons for the proposed cut-off and an opportunity for the recipient to be heard and to confront any witnesses against him or her. An HEW regulation later extended the right of prior hearings to people faced with reductions in payments.

In the decision, the Court said, "It may be realistic today to regard welfare entitlements as more like 'property' than a 'gratuity.' Much of the existing wealth in this country takes the form of rights which do not fall within the traditional common-law concepts of property."

It mentioned the doctor's and lawyer's license to practice, a worker's union membership, subsidies for farmers and businessmen, routes granted to airlines, channels assigned to television stations, long-term contracts for defense, space and educational programs, and social security pensions.

It asserted that such public and private benefits were not considered charity by their recipients, and that only the entitlements of the poor have not been enforced effectively.

In 1971, the Supreme Court struck down an Illinois law which banned aid to children between eighteen and twenty-one who were attending colleges, but not to those in high school or vocational training. The lower court had noted that the existing labor market was one in which "the skills of manual laborers are in short supply" and had ruled that "as a means of utilizing limited state funds in an effort to channel persons into those employment positions for which the society has great need, the statutory discrimination between college students and post-high school vocational training is not purely arbitrary but rather a rational approach designed to correct a perceived problem."[17]

In 1971, the Supreme Court ruled that citizenship cannot be a qualification for welfare benefits, and a year later it ordered Florida to make retroactive payments to aliens who had been illegally denied assistance. In 1972, the Court also ruled against a California law that denied aid to children who were needy because their fathers were away as the result of military service.

It also affirmed a lower court ruling that states may not under existing regulations deny welfare benefits to families of workers who are unemployed because they are on strike or were fired for misconduct.

In 1967 the Supreme Court ruled against the constitutionality of "midnight raids." The suit involved a blind caseworker who refused to make the visits and was fired.

The significance of these cases was that the federal not the state government would define eligibility. The federal law had established certain categories of eligibility and said that within those categories (aid to aged, blind, disabled, families with dependent children) only need could determine eligibility; the states could not set additional requirements or limitations. Welfare-rights lawyers saw the decision as a way to expand the numbers of those eligible for aid.

Not all the decisions of the Court were favorable to welfare-rights challengers. In 1971, the Court rejected a Fourth-Amendment suit against home visits by caseworkers. The suit citing the decision in the midnight raids case, had said the visits constituted an illegal search; the Supreme Court said they were a "reasonable administrative tool."

In 1972, the Court also ruled that the state of Texas did not violate the Constitution or the social security law by granting lower benefits to AFDC recipients, who were mostly black and Mexican-American, than it did to recipients of programs such as aid to the aged and the disabled where the beneficiaries were largely white. Texas provided 75 percent of need to AFDC recipients, of which 87 percent were minorities, and 95 to 100 percent of need in the adult categories, where 62 percent of the aged and 53 percent of the disabled were white.

A more significant aspect of this decision was the Court's

ruling that states could deduct applicants' incomes from the payment level rather than the standard of need.

Discrimination Against Women Banned

In a lower-court decision, a Seattle judge in 1971 ruled in favor of a welfare mother who had been put on a waiting list for WIN training because of the priority given to men. A similar suit was brought by the Chicago Welfare Rights Association. As a result, the office of Health, Education and Welfare did away with the male priorities and the judge ordered that women who had previously been refused enrollment in the program would be admitted in order of application.

In 1971, a federal court in Chicago struck down two Illinois regulations requiring welfare mothers to identify the fathers of their children and to initiate court action for support before they could get aid.

A federal court in Oregon struck down a regulation that required AFDC mothers to cooperate with law enforcement officers in efforts to secure support from the fathers of their children.

And in California, the court ruled that women on relief did not have to prosecute their husbands for criminal nonsupport. The Supreme Court affirmed all three rulings.

In the early 1970's, numerous other cases, most of them brought by antipoverty legal-services programs, were still in lower state and federal courts. They challenged government rulings on eligibility, amounts of grants, clients' rights, and work requirements.

1972 was a year for political action. On March 25, 1972, 50,000 people went to Washington, D.C., on a "Children's March" to protest President Nixon's policies on issues that affected children—welfare, day care, nutrition, and health. The demonstration was sponsored by a coalition of liberal and civic groups brought together by NWRO.

In the summer of 1972, NWRO went to the national political conventions. It organized a coalition at the Democratic Convention with the Southern Christian Leadership Conference and the National Tenants Organization. Six out of eight of its "Poor People's Platform" demands were adopted by the Democrats but not, importantly, the plan for a $6,500 minimum income. However, that was brought to the convention floor as a minority report, and on a roll call, it got 1,000 votes, a third of the convention.

The issue of a "guaranteed income" had been the focus of controversy for nearly a decade.

The debate at the beginning of the 1970's was one that went back to the essence of the conflict over welfare, a conflict that has existed since the British poor law of 1601 and which has figured centrally in virtually all the decisions about public assistance that have been made in the past four hundred years.

It is the debate over whether public assistance policies should be aimed at getting people out of dependency and into jobs, with minimal aid and punitive rules to discourage "pauperism," or whether the society has an obligation to guarantee all people a minimum decent standard of living whether or not they work.

Through the centuries in which the poor law has operated, the notion has been that people need the threat of starvation to make them work and that, in view of society's need for workers, it should not give aid to anyone who is in any way employable. However, in the past decade, economists and social thinkers have declared that today, economic conditions and technological changes make it necessary and possible to guarantee all people a minimum income.

Some of those thinkers believe, in fact, that work may be obsolete for growing parts of the population and that the guaranteed income should thus be an adequate one. Others agree that many people have been shut out of the work world, but they propose plans that would not reduce the financial incentive to work for those who can do so. Some of the plans propose incomes below the poverty line, while others would

8

GUARANTEED INCOME

continue payments even to those who have worked their way out of poverty.

There had been proposals for some form of guaranteed income before the sixties. In fact, Lady Juliette Evangeline Rhys-Williams proposed in 1943 that a "social dividend" be paid to everyone in England in a plan tied to the tax system. However, now, when the welfare crisis has become a national issue, there is widespread discussion of the idea.

Theobald Plan

One of the first in the last decade to propose a guaranteed income plan was Robert Theobald, a socioeconomist, who in 1963 announced in *Free Men and Free Markets* that American society had to do away with the link between jobs and income.[1]

The chief cause of the revolution in work, Theobald said, is cybernation, the use of computers to run automated equipment. In cybernation, computers replace people in thinking and decision-making. They are being used to analyze stock market portfolios for investors, to compute the best conditions for crops and livestock, to design airplanes, and to keep inventory records up to date. Theobald said we are coming to a period when we will not need financial incentives for production. Machines will do the work.

He wrote that "many experts have concluded that the continuing impact of technological change will make it impossible to provide jobs for all who seek them." "Those with inadequate education and training," he continued, "will not find jobs in the future because their toil will not be economically competitive with that of the machine. Even more seriously, it now seems fully clear that in today's socioeconomy the children of the poor are almost inevitably condemned to poverty because they do not receive an education that would enable them to hold jobs in the future."[2]

Income Not Related to Effort

Theobald asserted that in this society, income was no longer a reward for hard work and effort. The distribution of income was "primarily dependent on power rather than on economic contribution," the power to create artificial scarcity, and he pointed to the relative earnings of teachers, doctors, construction workers, truckers, garbage workers, and film stars. Furthermore:

"As long as our socioeconomic system needed all the available workers and provided for them, we were behaving reasonably in continuing a system in which the non-workers received substantially lower incomes than those who carried out required tasks. Today, our socio-economic system neither needs all the available workers nor can it provide work opportunities for them.

The non-workers have become a group living essentially outside the society whose interest their unenviable existence is presumed to be safeguarding. It is clear that we need to change our attitudes about all these matters: about the value of work, when it is merely repetitive toil, easily performed by a machine; about our responsibilities to those who are no longer needed to perform this toil, and how they should be included in a society of abundance as full participating members. . . .[3]

Our present system is postulated on the belief that every individual who desires a job will be able to find one and that the jobs thus obtained will pay well enough to enable the individual to live with dignity.

However, he countered, the notion that society can and should provide jobs for everyone is no longer valid. It should instead provide a guaranteed income.[4]

This income should be an absolute constitutional right, not one that would allow the government to withdraw it under certain circumstances. That could lead to tyranny, said Theobald.

He proposed a two-part plan. First an income of $1,000 a year for every adult and $600 per child would be provided as a matter of right. An alternative might be to bring all incomes up to an adequate level, with an added incentive to work. A family might get $3,000 a year; if it had earnings of $2,000, it might be allowed $1,000 to reach the minimum income plus another 10 or 20 percent of its earned income.

He agreed that his plan might make it more difficult to find workers to do unpleasant jobs, but this would force up wages for dirty work. In other cases, the work would be cybernated.

He also proposed a higher subsidy for people in the middle class who lost their jobs through cybernation and who would find themselves suddenly unable to continue at their customary standard of living. He said society needed this class as "a source of initiatives and drive to move it toward its goals."[5] Such people would get payments related to their past incomes. A person's grant might be 50 percent of past earnings if unemployment came at age thirty with percentage points added until the figure reached 85 percent if unemployment came at age 65.

The amounts would not exceed a certain limit, perhaps three times as much as families getting the lower grant.

The Negative Income Tax

A completely different kind of guaranteed income was proposed by conservative economist Milton Friedman in *Capitalism and Freedom,* a book published in 1962, which proposed a negative income tax.[6]

Friedman attacked the existing welfare system for depriving people of personal liberty, freedom, and dignity by subjecting them to humiliating investigations and seeking to manage their lives. "It would be far better to give the indigent money and let them spend it according to their values." And he noted that the vast majority of welfare spending did not go to people who were poor. (Elsewhere, he criticized farm subsidies as a "free lunch program for rats and mice.")

Friedman based his plan on the income tax which provides exemptions of $750 per person for taxpayers and their dependents. A family of four would have $3,000 in exemptions, and if its income were $3,000, it would pay no tax. If its income were $4,000, its taxable income would be $1,000, and at a rate of 14 percent, it would pay $140.

However, if the family income were $2,000, it would have an unused exemption of $1,000. Under the negative income tax, it would *receive* $140, using the tax rate of 14 percent. If the negative income tax rate were 50 percent, a figure Friedman used in his calculations, it would receive $500. If the family had no income, a 50 percent rate would yield $1,500.

Friedman said that the plan "would concentrate public funds on supplementing the incomes of the poor—not distribute funds broadside in the hope that some will trickle down to the poor. It would help people because they are poor, not because they are old or disabled or unemployed or farmers or tenants of public housing."

In addition, he said the plan treats the poor as responsible people, not "incompetent wards of the state," it promotes the development of habits of independence and self-reliance, and it gives the poor an incentive to work since their grants would be reduced by only 50 cents for every dollar earned.

Friedman would have the negative income tax replace all social welfare programs. (Some people are suspicious of this since the cost of services like child care and medical care are far above what a person or family could afford on the grants that Congress would be likely to give. Tax exemptions are based on the amount of money a family is considered to need for subsistence and which therefore should not be taxed. Since his proposal calls for providing only a percentage of the value of the exemptions, it does not pretend or attempt to provide an adequate income.

Other Plans

Other proposals that followed the Theobald and Friedman plans were variations of the guaranteed income payment or the negative income tax.

A social-work professor named Edward Schwartz wrote an article called "An End to the Means Test" which called for payments up to a guaranteed minimum of between $3,000 and $5,000 for a family of four, to be administered through the income tax system.[7]

Since the subsidy was already at the poverty line or above, the plan would tax additional income at 60 to 80 percent which, using the lower figure, would provide some help to families with incomes above $3,000 until the combined income and subsidy reached $4,000.

James Tobin, an economist, proposed giving all families under the poverty line (then $3,130) an allowance of $400 for each parent and the first four children, and $150 each for the fifth and sixth child. No family would get more than $2,700. The subsidy would be cut only 40 cents for each dollar earned until the combined wages and allowance reached the point where the family was eligible for positive taxes.[8]

Tobin argued that half the poor benefited from none of the federal welfare and social insurance programs, and that "most of the public money spent to supplement personal incomes goes to families above the poverty line." His plan was designed to supplement other welfare payments which would not be counted as income if they were based on need.

Another economist, Robert Lampman, devised a series of alternatives that would set allowances of between $750 and $2,000 for a family of four with reductions of from 25 to 75 percent for outside income. He said the allowances would not take any family out of poverty, but they would fill half the poverty gap for people on public assistance.[9]

Lampman explained that the plans were "deliberately set low to make it clear to everyone that we are not inviting people to stop work." Existing social welfare payments would continue.

The Key Elements in All Plans

All of the guaranteed income plans made various decisions about certain key elements:

1. Should the payments seek to bring people up to the poverty line or only provide a partial subsidy?

2. How much income above that level would recipients be allowed to keep? If they could keep little or nothing, that would discourage work. If they could keep too much, the government might end up subsidizing people to a point above the poverty line.

The plans either set upper limits and provided all or part of the difference between that level and a family's income, or they provided money allowances for each member of the family. All the plans set a higher "tax" on earned income than exists for the general population; that is, recipients could keep only a portion of their earned income as long as they were getting allowances.

Plans that provided high minimum payments tended to have high tax rates on earned income. Those that gave lower grants naturally allowed people to keep more of their own earnings.

At a certain break-even point, the tax on income equaled the guarantee and the allowance was stopped. The variations were in the amount of the subsidy, the level of the tax rate and the break-even point.

Bringing payments up to the poverty line would discourage people from working at jobs that paid wages below that level. On the other hand, it might encourage employers to raise subsistence wages.

However, plans that provided 50 percent of the poverty level income and allowed people to keep a part of earnings above that line were better for the working poor than for people who could not supplement that limited guarantee.

Such plans might also subsidize low-wage employers who could keep workers at low pay with the knowledge that they were also receiving government allowances.

The proponents of the guaranteed income were not agreed about the effects of giving people enough money to live on without working. Economist George Hildebrand said, "We actually do small service to the cause of the working poor if we look tolerantly upon the possibility that they will work less if their incomes are fully guaranteed. To be or to become partly or wholly self-supporting is an essential step to a vitally needed strengthening of family life. It is also the route by which many of the poor can be more firmly integrated into the whole of society. Accordingly, the motivation to work must be strengthened, not weakened."[10]

James Vadakin countered, "Certainly the old notion that workers prefer indolence to a higher standard of living and will work only to the point necessary to stave off starvation, is not particularly credible in the United States today," and he cited the growing number of families where more than one person works, the widespread desire for overtime and the fact that "over recent decades almost 60 percent of our increased ability to produce has been taken in the form of more goods and services, whereas only 40 percent has gone to increased leisure."[11]

Harold Watts, director of the University of Wisconsin Institute for Research on Poverty, said, "Can we really believe that the threat of extreme deprivation is the linch-pin of our whole economic system? Or is the opportunity to move from a basic but viable minimum to higher levels by one's productive efforts the more important key to our present and future progress?"[12]

Children's Allowances

Another proposal for raising income in a totally different manner was the children's allowance that currently exists in sixty-two nations including Canada, the countries of Europe, and virtually all of the "advanced" industrial nations of the world.

A certain sum per child would be paid to every family in the country. Income tax deductions for children would be eliminated and the allowance would be taxable so that people who were not poor would not retain all of it.

Social-work professor Vera Shlakman called for children's allowances of $50 a month as a supplement to other welfare measures. She noted that AFDC excludes more poor children than it helps and that income tax deductions for dependent children are a recognition that government must provide some aid to such families but that they do not help families with the lowest incomes who pay little or no tax.[13]

One might want to limit the payments to the first three or four children, she said, adding that studies of other countries have shown that children's allowances do not push up the birth rate.

Social worker Alvin Schorr, now dean of the New York University School of Social Work, proposed a benefit of $50 a month for each child under six and $10 for each older child.[14] A family with taxable income between $4,000 and $8,000 and with school-age children would break even since they would receive a $120 benefit per child in exchange for a $600 exemption. Families with preschool children and all low and middle-income families would receive added income.

Daniel P. Moynihan, then an advisor to President Nixon, proposed $8 a month for children under six and $12 for those six through seventeen.[15]

An allowance of $50 would give some money to people with incomes as high as $44,000. Even if exemptions were removed and the allowance were taxed, the poor would get only one-third of the benefits paid out. Thus, another advocate of children's allowance, Professor Harvey Brazer, proposed a special children's allowance tax to cut down the payments to people who didn't need them. Thus, the value of the subsidy would go from $600 a year for the poor to $60 at levels of income over $12,000.[16]

Advocates of the children's allowance pointed out that half the nation's poor are children, and the most serious poverty exists in large families. In addition, paying out the allowances to everyone on the basis of children instead of income would avoid the stigma that has always been attached to subsidies based on need. They said that wealthy families who got allowances would pay the money back in taxes.

Critics said this plan would not aid individuals without children, and that large amounts of money would be paid out to people who are not poor.

Social-welfare consultant Elizabeth Wickenden points out that countries like England and France, with long-time family allowance plans "are finding it difficult to channel more money to the most desperately needy families in the face of pressures to raise the universal benefits."[17]

Guaranteed incomes, whether they be in the form of per capita payments, negative income taxes, or children's allowances, have won increasing favor in the past decade.

In 1966, the Advisory Council on Public Welfare recommended that all Americans be guaranteed a minimum income of $3,200 for a family of four—as a matter of right.

Jobs for Everyone

Elizabeth Wickenden, who was a member of that panel, was as concerned with the creation of jobs as the question of minimum income. "In the mid 30's," she said, "people were saying we would always have large numbers of unemployables. By 1938, people were pouring into the shipyards. During the war, people assembled electronics parts from their beds. Employability is a function of the market, and not of the individual."

Her solution was for government to "guarantee a job at standard wages to everyone willing and able to work," to "subsidize retraining and relocation for all those displaced by economic changes," to set up day-care programs and visiting-nurse services for those who need them, and to "pioneer in the development of new kinds of work for persons of all ages and backgrounds."

Government should also "place a value on work in the home"—a major bank recently evaluated the average housewife's labor at over $8,000 a year. And it should pay people enrolled in higher education.[18]

In his economic report to Congress in 1967, President

Lyndon Johnson suggested an exploration of proposals for guaranteed minimum incomes and announced that he would set up a national commission to do so.

Support and Opposition

In 1968, over twelve hundred economists, including John Kenneth Galbraith and Paul Samuelson, called for the establishment of a guaranteed income. They said it was "feasible and compatible with our economic system."

Some businessmen supported the concept too. That same year, Arjay Miller of Ford Motors, Joseph Wilson of Xerox, and M. L. Haider of Standard Oil announced their support of the guaranteed income.

However, all their colleagues were not in agreement. Edwin Parker, president of A. G. Spalding, said that part of the problem was that politicians and the courts had helped convince "these people that they must be supported in their insolence, their arrogance, and often in their immorality, in grand style, by the decent, hard-working, moral people of the United States."[19]

George Wilson, president of the Lone Star Steel Company, declared, "Furnishing economic assistance to the able-bodied inevitably destroys incentives and creates bums."[20]

The Office of Economic Opportunity in 1968 funded a project to see what would happen if families got guaranteed incomes. Selected people in New Jersey with income of no more than 150 percent of the poverty level were given allowances of from 50 to 125 percent of that amount with taxes on their earned incomes of from 30 to 70 percent. After more than a year, there was no evidence that people stopped working when they were given guaranteed incomes.[21]

Presidential Commission

In 1969, the commission appointed by President Johnson came back with its report and recommendation for a universal income supplement of $2,400 for a family of four with added income cutting payments by 50 cents for every dollar earned. Families of four would get some aid up to $4,800.

The President's Commission on Income Maintenance Programs said it recognized that, "Since $2,400 is below the poverty line for a family of four, the basic benefit would not meet the full income needs of families with no other income. This level was not chosen because we feel that it is an adequate income, but because it is a practical program that can be implemented in the near future. The level can be raised to an adequate level within a short period of time."[22]

The commission noted, "Any program which provides income without work may have some effect on labor force participation. Some secondary and part-time workers as well as primary workers [here the commission meant wives as opposed to husbands] may withdraw from the labor force or reduce their hours worked. However, we do not believe that work disincentive effects of the proposed program would be serious. The level of income provided is low, and we do not believe that the poor are anxious to receive less income rather than more."

It asserted, "Requiring low-income households to support themselves from earnings creates gross inequities because every able-bodied adult has not been assured of opportunities to develop skills fully, and to find employment." And it declared, "Since we do not now have employment for all who want to work, employability tests lose much of their meaning in the aggregate. But they allow abuses in individual cases."

NWRO Plan

That same year, the National Welfare Rights Organization announced its support for a guaranteed income, but it pegged it to Labor Department figures for the "lower living level" for a family of four, $5,500 in 1969. In 1971, the NWRO revised its proposal to account for the increased cost of living and called for a $6,500 income for four, with $2,250 for single people.

Under its proposal, payments would rise as prices and the average family income of the country went up. People with jobs would be able to deduct the cost of child care, transportation, uniforms, tools, union dues, and other work expenses, and they could keep one-third of the rest of their wages. A four-person family would get some aid until its earned income reached $9,750, and families with incomes up to $11,461 would pay reduced taxes.

Its sample budget for a family of four called for $50 a week for food, $137 a month for housing, $76 a month for clothing and personal items like shampoo, $367 a year for medical care, $11 a week for transportation, and $7 a week for reading, recreation, and educational costs.

The plan would provide either benefits or tax relief to over half the country's population and would cost some $70 billion a year. As a result, the NWRO said, "the 20 percent of the people with the highest income would receive only 20 percent of the country's total income instead of the 43 percent they get now, and the bottom 20 percent would have about 15 percent instead of its present 6 percent."

The program would have no forced-work requirement, and jobs offered to recipients would have to meet minimum wage and fair labor standards.

The NWRO bill was introduced into the House and Senate, but failed to muster more than a handful of supporters. On March 25, 1972, some thirty thousand people participated in an NWRO Children's March for Survival to protest the Nixon Administration's policies on welfare, education and child care and to support the $6,500 minimum income.

However, it was evident that Congress was far more likely to pass a bill in line with the President's proposals. The House had already approved H.R. 1 which revised welfare drastically, and not in the direction desired by the National Welfare Rights Organization.

There are several major issues that are at the heart of the demands and protests of the welfare-rights movement and which are central to the debate over welfare reform.

First, the demands for a guaranteed income are set in the context of a society that actually pays out all kinds of subsidies to the middle class and the rich, but does not call them welfare. Income guarantees are nothing new except for the poor.

Second, the demands that welfare mothers work and the protests over illegitimacy are directly related to the role and status of women in this society. The fact that the majority of adults on welfare are women is itself significant. It should not be surprising that, in a society where most women are dependent on their husbands, they become dependent on the state when their husbands leave them. Or that in a society where women are underpaid and child-care facilities hardly exist, that they cannot earn enough alone to support their families.

Welfare for the Rich

The government provides far more in financial guarantees and assistance to people who are not poor than to those on welfare. In fact, some critics assert that the real "welfare crisis" has been caused by overpayments to the rich.

A study in 1971 by Senator William Proxmire's Joint Economic Committee reported that almost one-fourth of the

9
ISSUES – SUBSIDIES AND WOMEN

total federal budget, more than $63 billion, is spent on federal "subsidies."[1]

The government pays large amounts to aid companies in particular industries. About $5 billion a year goes to farmers for price supports and soil-bank payments.[2] The government also pays them to take land out of production which cuts down the supply and increases the price of food. All this adds up to a 15 percent tax for the consumer or $4.5 billion.[3] Only a fraction of the money goes to the 2 million subsistence farmers in the country. The poorer half of the farm population gets 9 percent of the total, and the wealthier 19 percent gets 63 percent.[4]

Mississippi Senator James Eastland has received well over $100,000 annually for years for *not* farming land he owns. Some farmers have received more than $1 million.[5] Seventy percent of rural Americans earn less than the poverty level.

Federal aid to transportation in the U.S. goes largely to build roads that aid the automobile, not for mass transit needed by the poor. Programs that aid colleges and universities help the middle class and the rich, since the poor lack the education or funds needed to enroll.

The federal government pays $224 million a year to fourteen shipping companies to subsidize the salaries of their workers (about $12,000 per seaman) and pays $238 million a year to subsidize the salaries of workers who build the ships (about $8,000 per worker).[6] The shipowners pocket the profits.

Government taxes pay about $640 million for the cost of air traffic control and the construction of airport facilities used by the owners of private airplanes. The subsidy comes to about $3,500 per aircraft.[7]

Even the government housing program for the poor aids the rich and middle class. A study for the House Banking and Currency Committee in 1972 revealed that as much as half of the money to subsidize housing for the poor ends up in the pockets of middlemen and speculators who make enormous profits off rehabilitated housing.[8]

Tax Breaks

Perhaps the major method of giving money to the rich and middle class is through the tax structure. Whatever one person does not pay in taxes leaves a deficit which must be made up by everyone else.

People who make their money by investing in stocks and bonds or property pay lower taxes than people who make the same amount by working. The "capital gains" rate is limited to 50 percent instead of 70 percent, which is the highest income tax. The savings from capital gains are worth about $13.7 billion a year to the one in twelve people who are investors.[9] In addition, estimates by the Internal Revenue Service are that 34 percent of private interest income goes unreported compared to 3 percent of taxable salary income.[10] According to HEW, in 1972, the incidence of welfare fraud was .4 of 1 percent.

A $27\frac{1}{2}$ percent "depletion allowance" amounts to $1.5 billion for the oil companies and their stockholders. The oil import quota, which restricts outside competition, is worth another $5 billion to oil companies—and higher prices to the consumer.[11] President Nixon's economic program has resulted in another $6 to $9 billion a year in tax benefits for corporations.[12]

The middle class and the rich benefit from housing subsidies through federal tax deductions for property taxes and mortgage interest payments. A couple earning $25,000 a year that buys a $50,000 house gets a benefit of $1,000 a year; a family with a $10,000 income and a $25,000 house gets a benefit of $350.[13]

Up to 70 percent of the aid goes to families with incomes of over $10,000. The subsidy, amounting to $9.6 billion a year, is more than twice the total budget of the U.S. Department of Housing and Urban Development and more than fifty times the amount of federal money spent directly on housing assistance to the poor. The property tax and mortgage interest deductions amount to more money every year than all the housing programs of the past twenty years.[14]

If one figures up all the federal funds distributed through social security, welfare, unemployment benefits, workmen's compensation, veterans' disability, and railroad retirement benefits, one would find that people earning below $5,000 get $296 a person and those with incomes of $25,000 to $40,000 get $1,146.[15]

Who Gets Aid

The "weekly welfare check" from all tax subsidies has been calculated to equal 31 cents to the poor, $12.52 to those earning $10,000 to $15,000; $229.07 to those with incomes of $50,000 to $100,000 and $13,854.78 to millionaires.[16] Some 3,000 families with incomes of more than 1 million dollars a year enjoy tax loopholes that allow them to avoid paying $2.2 billion in taxes while the 6 million poorest families have tax deductions that save them $92 million in taxes. The loopholes in the tax law resulted in 112 people with incomes over $200,000 paying no taxes at all in 1970.[17]

The members of the welfare-rights movement are well aware of these facts. The first NWRO president, Johnnie Tillmon, said, "We say poor people in this country do not get welfare. Farmers get welfare. Middle-class homeowners get welfare. Airlines get welfare. Oil millionaires get welfare. Almost everyone in this country gets some kind of government handout. We get the crumbs!"[18]

Social Security

Even the social security program, which provides old-age pensions, turns out to benefit the middle class more than the poor. The social security tax is 11.7 percent on wages (including the employer contribution) and 8 percent on the earnings of the self-employed, up to $10,800 and to $12,000 beginning in 1974.

Since there are no deductions and since the tax is on a limited amount of income, those with smaller incomes end up paying a much larger percentage of it on social security taxes than the rich. Conservative economist Milton Friedman charges that social security programs "appear on balance to transfer income from the relatively low-income classes to middle and upper-income classes."[19]

Social security is not really a pension program in the sense that one gets out of it what one has put in. Benefits are weighted in favor of the poor and people with dependents. And unlike insurance, where you don't get higher benefits without paying higher premiums, Congress can decree high benefits for people no longer working and paying social security taxes. The added costs are picked up by those who are still in the work force.

Unlike pensions, social security benefits are dependent on what other income a person has. Some beneficiaries may have other income from stocks and bonds or from rents on property. Their benefits are paid in part by workers who have little income to spare. At the same time, old people who continue working have their benefits reduced or cut off entirely.

Friedman says that if the money spent on social security and welfare programs, public housing, urban renewal, farm subsidies, and similar programs whose cost was over $75 billion in 1969–70 was divided among the then more than 24 million poor people, it would come to over $3,000 *a person*.

He said, "The problem is not that the government is spending too little on redistributive programs, but that most of the money is not going to the poor."[20] His critics point out that Congress is much more likely to appropriate money for social programs than to give $3,000 apiece to the nation's poor.

Majority of Poor Are Women

Most of the money also goes to men. Two-thirds of the people in poverty and virtually all the adults on AFDC are women. They are condemned to poverty not only by the same economic conditions that bear down on the male poor, but by social mores and job discrimination that force into poverty or dependency most women who do not have men to support them.

To begin with, women are brought up to believe that their role is to get married and have children and that they will be supported by their husbands. If their husbands divorce or desert them, they often are left without the training or job experience that would enable them to support themselves. Since husbands rarely keep the children of broken marriages, the women are left to support not only themselves but their families. Departed husbands also rarely contribute to the support of their children.

In cases where the couple is not legally married, the woman is virtually always left to support and raise children on her own. The difficulty of securing abortions, which were illegal in most states until the Supreme Court struck down bans on abortion in 1973, and the lack of child-care facilities have made it almost inevitable that poor women who became pregnant out of wedlock were forced onto welfare.

There are at present 8 million children in families with

only mothers, and at least 60 percent of these families are on welfare. Even when women alone with children find work, they often cannot earn enough to support themselves and their families. About 14 percent of women on welfare work and still receive supplemental aid because of their low incomes. In New York City, a woman with three children can earn $2 an hour and still be eligible for AFDC. Many earn only the minimum wage at jobs that are seasonal or irregular.

The major welfare issues are also "women's issues." Illegitimacy is related to women's rights to birth control and abortion. Work problems are related to sex discrimination in employment and to the lack of adequate child-care facilities for working mothers.

Illegitimacy

Probably the most explosive issue is illegitimacy. In 46 percent of the families on AFDC, there is at least one illegitimate child. (The notion that children should be labeled "legitimate" or "illegitimate," as if the latter had no real right to exist, merely because their parents did not pay $3 to the state for a marriage license, is another important issue.) The largest single cause and fastest growing category of AFDC eligibility is now out-of-wedlock births.

Once the government establishes a program and sets certain eligibility standards, does everyone who meets those standards have a right to benefits regardless of whether they adopt the sexual behavior or life-style advocated by the majority? Assuming that the purpose of the welfare program is to keep people from desperate poverty or virtual starvation (it does not pretend to take them out of poverty) can there be regulations or even indignation relating to the marital status or sexual habits of the mother or the legitimacy or illegitimacy of her children? Do people ask the recipients of farm subsidies about their sex lives?

In a case that occurred over thirty years ago, a man was denied assistance because "despite all efforts to dissuade him, [he] insists upon his right to sleep under an old barn, in a nest of rags to which he has to crawl on his hands and knees."

The New York State Supreme Court ruled in 1941 that "he has no right to defy the standards and conventions of civilized society while being supported at public expense. This is true even though some of those conventions may be somewhat artificial. One is impressed with appellant's argument that he enjoys the life he lives in his humble "home" as he calls it. It may possibly be true, as he says, that his health is not threatened by the way he lives. After all he should not demand that the public, at its expense, allow him to experiment with a manner of living which is likely to endanger his health so that he will become a still greater expense to the public."[21]

The Rights of Recipients

The question is whether a person must order his or her life so as to be able to demand more of the aid that is his or hers by right and whether the government can impose certain requirements, including a life-style, on people that receive government aid, when it cannot impose the same requirements on the population at large.

People protest that unmarried women who have children are doing so purposely with the knowledge that they can live on welfare. Or they are having children, knowing full well that they cannot support them. Or, at the very least, while already on welfare, they are failing to exercise the caution, generally translated as abstinence, that ought to be required of anyone living off government handouts.

The issue here is whether women or couples on welfare have the same right to have children as anyone else or whether people have the right to have children only if they can support them. If welfare is aimed at providing some of the decencies of life to people who have little or no income, is one of the decencies of life the right to have children?

Related to that is the question of whether the right to welfare assistance under the law is a property right, and thus equivalent to the ability to provide support, or is a charity and thus to be meted out to the deserving. One of the marks of the "deserving" has always been the effort to become independent of assistance, to do whatever one can to avoid claiming the aid of charity.

No one objects to people claiming their property rights. If a farmer who gets payments from the government to take land out of production buys more land to take out of production and thus gets more money from the government, no one protests, even though he is getting money from the government for not working. Does the farmer have an obligation to stop being eligible for soil bank payments? Should he have tried to avoid claiming them in the first place?

Morality and Divorce

Part of the attack on unwed mothers who claim welfare benefits is related to conventional notions of morality that say that people should not have children unless they are married to each other. A major problem is that for the poor, desertion and living together without marriage is often the result of the high cost of divorce. Poor people can rarely afford the $200 or $300 it costs to get a legal divorce.

One recent study in California showed that only 2.6 percent of the children on AFDC were the result of casual, short-term relationships.[22]

Another part of the "morality" question is that public disapproval of sex outside of marriage is directed against women, not men, and only if it leads to children born out of wedlock. The NWRO points out that "the illegitimate behavior of affluent people is more easily concealed through quick marriages, privileged abortions and contraceptives" and that "poor peoples' illegitimate babies are more likely to be recorded for public condemnation."[23]

Middle-class and wealthy whites who do not have abortions are more likely than minority women to place their children for adoption. Two-thirds of white babies born out of wedlock are put up for adoption compared to 7 percent of black babies.

According to the Department of Health, Education and Welfare, one-third of all firstborn American children born between 1964 and 1966 were conceived out of wedlock, but by the time the children were born, nearly two-thirds of the mothers had married, making the children "legitimate."

Birth Control

Poor women have much less access to contraception and abortion than women of the middle and upper classes. A recent government study showed that over half the counties in the U.S. offered no public family-planning services at all and that a large number of nonprofit hospitals, in which 60 to 65 percent of low-income mothers deliver their babies, offered no contraceptive programs either.

A study in Chicago showed that nearly half the mothers whose youngest children were born out of wedlock said they had no information about how to prevent contraception or that they used ineffective home remedies. One woman said, "When you are a country girl or a country boy, you have to be in the city for quite a while before you get the word that you should get hip. I didn't know nothin' about nothin' to use no more than just the ordinary things men buy at the drug store."

Her children had been born in the county hospital in Chicago. She said, "At this particular time they didn't tell you nothin' about using nothin'. Now when I did get hip to myself I asked the doctor if he could space my children for me or stop me from findin' kids. And he told me that if they would stop me from findin' kids I'd lose my health and findin' kids hasn't done anything to me and for that reason 'we wouldn't stop you unless it was doing something to your health.' This was fifteen years ago, so in due time I just kept having them."[24]

The 1967 social security amendments made it mandatory for states to provide contraceptive information, with the federal government paying 75 percent of the cost. However, by 1970, services were provided to little more than a hundred thousand women. Only a handful of states reported reaching as much as half the welfare population. By 1971, HEW said that only twelve states had taken advantage of the grants to set up family planning programs for AFDC recipients.

Laws also have set minimum age limits for contraceptive patients, although almost half the out-of-wedlock births are to mothers under twenty. Most school districts do not allow pregnant students to remain in school nor to return after their babies are born. Thus, the girls' educations are stopped and they have virtually no chance of getting the training they need to earn a living.

The President's Commission on Population Growth in 1972 recommended that states make contraception available to teen-agers and that they make abortions available to all women who want them, the latter not as a means of population control but to expand individual freedom, giving women "freedom from the burden of unwanted child-bearing."

Nixon Statement

President Nixon rejected both proposals. Regarding contraception for minors, he said, "Such measures would do nothing to preserve and strengthen close family relations." He repeated his own view that abortion is "an unacceptable means of population control" and added that he believed "in the right of married couples to make these judgments by themselves." Critics found the statement somewhat contradictory.

In a few states, legislators have made unsuccessful attempts to force sterilization on unwed mothers who applied for welfare. In 1959, lawmakers in North Carolina proposed to sterilize mothers of illegitimate children. In 1971, a Tennessee legislator introduced a bill to sterilize unwed mothers who applied for welfare and, if the women refused to undergo the operation, to declare their children orphans and make them wards of the state.

In 1972, the California Social Welfare Board, an advisory group appointed by the governor, proposed that any woman who had a third illegitimate child should be declared unfit and morally depraved and forced to hand the third child over to the state. If the mother was under sixteen, the first child would make her unfit.

Such proposals were sometimes put forth with the charge that if women did not get money for children born out of wedlock, they would not have them. Louis Kriesberg, the author of *Mothers In Poverty,* wrote recently, "If children were born in order to maintain and increase assistance benefits, then one would expect husbandless mothers to remain on the welfare rolls for a very long time. In a national study of closed AFDC cases, however, the median length of the time payments were received was less than two years." He said, "There seems to be no evidence that husbandless mothers desire to have illegitimate children."[25]

Women on welfare reject the notion that they have children to earn more money. They say the added benefits, an average of $35 a month, are not enough even to care for their children properly and that no one would bear and raise a child for the sake of an added $9 a week from the welfare department.

Need for Child Care

The next major issue in welfare is work, and for mothers that means a need for child care. During World War II, the Lanham Act created child-care facilities for some 1,600,000 children of working women who were employed in war plants. The children were cared for in vacant stores, churches, private homes, and wherever space was available. At the end of the war, the federal aid ceased, and the centers were shut down. Only New York City and California continued to provide public funds for day care.[26]

Today, there are only some 640,000 spaces in child-care centers for the 6 million preschool children of women who work. The government recognizes that the lack of child care is one of the chief obstacles to getting women off welfare and into jobs. Study after study by government and private agencies have shown that the vast majority of women on welfare want to work but have no adequate child-care arrangements. Sixty per cent of AFDC mothers have at least one child under six, and half of them have two. Eight out of ten have children under eight. Since federal funds for day care help less than 5 percent of the poor children who need it, most of the children of welfare mothers who work are cared for in informal arrangements with relatives, neighbors, and older children. Some are "latchkey kids"; they have keys to the house and take care of themselves.

In 1971, Congress set further limitations on child care by imposing a ceiling on the 75 percent federal matching grants for social welfare programs.

Middle-class women suffer from the lack of child-care facilities as well. President Nixon in 1971 vetoed a bill to provide child care for large numbers of American children, not only the poor, and declared that he was against committing "the vast moral authority of the national Government to the side of communal approaches to child rearing over against the family-centered approach."

However, Nixon's opposition to child care for the majority

of Americans made welfare recipients suspicious about the government's plans to put *their* children in child-care centers so mothers can work. Many of them disagreed with the President's ideas about child-rearing, but they viewed his double standard for welfare families as an indication of contempt and lack of concern for the well-being of their children.

Welfare mothers, in fact, are well aware that, although 30 percent of American mothers with children under six and also half the mothers with school-age children work, the dominant belief of the country is that it is better for women to stay home and take of their children. They resent the notion that they and their children should not have the same right.

The NWRO said, "Whether or not one accepts the notion that child-raising should be 'woman's work,' the fact is that in most American families child-raising is woman's work—and hard work, at that. If a woman's husband dies or leaves home, does child-raising suddenly cease to be 'work'?"[27]

The NWRO supported the idea of child care for all women who chose it for their children. It condemned the President's veto of the child-care bill and his support of the "custodial" kind of care proposed in his welfare reform bill.

However, it added, "It's at least paradoxical, perhaps cruel, that a society which traditionally extols the virtues of motherhood is simultaneously forcing some mothers to leave their homes and children for low-wage, dead-end, outside jobs."[28]

Women and the Work Ethic

Johnnie Tillmon, the first NWRO president and, beginning in 1973, its national director, said in the feminist magazine *MS.:*

In this country, we believe in something called the "work ethic." That means that your work is what gives you human worth. But the work ethic itself is a double standard. It applies to men and to women on welfare. It doesn't apply to all women. If you're a society lady from Scarsdale and you spend all your time sitting on your prosperity, paring your nails, well, that's okay. Women aren't supposed to work. They're supposed to be married.

But if you don't have a man to pay for everything, particularly if you have kids, then everything changes. You've "failed" as a woman, because you've failed to attract and keep a man. There's something wrong with you. It can't possibly be the man's fault, his lack of responsibility. It must be yours. That's why Governor Reagan can get away with slandering AFDC recipients, calling them "lazy parasites," "pigs at the trough," and such.

She declared that many of "the 'employable' mothers are already employed—many full time—but at such pitifully low wages that we still need, and are entitled to, public assistance to survive." And she added, "There are some ten million jobs that now pay less than the minimum wage, and if you're a woman you've got the best chance of getting one."[29]

Women in poverty are likely to have had less educational opportunities than people in the rest of the population. Only 16 percent of the women on AFDC have completed high school, and 43 percent never went beyond the eighth grade.[30]

Nevertheless, 15 percent of the women on welfare work, and 75 percent have worked in the past, usually before the birth of their first child. Nearly half worked afterward.[31]

Women Get Lower Wages

However, the low-wage, dead-end jobs available to women on welfare are a central factor and reason for the welfare crisis. Even if women have child-care centers for their children, the extent of sex discrimination (and, for many, racial discrimination) in employment and wages makes it virtually impossible for them to support themselves and their families. NWRO President Beulah Sanders declared, "We have no problem with mothers working. We do have a problem about not paying them adequately."

Women in the population as a whole have fewer job opportunities than men, earn less money for the same work, and have a higher unemployment rate. For example, in 1972, women salesworkers earned $4,188 compared to $9,790 for men. Women service workers were paid $3,953 compared to $6,955 for men.

In 1970 the full-time year-round median wages of workers were: white men, $9,373; minority men, $6,598; white women, $5,490; and minority women, $4,674. And the difference between men's and women's wages had increased in the past five years. In 1965, women earned 64 percent of what men earned; by 1970, their incomes had been reduced to under 60 percent of men's wages.[32]

The wages poor women earn often turn out to be less than they would be entitled to on welfare. One woman in New York took a government training course to learn bookkeeping. She reported, "Then the only job I was offered was $71 a week as a cashier clerk. I would have lost my Social Security, and with five kids to support, I couldn't take it. So I went back on welfare."[33]

Another in Indiana tried supporting three children by working at two jobs, at a tavern until 2 A.M. and in a radio parts factory beginning at 7 A.M. "I ended up in the hospital with nervous exhaustion," she said, "and for the next six months we lived on a $12 weekly grocery order until they finally accepted me on welfare."[34]

For the most part, the women on welfare have worked in the past at clerical, service, and factory work. Most of the women who worked full time as maids had incomes of under $2,000 a year.

Although lack of education is often the cause of poverty, 18 percent of college-educated women who have children and no wage-earning husbands are in poverty. Women with college degrees on the average earn less than men with eighth-grade educations.[35]

Less than a third of divorced fathers pay any child support, and the typical payment in California is $75 a month. One recent study of fathers who failed to help support their children at all showed that nearly one in five was a professional, semiprofessional, owner, manager, official, or crafts worker.[36]

Sex Discrimination in Federal Training

Women even faced discrimination in the WIN program designed to get them off welfare and into self-supporting jobs. Government policies have supported the same notions of priority for male workers that helped cause the welfare problem in the first place. Although some 95 percent of the adults on AFDC are women, 37 percent of the people in the WIN program are men.[37] Department of Labor regulations established the following order of priority: unemployed fathers, mothers who have participated in government work or training programs, youths sixteen and over who are not in school, mothers with only school-age children, and mothers with preschool children.

In 1970, a Seattle woman with two school-aged children tried to get into a training program, but was put on a waiting list because priority was being given to training and hiring men. A year later, Shelley Thorn, another woman in the same city filed a suit against HEW charging sex discrimination because she too had been forced onto a waiting list.[38]

Even when they get into WIN and other government training programs, women are trained as clerks or typists, while men are taught higher paying crafts and skills.

In the decade of the 1960's, the number of poor families with fathers present was reduced by 50 percent to about 3.3 million. The number of poor families with only mothers remained the same, 1.9 million. In 1971, when the number of poor people increased by over a million for the first time in ten years, half the increase was due to the poverty of families with only mothers present although these families are only 14 percent of the population. Such families accounted for virtually all the increase in poverty among blacks. Nearly six out of ten poor black families are headed by a woman alone.[39] And the incomes of low-income families headed by women are much farther below the poverty line than those headed by men.

The poverty of Americans is increasingly becoming the poverty of women, as shown in the following table:

People in Poverty by Family Head*

(Including Unrelated Individuals)

White male	10,635,000	(6.8%)
Black male	3,267,000	(21.2%)
White female	7,145,000	(32.1%)
Black female	4,129,000	(55.8%)

* The notion that when males and females are present, the males "head" their families and that females do so only when males are absent is a sexist Bureau of Census peculiarity that distorts statistics by ignoring the existence of families where both wife and husband work.

The Changes, by Family Head, of People in Poverty

from 1960 to 1971

	Male Head (and Unrelated Individuals)		Female Head (and Unrelated Individuals)	
1960	29,188,000	(18.5%)	10,663,000	(49.5%)
1965	22,127,000	(13.2%)	11,058,000	(46.0%)
1971	14,151,000	(8.1%)	11,409,000	(38.0%)

Bureau of the Census, July 1972

President Nixon's welfare reform proposal was a major step backward to the notion that no one, including the mothers of small children, ought to get public assistance without working for it. The bill eliminated the matching payments incentive to states to add to the minimal federal grants which were below what 90 percent of families had been receiving under AFDC. At the same time, it raised both social security payments to the aged and public assistance to the aged, blind, and disabled.

The President's welfare bill was first introduced in 1969. It passed the House but died in committee in the Senate a year later. In a new session of Congress, it was introduced in the House as H.R. 1, passed in 1971, and sent to the Senate.[1]

The bill, nicknamed FAP for Family Assistance Plan and called Workfare by the Administration, did away with the categories of public assistance established in 1935 and substituted three programs, one for families with dependent children with employable parents, one for such families without employable parents, and one for the aged, blind, and disabled.

The family programs were no longer limited to those where the father was absent or unemployed. Single people and childless couples still could not get aid, but any family with a child under eighteen or under twenty-two and attending school and not married was eligible if its income was low enough.

10
WORKFARE

Eligibility

The eligibility level and the income guarantee were the same: $2,400 for a family of four ($800 each for the first two people, $400 each for the next three, $300 for the next two and $200 for the eighth.) The grant would be only $1,600 if the mother refused to work.

Eligibility was no longer determined by a family's immediate need—its lack of any resources at the time of application—but by its income in the present and past three calendar quarters of the year. For example, if a family of four had no income for the current three-month period and none for the prior nine months, it would get the full $2,400 in monthly payments of $200 as long as it continued to have no income.

However, if it had income over $600 in any of the preceeding three quarters, that "excess" would be deducted from present payments. If it had no income in the previous nine months but some in the present period, the grant would still be reduced by the current income.

Any excess over $600 a quarter was assumed to be available to pay for future expenses but not needed to pay for past costs in periods where earnings were under $600.

In effect, a family with an adequate income which was suddenly faced with unemployment, illness, or other financial disaster might have to wait as long as nine months before it became eligible for aid.

The family would be allowed to keep $1,500 in property plus a home of reasonable value, a car needed for work or medical purposes, and a reasonable amount of clothing and household goods.

The law specified that application would not be by declaration, a method that had begun to be used under the old law, and it called for special investigators to check on eligibility. It also provided for vendor payments (mailed directly to landlords, grocers, etc.) when that was deemed necessary to prevent people from spending grants on unauthorized items.

Families would have to report their incomes every three months and fines of $25, $50, and $100 would be levied against those who failed to do so within thirty days after each quarter. Families would have to reapply for benefits every two years. Full-time college students would not be eligible for aid, nor would pregnant women, who were eligible under AFDC rules, be able to get assistance on the basis of their unborn children.

The House Ways and Means Committee report on the bill said, "Every possible step will be taken under the new programs to assure that only those eligible for the benefits will get them." It said it was convinced that thousands of people on AFDC rolls did not belong there and that there were people on welfare who did not report their earnings.

"Opportunities for Families" Program

Families with employable members would be assigned to the Opportunities for Families Program. Everyone would be required to register for work or training except children under sixteen, students under twenty-two, people, or caretakers of people too old, ill, or incapacitated to care for themselves, and mothers of children under three (under six for the first two years of the program). If a male adult in the family registered, the mother was exempt.

About 2.6 million families were expected to be assigned to the OFP category.

The bill made registration of all other people voluntary and did not permit the states to establish other exemptions. The House Committee report said, "The weakness of the 1967 welfare amendments was that the clear congressional intent of getting able-bodied welfare recipients (including mothers where there was adequate day care available) into work and training was effectively diluted by federal and state officials who did not share this objective with equal enthusiasm."

People would have to take any jobs available unless the wages were below the federal, state, or local minimums for that kind of work. If the job was not covered by a minimum wage law, they would have to work for as little as three-quarters of the federal minimum, $1.20 an hour. People also could be referred to public service jobs that would have to pay at least the federal minimum of $1.60 or the prevailing wage, if that was higher. The bill called for $800 million to provide 200,000 public service jobs.

People in training would get an additional $30 a month as an incentive. People who worked would keep the first $720 a year of their income, plus a third of the rest.

Families also could disregard income earned by students, and irregular gifts or earnings (from babysitting, etc.) and child-care costs of up to $2,000 for a family of four, with an increase of $200 for each additional person up to a limit of $3,-000. After a family of four had an earned income of over $4,140, it would no longer get a federal subsidy.

Anyone who refused training or employment without a good reason would cause the family's grant to be reduced by $800 a year.

The bill called for $540 million for 225,000 training slots in addition to the 187,000 authorized under the WIN program. There would be priority given in the training program to teen-age mothers who would be required to finish high school.

Family Assistance Plan

Families exempt from the work and training provision, an expected 1.4 million families, would get the same amount of aid under the Family Assistance Plan. However, individuals who were considered eligible for rehabilitation would be referred to state vocational rehabilitation agencies, would receive $30 a month for an incentive allowance and expenses and would have benefits reduced if they refused to participate in the programs. This requirement included alcoholics and drug addicts.

The drafters of the bill recognized that the lack of child care was an obstacle to mothers getting jobs or training.

H.R. 1 called for $50 million for the construction of child-care centers and $700 million to buy child-care services to take care of 291,000 preschool and 584,000 school-age children. (In 1971 there were 2.3 million AFDC children under six and 2.8 million from six to twelve). It allowed the centers to charge the mothers full or partial fees to pay the cost of the centers. (The average cost per child in child-care facilities is about $2,000.) It said also that care "should not be care of low quality, but should include educational, health, nutritional, and other needed services wherever possible. However, the lack of child care of that level would not be good cause for failure to take training if other adequate and acceptable care is available." The agency not the parent would decide what was adequate and acceptable.

The bill increased federal funds to help states find and obtain support payments from deserting fathers. Mothers would be required to help locate the fathers of their children and to file suit against them for support. As an encouragement, a third of alimony or child-support payments would not be counted as income in figuring out the welfare benefit.

Deserting fathers would be liable for the cost of welfare benefits given to their families or for the amount of court-ordered payments they did not make. The money could be deducted from their benefits under other federal programs such as social security or unemployment compensation.

The bill also called for family-planning services run by the federal government for all families receiving benefits, a program expected to affect $1\frac{2}{3}$ million women. The House report noted that "experience under the present WIN program shows that a substantial number of women drop out of training and employment due to unwanted pregnancies."

Numerous other sections of the bill were aimed at doing away with rulings favorable to welfare recipients that had been won in court decisions or past legislation.

It required that the resources of stepfathers or "men in the house" be included in determining a family's eligibility, regardless of the men's responsibility under state law.

It provided for no cost-of-living increases.

It said that the determinations of fact made in fair hearings would not be subject to review by the courts.

In a move thought to be aimed at welfare-rights groups, it said that individuals who represented recipients in fair hearings had to be, in the judgment of the welfare department, "of good character," able to "render claimants valuable services," and "otherwise competent."

State Participation

Under H.R. 1, there was no requirement for states to provide matching funds. In five southern states and Puerto Rico, the new federal grant would mean an increase in amounts paid to families of four with no other income. For 90 percent of welfare families, it would mean a reduction.

However, states could pay supplemental assistance if

they chose to do so. The federal government volunteered to administer those payments at no cost to the state and also to guarantee that, if the state did not raise the level of its payments, the federal government would pay, for five years, any increased costs over the 1971 appropriation that resulted from increased rolls. This would not apply to state aid given to families with employed fathers.

States were given the option of setting residence requirements for the recipients of their supplements and of excluding families with employed or employable members. States would have to apply the federal income-disregard formula—$720 a year plus a third of the rest; and the federal government would not administer special needs grants.

Change in Medicaid

H.R. 1 also changed eligibility and benefits for medicaid, the program of government payments for health care for the poor that had been instituted in 1966. Under the law, states had been required to give medicaid payments to all people eligible for public assistance.

However, the House report noted that under those rules, the new family-assistance plans would bring many thousands of additional people into the health-care program, and this would be expensive. It voted therefore to limit medicaid to families whose income fell below $133\frac{1}{3}$ percent of the payment level, i.e., $3,200 for a family of four. After the family's medical bills used up their "excess" income, they would become eligible for medicaid. The report said this would save the government $140 million.

Under the new medicaid rules, recipients also would have to pay for services previously paid for by the government. They would have to pay $7.50 a day after the thirtieth day of hospitalization and $15 a day after the sixtieth day. They would also have to pay for a third of the cost of nursing homes after the first sixty days.

The bill eliminated the requirement that all states provide comprehensive medicaid programs by 1971. States would not be required to spend more on medicaid than they did in 1971.

Changes in Other Categories

While it cut benefits to families with dependent children, H.R. 1 raised federal benefits to the indigent aged, blind, and disabled and added disabled children to the list of eligibles. It removed the program from administration by state welfare departments. Under H.R. 1, the federal social security department would send out the checks for those categories.

The standard of eligibility and level of payment would be $130 and, by 1975, $150 for an individual, and $195 and then $200 for a couple. Applicants would be allowed to have the same resources as people in the family programs and could claim similar exemptions.

However, if a person lived with a friend or relative, the value of the room and board would be considered equivalent to a third of the benefit, and the payment would be reduced accordingly even if the person had to pay for the accommodations. There would be no reduction if the person lived in a rooming or boarding house.

Disabled persons, including alcoholics and drug addicts, would be required to participate in rehabilitation programs or lose their benefits. The bill had a more liberal income-disregard provision for the disabled and blind than for the aged with the aim of encouraging the former to return to work. They could keep the first $85 a month of income plus half above that. Blind recipients could also keep work expenses. The aged could keep the first $60 a month plus a third of the rest.

The bill also allowed disabled recipients trial work periods of nine months in which to see whether they could hold a job. During this period they would not be removed from the welfare rolls; although, ordinarily, the ability to work would have made a person ineligible for aid. At the end of the nine months, the work would be evaluated to see if the person could be self-supporting or was eligible to remain on welfare.

As in the family programs, the states could choose to pay supplements which the federal government would administer, and they could set residence requirements. HEW estimated that as a result of higher eligibility levels, some 6.2 million people could get aid under the new adult program in 1973, 2.8 million more than received assistance from the old ones.

However, there was no *requirement* that the states pay supplementary assistance in order to get the grants. (The old program had been a matching one; states were required to pay their share.) Half the people on old age assistance had been getting as much or more than the new federal minimum, and many would stand to lose under the new law. In early 1973, no state had yet enacted legislation to provide state supplementation.

The requirement for quarterly income reports would be eliminated in the case of the very old, blind, or extremely disabled, where changes in income were unlikely.

The 1972 bill also made changes in social security benefits, raising them by 5 percent. (Congress later that year acted to increase old-age pensions by 20 percent even before the Senate had considered H.R. 1.)

Under the same bill, social security benefits were to be increased automatically whenever the cost of living rose 3 percent or more; widows and widowers would get 100 percent instead of $82\frac{1}{2}$ percent of their spouses' benefits, and the amount that people could earn without having benefits reduced would be increased. (These changes all were enacted.)

Nixon on the Work Ethic

The President, in an address before a joint session of Congress in 1971, urged action on H.R. 1 "so that going on welfare will not be more profitable than going to work—so that we can bring under control a system that has become a suffocating burden on State and local taxpayers, and a massive outrage against the people it was designed to help."

He said, "Hard work is what made America great. There could be no more dangerous delusion than the notion that we can maintain the standard of living that our own people sometimes complain about but the rest of the world envies, without continuing to work hard. The 'good life' is not the lazy life, or the empty life, or the life that consumes without producing. The good life is the active, productive, working life—the life that gives as well as gets."

He concluded, "Let us recognize once and for all that any work is preferable to welfare."[2]

President Nixon may have suffered some embarrassment

when it was revealed that his cousin Philip Milhous and Milhous' wife Anna were on welfare in California. The Milhouses were forced to turn to the California Rural Legal Assistance program for help when their check was cut in 1969. Mr. Milhous had a heart condition and Ms. Milhous suffered from arthritis. In 1972, Anna Milhous organized the Low Income Welfare Rights Organization of Nevada City, California.

Congressmen Explain the Bill

The House Ways and Means Committee report explained the motivation of the bill's supporters in Congress. It cited the sharp increase in AFDC recipients. From 1969 to 1970, the increase in the rolls had been 32 percent, From 1967 to 1972, the cost of AFDC had gone from $2 billion to nearly $7 billion.

The report declared, "Your committee believes that the American people do not want a system which results in promoting welfare as a way of life" and "your committee has developed a program which is in the interest of the taxpayers as well as the needy."

It said it believed that the bill would "reduce the number of families which are eligible for assistance and slow down the rate of growth of those which are receiving assistance."

The committee also explained why it had required people to accept jobs at 75 percent of the minimum wage: "There are about five and one-quarter million persons who now work for less than the Federal minimum wage of $1.60 per hour. It would be inequitable to excuse adult family members from such work when so many people are working at wages below that level."

In 1972, a proposal to raise the minimum wage was killed when the House refused to go into conference with the Senate to work out differences. The House had proposed raising the minimum to $2 an hour, but refused to extend coverage to domestic and farm workers and others not covered. The Senate had voted for a $2.20 minimum wage with coverage extended to 13 million new workers.

The Ways and Means Committee told why it required mothers with children under six to work. It said that about 5 million women, a third of all mothers with children under six, were in the labor force and "to require such women to support out of taxes on their earnings those mothers who choose not to work but to live on public monies would be inequitable in the extreme."

Four members of the House committee, Democrats Hugh Carey of New York, Charles Vanik of Ohio, William Green of Pennsylvania, and James Corman of California, voted for the bill but filed comments indicating some dissatisfaction. They said that $2,400, $1,500 below the government's official poverty line, was too low for families in the cities of the North and West. They noted, "It is no more than the $2,400 that the Ways and Means Committee itself considered necessary as a minimum payment to support an aged, blind or disabled family of two persons."

They said, "Unfortunately, the Committee rejected provisions to assure that no recipient would be worse off than under the existing law," and eliminated provisions it had passed in the first version of the bill requiring states to maintain their current payment levels.

The four also opposed "provisions that arbitrarily require all mothers with pre-school age children above three to work as a condition of receipt of benefits" and said that "both society and the family would be better served by a recognition that the work of the mother in caring for her children would be more meaningful than requirements which would separate her from vital family obligations."

They said minimum pay for jobs should be set at the minimum wage, not 75 percent of it. "Every effort should be made to avoid providing a captive work force to employers who offer jobs at substandard wages or working conditions."

They pointed out that provisions permitting states to reduce the scope of medicaid benefits, to require premium payments and impose cash deductibles on the medically indigent, will result in their exclusion from benefits or the transfer of the cost of their medical care to the already financially burdened cities and states.

Their criticism of the social security measures was that the increased benefits should have been raised at least partly by taxation rather than by increasing social security contributions, a burden which falls most heavily on low-wage earners.

NWRO Criticizes Bill

More angry criticism came from the welfare-rights movement. The National Welfare Rights Organization opposed the bill, charging that "there is no commitment to adequate income or to maintaining present payment levels in the 45 states where payments are now above $2,400."[3] It noted also: "Half of the families on welfare are black. Only one-fifth of the aged, disabled and blind recipients are black. The program that is largely black will pay half as much as the program that is largely white."

It condemned the forced-work requirements and said, "In the light of growing unemployment (nearly 6 percent in 1972) these provisions will only serve to deny benefits to needy people, harass innocent citizens, destroy family life and deny real opportunities for advancement." It declared, "The lack of adequate training, child care and employment provisions means no real opportunities for meaningful jobs, only harassment for poor people."

The NWRO asserted that "the purpose of F.A.P. is to subsidize low wage paying employers rather than enable poor people to become self-supporting. Families headed by a college or university student will not be eligible for benefits. Under current law, welfare mothers are regularly attending college in the WIN program. Under F.A.P., family heads will be denied the opportunity to receive the training necessary to enable them to advance to the limit of their capabilities."

They protested the change in child care regulations. "Under present law, a mother has the right to be consulted about the adequacy of the child care arrangements. No standards for child care arrangements to meet are written in the bill. Authorization of funds for child care in this bill are totally inadequate. Families may be asked to pay all or part of the child care costs." It noted, "Child care authorities estimate the actual cost at over $2,100 a year for the care of just one pre-school child, but the bill allows a total exemption of $2,000 for a family of four for all child care plus earnings of school children."

The NWRO protested, "The Federal government will not provide jobs. Public service employment authorized by F.A.P. would receive Federal funds for only three years."

It objected to the fact that aid was based not on current need but on past earnings. "A family could be denied assistance for six to nine months under this provision."

The NWRO opposed the inclusion of stepfathers' incomes. It protested the allowance of residency requirements by the states.

In a paper prepared for the Columbia Center on Social Welfare Policy and Law, welfare expert Elizabeth Wickenden expressed concern over the elements of coercion present in H.R. 1.[4]

She said it would be "an instrument of control and coercion" over the "employment, child rearing, family relationships, health care, drug use and other behavioral patterns" of the poor, that the authority for states to impose residency requirements was "a clear invitation to the control of free movement," and that for those assigned to Opportunities for Families, "the Labor Department assumes virtually complete control over their lives," penalizing them if they violate its directives.

The allowable wage of $1.20 an hour poses "an outright and virtually unlimited subsidy for employers of domestic labor as an answer to the so-called 'welfare mess.' This is at best a form of indenture," she asserted.

"The arbitrary and discriminatory character of the job obligation on single mothers is evidenced by the exemption from obligation on the wives of male beneficiaries still in the home. The prohibition against benefits to family heads who are full-time students is also an example of short-sighted punitive controls," she said.

According to Ms. Wickenden, "the prohibition of payments in behalf of an unborn child, long permitted under Federal AFDC regulations, assumes both that the pregnant woman is employable up to the fact of her delivery and is to be punitively restrained from those measures which might be necessary to her own and her child's health."

She declared that "the primary purpose of this so-called 'welfare reform' is not to improve the well-being and dignity of the beneficiary, it is to so control and harass his behavior at every point that he (and more often 'she') will be either coerced into conformity or driven from the program altogether. While the alternatives for survival in a period of growing unemployment and polarization between the haves and the have-nots (quaint terminology from another day) are not bright, for many they may well offer more dignity than these controls."

Feminists viewed the bill in the light of the role and status of women in the society. The National Organization for Women, testifying in opposition to H.R. 1, noted that, "the AFDC program was founded on the premise that any woman faced with trying to support children alone is going to have a difficult time. This premise continues to be true."[5] "Virtually all AFDC mothers," it said, "before they became economically dependent on the state were economically dependent on a man."

NOW said, "We still hear the argument that this country wouldn't have such an unemployment problem if women would stay home and mind the kids, and let the men earn the money." It asked, "What is it that makes cooking and cleaning the house and washing clothes and getting the kids off to school and taking care of the baby *normal,* in fact *ideal,* when these activities are supported by the income of a husband/father, yet *deviant* when supported by public funds?"

It opposed the "exploitation" of the requirement to accept jobs at 75 percent of the minimum wage, and pointed out that, "One of the reasons that many of these women are on welfare in the first place is that the wage structure for women is so low."

It said that the poverty of AFDC families was due to the fact that the women had not been economically independent but had been dependent on men. The solution, it said, was in changing the economic status of women.

The National Welfare Rights Organization sought support for its own bill for a guaranteed income of $6,500 for a family of four.

While public debate continued over H.R. 1, and while the Senate Finance Committee considered its own version of welfare reform, the Congress passed two other bills dealing with welfare, both reinforcing the notion that nobody should get anything without working for it.

The Food Stamp bill of 1971 for the first time established a work registration requirement. After protests, the rules were modified to exclude mothers with children under eighteen; however, anyone between nineteen and sixty-four who did not work at least thirty hours a week, was not incapacitated or caring for incapacitated members of the household, and was not a student, had to register.

They were required to accept jobs that paid at least $1.30 an hour or the state or federal minimums that applied. If a married couple without children applied for stamps, they both had to be either working or registered for training or work.

Talmadge Work Rules

In 1971, by voice vote and without having a written copy of the bill available, Congress passed the Talmadge amendments which had been tacked onto a bill dealing with payments for burial expenses.

The amendments repealed the section of the welfare law that allowed states to determine who was "appropriate" for referral to jobs and training. Some states had excluded mothers of small children. The new law requires all AFDC recipients to register for work or training except children under sixteen, mothers with children under six or with husbands who registered, anyone who was taking care of an ill or incapacitated member of the household or was too ill, old, or disabled to work himself or herself and people living too far from project sites.

States that did not refer for jobs or training at least 15 percent of the average number of people registered during the year would be penalized by subtraction of one percentage point from its matching percentage for AFDC for each point that referrals fell below 15 percent.

Referrals would be made in a priority order starting with unemployed fathers, then mothers who volunteered, then mothers and pregnant women under nineteen, then children and relatives sixteen or over not in school, work, or training. (The Thorn case banning priorities for men arose under the old WIN program; Talmadge raised the issue all over again.)

Wages in public service employment or on-the-job training would reflect the "applicable minimum wage for the particular work concerned." The NWRO charged, "Jobs not currently protected by the minimum wage, such as domestic work, will only have to pay what the minimum rate of pay for that job is. There is not even language in the amendment about prevailing wages—only minimum wages."[6]

Some 2.6 million heads of families were eligible for

registration under the amendment. If the states referred the minimum of 15 percent, 390,000 jobs and training spots would have to be made available. The states were required to put up 10 percent matching funds and the law required that a third of new WIN budgets be spent for on-the-job training and public service employment. There would be no income disregards in public service employment; recipients would be working for their grants alone.

Furthermore, under the old WIN program, the emphasis was on institutional and classroom training. Under Talmadge, the emphasis was on job placement. In the State of Washington, the welfare agency sought in late 1972 to eliminate several hundred college students from the rolls. And in Brooklyn, New York, a woman taking courses for a high school diploma was told to drop out or lose her grant.[7] The development of administrative procedures delayed the program so that completion of registration was not required until the end of 1972.

The NWRO pointed out that if states spent a third of the $137 million WIN appropriation for those purposes, at an average cost of $4,400 per person, they would be able to accommodate fewer than 10,500 out of the 1.5 million adults on AFDC. It charged that the Talmadge registration requirements were at minimum a form of harassment and that the government had failed to appropriate enough money to provide meaningful jobs or training.

Effect of Federal Economic Program

Furthermore, President Nixon's anti-inflation program was calculated to bring down prices by limiting wages and spending, a move he and his advisors knew would also result in increased unemployment. He did not propose any programs to take care of the workers who would be thrown out of work because of his decision, nor did he explain how welfare recipients could be expected to find jobs when the government adopted a program that was certain to increase unemployment.

Even before the Senate considered H.R. 1, the Nixon Administration gave the go-ahead to two states that wanted to put into effect more restrictive work rules within the current system. The Department of Health, Education and Welfare granted "waivers" of the social security laws for purposes of "demonstration."

In California, Governor Reagan said the goal of the project was to "reintroduce the principle of the work ethic to our way of life." In April, 1972, up to thirty thousand welfare recipients between eighteen and sixty-five in thirty-five of the state's counties were ordered to work at unskilled jobs with local schools, government agencies, and nonprofit organizations. They got no pay for their work as provided for in the WIN program; they received only their regular grant. Work was limited to eighty hours a month. Physically handicapped people and mothers of children under six were exempt.

The NWRO charged that the program was not really an experiment but an illegal device to force welfare recipients to work in violation of the social security rules. The State of California, which did not want to begin the program while its legality was unresolved, filed a suit against the California Welfare Rights Organization for a declaratory judgment upholding its right to do so. In early 1973 it was still unresolved.

Public Work Rules

The New York State program had two parts: Public Service Work Opportunities Program and Incentives for Independence.[8] The programs were delayed because of a court order obtained by NWRO and by welfare groups' threats to disrupt the operations of welfare offices if they were put into effect.

The PSWOP declared that every member of a recipient family deemed available for work by the welfare agency would be required to work off his or her grant in public service employment if regular employment was "not available or appropriate." The rule included nonstudents over sixteen and mothers of children six or over. Women in families with an adult male were exempt. In order to insure availability of mothers for work relief, recipients would be encouraged to work off their grants by running day-care centers in their homes.

The purpose of the program was to insure that every "mother and other female caretaker will be employed in the regular economy, or be in training, or be in a public service program or be providing 'in home' day care to children of other recipients."

The hourly rate for work projects would be the state minimum wage, $1.85 an hour, *or* the wage paid employees in comparable work. The project was designed to cover some eighty-eight thousand families.

Brownie Point Program

The other state project, Incentives for Independence, was aimed at the use of increases and cuts in grants to enforce behavior believed to be in the best interests of the recipients. It was nicknamed "the brownie point program."

In the original version of the plan, the grant levels of all AFDC and home-relief recipients would have been reduced to $2,400 for a family of four as opposed to the existing state grant of $3,763 (the state was paying 90 percent of "need," as defined by 1968 prices, a time when living costs were 15 percent lower). However, families could earn up to (but not above) their previous grant levels by winning incentive points.

For example, a family would get $25 a month if the parent made sure her preschool child was vaccinated during the preceeding six months; another $25 if the parent of a child five to fifteen years old cooperated with school authorities; $25 if a child participated up to thirty hours a week in a summertime community service project; and $25 if an unemployed adult on assistance for over four weeks reported to the State Employment Service and participated in manpower training. The family would get $12.50 a month if the parent of a student over fifteen cooperated with school authorities.

Families also would get "brownie points" if unemployable adults improved their housekeeping by cleaning up or repairing their homes, had their children participate in "citizen building" programs like the Boy Scouts, participated in activities designed to improve money or home management, attended family life education programs, used community resources to deal with child delinquency problems, provided home day care for a child of another welfare family, named the father or secured support for children born out of wedlock, located or got financial support from a deserting father, secured a satisfactory day-care plan for the children in order to get a job or training, used medical services designed to enhance employability, participated in a program of self-rehabilitation to improve economic independence, participated in an adult basic education or high-school equivalency program, attended a health education program, provided a child with foster care or served as a social services agency volunteer.

A paper by attorney Adele Blong of the Center on Social Welfare Policy and Law at Columbia University charged that the government was trying to "use public assistance to control individual behavior."

Widespread opposition resulted in a modification of the plan. The across-the-board reductions were abandoned, but families still would get reduced grants because of the failure of the "employable" members to participate in work or training selected by the welfare agency or the failure of a teen-ager over fourteen to participate in a "community service project." There would be a $12.50-a-month reduction for each child that refused to participate.

Ms. Blong also noted in her critique of PSWOP the effects of existing unemployment and cited a state report on the WIN program which said, "1970 accomplishments of this program have been disappointing. The program has been adversely affected by a lack of employment opportunities caused by the general business slowdown during the past year and by a shortage of day care facilities." In 1970, less than three thousand people were placed in the nearly fifteen thousand WIN training slots in New York State.

Ms. Blong asserted that rather than receive training or adequate employment, recipients would be "placed in work relief where they will work off their grants in jobs for which state and local governments are not willing to pay a living wage."

Court challenges and demonstrations delayed the program so that it had not gone into effect by mid 1973.

State Work Law

Meanwhile, a New York State law that took effect in July, 1971, required able-bodied AFDC and home-relief recipients to pick up their checks in person at state employment offices. If they could not be placed in regular jobs or training in thirty days, they were to work in public service agencies for enough hours to offset their relief checks.

The court said that the state could not put AFDC recipients in work relief and continue to get federal funds for them. The money they received would be considered wages, and the state would not qualify for matching grants. However, the state could require AFDC recipients to pick up their checks at employment offices and be interviewed for jobs.

The law was challenged by the Buffalo Legal Services project which charged that it violated the involuntary servitude provision of the Bill of Rights. It also said that there already was a federal work program (WIN) and that the state could not run a contradictory one.

The brief presented by the Center on Social Welfare Policy and Law on behalf of welfare-rights groups noted that the state had placed some people in jobs paying less than the state minimum wage of $1.85 and that it was using relief recipients' "dependence to subsidize the continuation of industries and employers who pay substandard wages."

Sixteen major social-work organizations joined the suit saying that the law was "an instrument of coercion and intimidation" and represented a "total repudiation of humanitarian values."

A year after the law went into effect, a panel of three federal judges ruled that it would not be applied to AFDC recipients, though it did not accept the "involuntary servitude" argument. The state could continue to assign work relief to general-assistance recipients not covered by the federal law.

The local unit of the American Federation of State, County and Municipal Employees and the New York Civil Liberties Union filed suits in 1972 to prevent New York City from assigning home-relief clients to city jobs. Some six thousand recipients in those jobs received no pay but their regular state-city welfare checks.[9]

The suits charged that the program undercut the regular pay scale with wages that frequently were less than half the regular rates.

Critics charged that the program was politically motivated and led to little but harassment. A joint state-federal study nearly a year after the law went into effect showed that it had had little effect on the state's welfare rolls and that a far smaller percentage of employable people were on relief than had been estimated. The study said that only four out of every fifty people referred to jobs by the state employment service had been placed.

Ten percent of eligible recipients failed to report to state employment centers and 12 percent did not comply after reporting.

However, the New York City welfare commissioner pointed out that "one-third of the clients placed in jobs lasted for only one week or less and nearly two-thirds lasted for 10 weeks or less. And despite a 96 percent increase in registrants, there was a 14 percent drop in placement."[10]

In another study, the Community Council of Greater New York reported that some relief recipients were filling jobs left vacant by the government when regular workers left and that this situation blocked real employment and the union wage scale and lowered the morale of recipients who knew that they were not getting the same salary or benefits as others who did the same work.[11]

The report said that most relief clients "enjoy working and want to work" but that they "realize they are not likely to get real jobs through the program" and that "training opportunities are very limited, if existent at all."

The Nixon plan did not sail through the Senate after its second passage in the House, but hardly for the reasons that welfare-reform advocates would have preferred. The Senate Finance Committee refused to report out the bill on the grounds it was too liberal, and they voted instead for a program that Republican Secretary of Labor James D. Hodgson called a step toward "convict-type labor."[1]

The plan, devised by Committee Chairman Russell Long of Louisiana, would retain existing payments for families with preschool children—about 1.8 million. However, the adults who headed the other families would be required either to find jobs in private industry or sign up with a new Federal Employment Corporation.

Those with jobs at the minimum wage of $1.60 an hour would also receive $6.40 from the government as a rebate for the social security taxes they paid. Their income would come to $70.40 a week. (Blue-collar and nonsupervisory sales and clerical workers in 1972 averaged $137 a week. The poverty line for four was about $80 a week.)

People would be required to work in private industry for as little as $1.20 an hour, 75 percent of the minimum wage. They would get an additional $12 from the government plus $4.80 for their social security, adding up to $64.80 a week.

Anyone who could not get private employment would be required to work for the corporation at jobs paying $1.20 an hour, with nothing above their $48 a week. The corporation could use them in public works or hire them out at this rate

11
THE NEW LAW

to private citizens who needed maids, yardworkers, or other help. (Senator Long at one point in the hearings shouted at a witness, "I can't get anybody to iron my shirts!")[2]

Payments to unemployables would be related to each state's 1972 welfare costs instead of being figured on the existing open-ended matching plan. Grants would be increased only in proportion to population growth.

The welfare agency could require unemployables to undergo rehabilitation. Those that refused would lose their grants. No money would be given to drug addicts or alcoholics who were not in treatment programs.

Birth Control

The bill provided for 100 percent federal payments for birth control programs for all poor women of child-bearing age, including those not on welfare who might need public assistance if they had children. The states would be required to set up programs to reach at least 95 percent of all eligible women. Those failing to establish such programs within a year would lose up to 2 percent of federal welfare payments.

Parents who refused jobs or training would be denied welfare grants for themselves and their children who would be referred to local child-welfare agencies directed to make provision for their care.

The bill would allow federal, state, or local governments to intervene for mothers who were afraid to seek support payments from the fathers of their children and would allow women on welfare to count such payments as earned income, with the right to keep the first $30 a month and one-third of the rest without deductions in their welfare payments.

In an attempt to put pressure on states to cut ineligibles off the rolls, the federal government would reduce matching funds 1 percent for each percentage point of ineligibility over 3 percent.

The Senate Finance Committee also voted to combat fraud by requiring the issuance of social security numbers to all children entering the first grade. Various relatives thus could not claim the same child as a dependent.

"Man in the House" Rules

The bill counteracted the 1968 Supreme Court decision against "man in the house" rules by permitting states to refuse benefits to mothers and children living with men who were not legal relations.

And finally, in an effort to make sure that welfare recipients could not use antipoverty resources to combat the effects of the bill, it banned the use of federal money for welfare suits against the U.S. government without specific authorization from the Attorney General. Most of the suits brought on behalf of welfare recipients have been handled by poverty-program lawyers.

The restrictions in the AFDC provisions of the bill were in sharp contrast to the sections dealing with aid to the aged, the blind, and the disabled. In these categories, the government would pay 95 percent of $130 a month for each adult recipient, $195 a month for each couple. The bill would thus move 4 million people out of poverty, with some 2.4 million of the aged only slightly below the poverty line.

Adult recipients would be allowed to keep $50 a month of unearned income, including social security and pensions, and another $50 of earned income, plus half the rest.

The poverty line in 1972 was $1,900 a year for a single person and $2,400 for a couple ($158 and $200 a month). Under the proposed rules, the 60 percent of people on aid to the aged who also get social security would have incomes of at least $180 a month ($2,160 a year) for single persons and $245 ($2,940 a year) for couples.

Social Security Raise

Action on the controversial welfare bill was delayed during the Presidential primaries and the campaign, but Congress acted without hesitation on the one public welfare measure that has long been a favorite of politicians—an increase in social security benefits. It also voted to raise welfare payments to the aged, blind, and disabled poor.

In June, Congress voted to raise social security payments by 20 percent, a move that meant more money for nearly 28 million people. President Nixon had wanted only a 5 percent increase, on the grounds that anything higher was inflationary, and Republicans in Congress supported a 10 percent hike. However the bill's proponents attached it to a debt-ceiling bill which was needed immediately to authorize funds to pay the normal expenses of government.

The bill passed the House by 302 to 35 and the Senate by 82 to 4; the President signed it.

The law raised the average social security payments for individuals from $133 to $161 a month and the average for couples from $223 to $270. It also raised minimum payments from $70.40 a month to $84.50 and increased maximums from $216.10 to $259.70 for individuals. Under the law, benefits would increase automatically whenever the consumer-price index rose by 3 percent or more.

In October, Congress passed another social security increase, raising monthly payments from $84.50 to $170 for 150,000 people who have worked for thirty years or more in low-paying jobs. It raised survivors benefits by $1 billion, and increased from $1,680 to $2,100 the amount a recipient can earn each year without deductions. The social security tax went up to 5.85 percent.

The law also raised federal guarantees to the indigent aged, blind, and disabled to $130 a month for one person and $195 for couples. Those receiving social security would be guaranteed a total of $150 per person, $4,215 per couple. They could keep up to $65 a month in earned income. The federal government would pay the full cost of these guarantees beginning January 1, 1974. States could add their own supplements—and set residence requirements for the additional benefits.

President Nixon hesitated in signing the bill on the grounds it was inflationary, but finally did so a week before the election.

Then, in June 1973, Congress overwhelmingly approved a 5.6 percent cost-of-living increase effective the next year. Average monthly benefits for individuals were raised to $170; couples now averaged $297. Minimum benefits increased to $89.30. Recipients under seventy-two could earn up to $2400 without a reduction in payments. (Benefits paid the aged, the blind, and the disabled poor also went up to $140 for individuals and $210 for couples.)

The increases were financed by an increase in the tax rate from 5.2 percent to 5.5 percent and in the wage base from $9,000 to $10,800 in 1973 and $12,600 in 1974. Critics had long pointed out that lower-wage earners had been forced to carry an unfair burden in the program since they were forced to pay a larger percentage of their total incomes in social security taxes than people whose earnings were above the cutoff point. The 1972 amendments attempted to shift some of the costs to the middle class and wealthy. After 1974, the wage base would rise as the general wage level of the economy did.

Cost-of-Living Formula

Other major changes in the law were the establishment of automatic cost-of-living increases and a substantial rise in taxes for people with incomes above $9,000. (Government figures show that half the families in the country have incomes of $10,000 or more.)

In contrast to these widely supported efforts to bring the aged out of poverty, the electoral campaign was a contest between two men who sought to convince the public that they were not going to give the "undeserving poor" too much.

Democrat George McGovern had been an original sponsor of the NWRO bill that called for $6,500 for a family of four. He repudiated this plan after critics accused him of being a radical and proposed instead a guarantee of $1,000 a year for every person in America. When that too was denounced as "radical," he proposed a national income insurance plan that would "guarantee a job opportunity to every man and woman in America who is able to work" at minimum or prevailing wages. Social security would be expanded to cover the aged on welfare, and a minimum of $4,000 in cash and food stamps would be given a family of four with no other income and no employable member. There would also be income supplements for the working poor.

President Nixon reiterated support for the concept of a guaranteed income, although the Republican party platform he ran on declared, "We flatly oppose programs or policies which embrace the principle of a government-guaranteed income. We reject as unconscionable the idea that all citizens have the right to be supported by the government, regardless of their ability or desire to support themselves and their families."[3]

However, the term "guaranteed income" had long before begun to be an ironic misnomer. What started out as a proposal by people who believed that society had to begin to break the link between jobs and income by guaranteeing everyone enough money to live on had become a meaningless label for everything from the NWRO proposal, which itself included work provisions, to the President's plan to give families less money than they were getting under the old system.

The Bill in Congress

Senator Abraham Ribicoff of Connecticut had introduced, with the backing of twenty-two co-sponsors, a bill to provide a $3,000 annual income for a family of four, rising in five years to the $4,000 poverty line. He was the chief spokesman for congressional liberals on welfare reform, and for a while it appeared that the Administration would work with him to get some bill passed.

Initially, it appeared as if a compromise would be worked out, though most of the compromising appeared to be on the part of the liberals. What emerged was a $2,600 minimum income, with yearly cost-of-living increases, and a 60 percent tax on earnings. Benefits in higher-paying states would be maintained and the rights of recipients would be better protected than in the Nixon version. Several million working poor would be helped by the measure.

The Administration had insisted to the liberals that H.R.1 was a liberal bill, and it had told conservatives that FAP was a conservative measure. In the end, it was a combination of liberal and conservative votes that killed it.

There had been some disagreement over strategy among the liberals. George Wiley and the NWRO thought it was unwise to let the bill out of the House committee. The AFL-CIO and other liberal organizations said it would be better to vote the bill out and try to improve it in the Senate. Thus most liberal congressmen, with the exception of the Black Caucus members, voted for it in the House.

In the Senate, liberal forces joined to support the Ribicoff amendments. However, the NWRO and most church groups concerned with welfare reform believed that even if the Ribicoff amendments passed, they would be thrown out in the conference committee.

Conservatives disliked the bill because it provided supplements for the working poor. The poor of the South would have benefited most from the bill. Southern Senators opposed it for fear that the higher welfare standard might push up wage levels.

The Election Campaign

After McGovern's proposal for $1,000 a year per person met widespread criticism, Nixon decided that it was more valuable to have welfare as an election campaign issue than to pass a bill. Mitchell Ginsberg, dean of the Columbia School of Social Work, said, "If a bill had passed, it would have appeared to solve the welfare problem, and that would let McGovern off the hook."[4]

Some parts of the Long bill passed the Senate and House and were signed into law. They related to the adult categories which had not been the prime focus of NWRO lobbying. For example, the aged, the blind, and the disabled now must pay to obtain the welfare manuals that detail agency rules and practices while AFDC recipients still get the manual free. People in the adult categories must wait ninety days before local welfare agencies have to grant them fair hearings; AFDC recipients are still covered by the thirty day rule.

Wiley said the exclusion of AFDC from the new provisions attests to the effectiveness of its lobbying. He pointed out that a section that would have denied government-supported legal service attorneys the right to handle welfare rights cases without permission from the U.S. attorney general was defeated as a result of NWRO efforts. The organization got Senators Edmund Muskie and George McGovern and Democratic party leaders to intervene to prevent House acceptance of that Senate measure.

In a Labor Day campaign speech, President Nixon brought the country full circle back to the philosophy of the seventeenth-century British poor law. He charged that the country was faced with a massive challenge to the "work ethic" that threatened to "weaken the American character." He cited the character-building effects of work, asserting that the work

THE NEW LAW

ethic "puts responsibility in the hands of the individual in the belief that self-reliance and willingness to work make a person a better human being." He said, "It is wrong for someone on welfare to receive more than someone who works."

Nixon warned against the effects of pauperization: "I believe that a policy of income redistribution would result in many more Americans becoming poor, because it ignores a human value essential to every worker's success—the incentive of reward."[5]

After his re-election, the President reiterated his attitude toward welfare, declaring that "because of varying standards and because the amounts for food stamps and other fringes have gone up so much, we find in area after area of this country it is more profitable to go on welfare than to go to work. That is wrong. It is unfair to the working poor."[8]

He pledged himself to stop that "unconscionable situation." However, what he had in mind was not raising the low wages of the working poor (he was opposing efforts to increase the $1.60 an hour minimum to $2 or $2.25) but cutting back the aid given to people on welfare.

The Senate failed to act on the House-passed Family Assistance Plan, and the measure died again. Observers believed that neither President Nixon nor Congress were likely to give welfare reform a high priority in the new session. And Nixon seemed determined to accomplish by administrative order what he had not been able to get through the legislature.

In December, 1972, HEW announced that it would withhold matching funds for payments made to people found to have been ineligible or overpaid. It declared that it would withhold over $230,000,000 from the 50 states for mispayments it said were based on a federal sampling of cases. It said an April, 1971 study indicated that one out of every 20 welfare recipients was ineligible and one in four was being paid too much. It added that less than 1 percent of the cases involved any fraud by the recipients; most were errors by the welfare agencies.[6]

Thirty-four states hired a law firm to fight the new ruling. (A recent regulation had allowed states a 3 percent ineligibility rate before Federal grants were cut. Before that, there were no similar rules.) Neil Cruikshank, president of the National Council of Senior Citizens, commented: "Getting welfare cheats off the rolls is all well and good, but I notice that the proposals don't call for locating 150,000 families that are known to be receiving underpayments and hundreds of thousands of others that are eligible but not receiving anything at all."[7]

At the same time, the federal government acted to cut back the social services that had been available to welfare recipients. The revenue sharing bill set a ceiling on federal grants for day care, homemakers, and children's services.

Under new regulations, only local governments could sponsor day care and receive federal matching funds. Programs where the local share was put up by churches, community funds, or social agencies could not receive aid. The ruling threatened to completely abolish day care in Texas where the local money was provided by the United Fund.

The new rule also limited federally aided day care to children of women on welfare. Working mothers who needed the services to keep their jobs would be forced to quit and go on relief. Widespread protests by childcare supporters, elected officials, and others forced the Administration to back down on these rulings.

At the beginning of the 1970's, the notion that one would have to provide guaranteed incomes because work would no longer be available for large numbers of people was under challenge. Urban planners pointed out that society had large unmet needs in areas like housing, health care, and pollution control and that the real problem was that the public was not willing to have the government spend money to solve these problems. They charged that all the guaranteed income programs were nothing but guaranteed poverty and that much of the welfare problem could be solved if the unemployed and underemployed received training for work at decent wages aimed at meeting real national needs.

The Future

However, one big-city official noted, "There is no market now for liberal welfare reform. Current efforts are based on the notion that the welfare problem can be 'managed out of existence,' that cutting and tightening the rolls through management reform will take the question of ineligibility out of the welfare debate and set the stage for real reform."[9]

The 1960's had been a period of liberal social attitudes, civil rights laws, antipoverty programs, and sympathy for the poor. It also was a period of expanding economic opportunity. The National Welfare Rights Movement reached its peak strength in 1968.

However, by 1969, state legislatures began to react to the rising welfare rolls by cutting grants. State legislators found that taxpayers' anger at the growing rolls was more significant to their political futures than the welfare-rights groups' threats of disorder.

In the 1970's the NWRO declined in membership. It had over 100,000 local members at its height, although members paying dues to the national organization numbered closer to 25,000, a figure indicated by subscriber information filed for its national newspaper.

George Wiley, until 1973 NWRO National Director, attributed the decline to the "repressive nature of the welfare system," and its discouraging effect among welfare rights organizers and leaders.

The nation still has not come to grips with the answer to the question, Why are people poor? There continues to be an unspoken agreement that the question somehow relates to the "pathology" of the poor. Yet, at every period of American history, different groups have been attacked as inherently lazy and immoral.

The reason for poverty is the lack of skills and job opportunities that pay living wages for large numbers of the population. Representative Wilbur Mills said he opposed supplemental aid to working people because it would prove that the American system does not provide adequate income to its workers. In fact, the American system does not provide adequate income to one out of eight of its citizens, the 25 million who are poor.

Unless public sentiment shifts drastically, it is unlikely that any new welfare "reform" will represent any move away from the old poor-law philosophy that has existed since Elizabethan times. Even if Congress chooses to keep calling welfare bills "guaranteed income plans," it is more likely to return to the philosophy that was shelved temporarily by the public-assistance law of 1935—that people on welfare must be put to work at whatever menial or make-work task can be devised, that giving them money without making them work for it is bad for their character, that our economy works because people work hard, and that they work hard because they know that idleness can lead to the misery and humiliation of being dependent on public welfare. There is no place in that philosophy for the realities of unemployment or the need for training and child care.

The American poor law has hardly changed in spirit from its antecedents. Beggars are no longer branded, nor are children sold by the dozen to manufacturers, yet poverty is still looked on by many as a personal failure, and dependence on government welfare is enough to cancel out anyone's right to dignity and the kind of decent living conditions the country can easily afford. And, like their predecessors, today's overseers of the poor explain that it is all really for the benefit of the poor — to inspire them to be self-supporting and to protect them from the evils of pauperism.

GLOSSARY

AFDC Aid to Families with Dependent Children; federal program aiding families where, in most cases, no father is present and the mother cannot earn enough to support the family.

AFDC-UF Aid to Families with Dependent Children and Unemployed Father; program which extends AFDC aid to families with fathers who are present but jobless. Program is optional and twenty-six states have put it into effect. It used to be the AFDC-UP (for Parent) but the name was changed when mothers were excluded.

Bound out Indentured or apprenticed to work for someone for a period of years.

Budget deficiency Difference between what an individual or family has and what it needs to live on; this was used to fix wages by the Emergency Work Relief Program during the Depression. A person would work for the number of hours needed to earn that amount.

Chargeable Eligible for and in need of relief.

Children's allowance A sum of money given to every family according to the number and ages of their children.

Direct relief Money aid (as opposed to work relief).

Dole Public assistance.

FAP Family Assistance Plan, also known as Workfare and H.R.1; proposed by the Nixon Administration to establish a minimum income for families ($2,400 for a family of four), including the working poor, with the proviso that employable parents, including mothers with young children, work.

Food stamps Vouchers for the purchase of food, these stamps are sold to eligible families and individuals at less than their face value (usually about two-thirds or more, depending on the recipient's economic status, number of people in the family, etc.).

Guaranteed income A sum which is guaranteed, by the government, to citizens or families. If an individual or family earns below the guarantee, the government will make up the difference.

General relief Public assistance given by the states (or cities) without matching grants from the federal government, usually to people who do not fit into federal categories. It generally aids single people, childless couples, and the working poor.

Grocery orders Vouchers that can only be cashed in food stores, and often only for certain specified foods.

Impotent poor or impotent beggars Those unable to work.

Income disregard Deduction of only part of a welfare recipient's earnings from his or her welfare check. Under the law, the recipient can keep $30 a month plus one-third of the rest; anything above that is deducted from the welfare benefit. If all earnings were deducted, this would leave little incentive to work, since the jobs welfare recipients can get generally are low paid and often below the level of their welfare benefits.

Indoor relief Aid given to people in almshouses.

Less eligibility The principle that people getting public aid should not receive more money than the lowest paid worker; the stated purpose was to prevent the able-bodied from accepting poor relief instead of jobs.

"Man in the house" rule Requirement that a woman receiving AFDC for herself and her children not have any man staying or visiting at her house. It was assumed that such a man would be supporting her; thus she would not be entitled to aid.

Means test An investigation of a welfare applicant's financial resources to determine whether she or he is eligible. It may involve extensive digging into the applicant's personal life, interviews with neighbors, etc.

Medicaid The federal program of partially reimbursing hospitals for the care of welfare recipients and of those certified as "medically indigent"—usually with incomes of up to 133 percent of the welfare eligibility line.

Mother's pension Aid given by local governments in the early 1900's, generally to "deserving" white widows.

Negative income tax A form of guaranteed income; people with no incomes or with incomes below the taxable level would file tax returns and get money back from the government.

NWRO National Welfare Rights Organization, a coalition of local groups of welfare recipients which aims at protecting the rights and increasing the benefits of recipients.

Outdoor relief Aid given to people who continue to live at home (as opposed to *indoor relief* given in almshouses).

Overseers of the poor Individuals (often local clergy, landowners, or businessmen) who were responsible for the administration of local charity and later of tax-supported assistance to the poor.

Pauper Person dependent on public charity for support.

Pauperism The condition of poor people being dependent on public support.

Poverty line An amount of money based on a low-cost food budget multiplied by three which the U.S. Department of Labor considers the minimum a family can get along on. (It assumes that food is one-third of a low income family's budget.) The amount the Labor Department considers necessary for a *decent* living standard is about 50 percent higher.

Public service employment Government jobs in hospitals, schools, parks, and government offices that are financed more to provide jobs than to do needed work.

Security wage Amount paid to compensate for a worker's budget deficiency (what the worker needs); the worker's hours were limited to the number required to earn the security wage.

Settlement Residence settlement often referred to the amount of time required to gain *legal* residence in a community.

Social Darwinism The application of Darwin's 'survival of the fittest' theory of evolution to economic life.

Special needs Certain needs of a family that are occasional and thus are not included in budgets paid for by semi-weekly government checks. These needs include furniture, kitchen utensils, bedding, and winter clothing.

Sturdy vagabond A person who was sound in body and did not have a job (also *valiant beggar*).

Substitute father A man whom the welfare department considers to be playing the role of the father in a family (sleeping with the mother, relating to the children, giving the family money, etc.).

Suitable home Prerequisite for aid to mothers set by the states; a suitable home generally meant that the woman, who was either a widow, divorced or separated, should not have a boyfriend or a sex life.

Supplemental relief State or local aid given to families of workers whose wages are too low to support them.

Survivor's benefits Under social security, a worker's spouse and children can collect if he or she dies; this amendment to the social security law removed many widows from the AFDC lists.

Talmadge Amendment Addition to the welfare law passed in 1971 that requires welfare recipients to register for work; exceptions include mothers of children under 6 and women whose husbands are registered.

Voucher A government promise to pay the supplier of a service rendered to relief recipients; vouchers have been given to recipients for groceries, rent, medical services, clothing, fuel, etc.

Warning out Practice of ordering out of town new arrivals who officials thought might become needy of public assistance.

WIN Work Incentive Program established by Congress in 1967 which required states to register appropriate welfare recipients for jobs and training. It was superseded by the Talmadge Amendment but the program is still called WIN. (The original program is referred to as WIN 1, the new one as WIN 2.)

Work ethic The notion that nobody should get anything without working for it and that hard work improves one's character.

Work incentives *See* Income disregard.

Work relief Government financed jobs given to people who are unemployed and who would need government assistance in order to live; the jobs do not necessarily pay standard wages. Sometimes they are a way of requiring people to work off their welfare checks.

Workhouse test The test of need for an applicant for aid. The theory was that no one who did not really need assistance would submit to the humiliation and misery of the workhouse. It also aimed to eliminate anyone who had sought aid because of a disinclination to work.

WPA Works Progress Administration, the major work relief program of the Depression; at its peak, it hired a fourth of the nation's unemployed.

BIBLIOGRAPHY

Books, pamphlets, magazine and newspaper articles, and unpublished papers, with notions that focus on the material used in this book.

Books

Bell, Winifred. *Aid to Dependent Children.* New York: Columbia University Press, 1965. Classic work which details the history of AFDC from mother's pensions to the present, including discrimination against blacks and unsuitable home rules. Highly recommended.

Bird, Caroline. *The Invisible Scar.* New York: David McKay and Co., 1966 (1972). Interesting social and political history of the Depression.

Brown, Josephine Chapin. *Public Relief, 1929–1939.* New York: Henry Holt and Co., 1940. Excellent history, including background of nineteenth-century almshouses, the charity organization movement, and detailed account of relief during the Depression.

Douglas, Paul H. *Social Security in the United States.* New York: McGraw-Hill Book Co., 1936. Story of the social security law, including its precedents in public assistance, and the political battle to win it.

Evans, Harry C. *The American Poorfarm and Its Inmates.* Des Moines, Iowa: The Loyal Order of Moose, 1926. Vivid picture of the almshouses of the early 1920's.

Hopkins, Harry. *Spending to Save — The Complete Story of Relief.* New York: W. W. Norton and Co., 1936. The beginning of the Federal relief system in the Depression, by the man who headed a major relief agency.

Leyendecker, Hilary M. *Problems and Policy in Public Assistance.* New York: Harper and Brothers, 1935. History, including the British Poor Law, relief in colonial America and the nineteenth century.

May, Edgar. *The Wasted Americans.* New York: New American Library, 1964. Account of the author's experience as a caseworker in Buffalo. Good data on welfare policies on birth control.

O'Neil, Robert M. *The Price of Dependency.* New York: E. P. Dutton and Co., 1970. Civil rights restrictions in AFDC, including substitute-father rules.

Piven, Frances Fox, and **Cloward, Richard.** *Regulating the Poor: the Functions of Public Welfare.* New York: Pantheon, 1971. Important new work that details the history of welfare from British Poor Law through the Depression and the present challenges to the welfare system to show how relief has been used to quell social disorder and enforce the low-wage system.

Tierney, Brian. *Medieval Poor Law.* Berkeley: University of California Press, 1959. Church law, the effects of the Black Death, and the enclosures; beginning of harsh laws against beggars.

Pamphlets

Coll, Blanche D. *Perspectives in Public Welfare: A History.* Washington, D.C.: U.S. Department of Health, Education and Welfare, 1969 (1971). Excellent booklet which in less than 100 pages tells the history of welfare from the British Poor Law through the mother's pension movement.

Poverty Amid Plenty, The American Paradox. Washington, D.C.: The President's Commission on Income Maintenance Programs, 1969. Excellent summary and analysis of the welfare problem, including description of present programs, with proposals for guaranteed income.

Shlakman, Vera. *Children's Allowance.* New York: Citizens' Committee for Children. Proposal and arguments for children's allowances.

Six Myths About Welfare. Washington, D.C.: National Welfare Rights Organization, 1971. Myths about employables, illegitimacy, and cheating.

Welfare Myths vs. Facts. Washington, D.C.: U.S. Department of Health, Education and Welfare, 1971. Basic facts about welfare families, payments, work and cheating.

Articles

Bruno, Hal. "Birth Control, Welfare Funds, and the Politics of Illinois." *The Reporter* (June 20, 1963). Arnold Maremont's fight for birth control for AFDC recipients in Illinois.

Cloward, Richard A., and **Piven, Frances Fox.** "Birth of a Movement." *The Nation* (May 8, 1967). Early days of welfare rights movement.

Cloward, Richard A., and **Piven, Frances Fox.** "A Strategy to End Poverty." *The Nation* (May 2, 1966). Welfare recipients meet with officials and make demands.

Cloward, Richard A., and **Piven, Frances Fox.** "We've Got Rights: The No-Longer-Silent Welfare Poor." *The New Republic* (August 5, 1967). Legal challenges against repressive practices of welfare agencies.

Greenfeld, Meg. "The 'Welfare Chiselers' of Newburgh." *The Reporter* (August 17, 1961). Story of the relief cuts.

Jernegan, Marcus Wilson. "The Development of Poor Relief in Colonial New England." *Social Service Review* (June 1931). Warning out, disputes over settlement, workhouses, auctioning off.

Jernegan, Marcus Wilson. "The Development of Poor Relief in Colonial

Virginia." *Social Service Review* (March 1929). Good brief background of British Poor Law, colonial workhouse, binding out of children, etc.

Rogin, Richard. "Now It's Welfare Lib." *The New York Times Magazine* September 27, 1970). Activities of NWRO.

Tillmon, Johnnie. "Welfare Is a Woman's Issue." *Ms.* (Spring Preview Issue, January 1972). Women on welfare trade in "a man" for "the man"; work ethic applies not to married women but to women on welfare who are forced to take lowest-paying jobs.

Welfare Reform: Problems and Solutions. Madison: Institute of Research on Poverty, University of Wisconsin, 1968. Valuable compilation of magazine and newspaper articles on welfare and the guaranteed income.

Unpublished Papers

Blong, Adele. "Analysis of Proposed New York Projects in Public Assistance Programs." New York: Center for Social Welfare Policy and Law, October 27, 1971. The brownie point program.

"H.R. 1: The Social Security Amendments of 1971, A Critique." New York: Center for Social Welfare Policy and Law. Analysis of benefit levels, eligi-. bility, work requirements, child care services, payments and budgeting procedures, fair hearings.

Wickenden, Elizabeth. "H.R. 1: Welfare Policy as an Instrument of Coercion." New York: Center for Social Welfare Policy and Law, March 1972.

FOR FURTHER READING

Books

Browning, Grace A. *The Development of Poor Relief Legislation in Kansas.* Chicago: University of Chicago Press, 1935. History from settlement in mid-1800's to the period before the Depression.

Dickens, Charles. *Oliver Twist.* New York: Signet, 1961. The classic about a young boy who is born in a poorhouse and forced to live among thieves.

Friedman, Milton. *Capitalism and Freedom.* Chicago: University of Chicago Press, 1962. The first proposal for a negative income tax (chapter 12).

Gaspey, William. *Poor Law Melodies and Other Poems.* London: Longma, Brown and Co., 1842. Poems about the sad effects of the poor law.

Gillin, John Lewis. *History of Poor Relief Legislation in Iowa.* Iowa City: State Historical Society of Iowa, 1914. Poor relief from the late 1700's through the beginning of this century.

Graham, James. *The Enemies of the Poor.* New York: Vintage Books, 1970. Medieval Christian background; denial of civil liberties; background of welfare philosophy.

Handler, Joel. *Reforming the Poor.* New York: Basic Books, 1972. Background of public assistance; charity v. rights, work policies.

Handler, Joel F., and **Hollingsworth, Ellen Jane.** *The Deserving Poor, A Study of Welfare Administration.* Chicago: Markham Publishing Co., 1971. Development of welfare philosophy; AFDC and changes in the law; the WIN program.

Heffner, William Clinton. *History of Poor Relief Legislation in Pennsylvania, 1682–1913.* Cleona, Pa.: Holzapfel Publishing Co. From the British Poor Law through colonial settlement laws, almshouses, binding out, and mother's pensions.

Johnson, Alexander. *The Almshouse.* New York: Russell Sage Foundation, 1911. Background of British Poor Law; philosophy of the almshouse.

Keith-Lucas, Alan. *Decisions About People in Need.* Chapel Hill: University of North Carolina Press, 1957. Control over recipients' lives and morality by caseworkers.

Kelso, Robert W. *The History of Public Poor Relief in Massachusetts, 1620–1920.* With English background and reports of nineteenth-century almshouses and auctioning-off.

Kershaw, Joseph. *Government Against Poverty.* Chicago: Markham Publishing Co., 1970. Social security, public assistance, and proposals for change.

Klein, Philip. *From Philanthropy to Social Welfare.* San Francisco: Jossey-Bass, 1968. Changing attitudes and practices.

Krosney, Herbert. *Beyond Welfare: Poverty in the Supercity.* New York: Rinehart and Winston, 1966. Challenges to repressive laws: work rules; Friedman's negative income tax.

Malthus, Thomas. *Essay on the Principle of Population.* 1798. The classic essay in defense of letting the poor die off as a natural check on excess population.

Russell, Charles Theo., Jr. *The Disenfranchisement of Paupers, Examination of the Laws of Massachusetts.* Boston: Little, Brown, and Co., 1878. Proposals to do away with voting rights for people on relief.

Seligman, Ben B., ed. *Permanent Poverty: An American Syndrome.* Chicago: Quadrangle Books, 1968. Includes British background and America before the Depression.

Seligman, Ben B., ed. *Poverty as a Public Issue.* New York: The Free Press, 1965. Articles on the effect of work programs, the working poor, and poverty and the law.

Schlesinger, Arthur M. *The Age of Roosevelt: The Coming of the New Deal.* Boston: Houghton Mifflin Co., 1958. Section on the development of relief in the Depression.

Stein, Bruno. *On Relief.* New York: Basic Books, 1971. Brief history of poor law, discussion of guaranteed income proposals and nature of income distribution in the United States.

Steiner, Gilbert. *Social Insecurity: The Politics of Welfare.* Chicago: Rand McNally & Co., 1966. Changes and issues of the 1960's, including birth control in Chicago, "the politics of eligibility," and "the social work syndrome."

Steiner, Gilbert. *The State of Welfare.* Washington, D.C.: The Brookings Institution, 1971. Current analysis, including adequacy of payments and effect of WIN program.

Theobald, Robert. *Free Men and Free Markets.* New York. Clarkson N. Potter, Inc., 1963. Description of how cybernation is changing the relation between income and work; proposal for guaranteed income.

Theobald, Robert, ed. *The Guaranteed Income.* Garden City, N.Y.: Anchor, 1967. The revolution of cybernation and the need for a guaranteed income and change in social mores.

Veeder, Fredric. *The Development of the Montana Poor Law.* Chicago: University of Chicago Press, 1938. Beginning in mid-1800's, poor farms, mother's pensions.

Weissman, Harold H., ed. *Justice and the Law in the Mobilization for Youth Experience.* New York: Associated Press, 1969. Poverty law cases, including results of Welfare Abuses Act.

FOR FURTHER READING

Pamphlets

Burns, Eveline, ed. *Children's Allowances and the Economic Welfare of Children.* Report of a Conference. New York: Citizens' Committee for Children, 1968. Series of articles with proposals for children's allowances.

Having the Power, We Have the Duty. Washington, D.C.: The Advisory Council on Public Welfare, 1966. Criticism of existing public assistance program and call for national floor on payments.

Hildebrand, George H. *Poverty, Income Maintenance and the Negative Income Tax.* Ithaca, N.Y.: New York State School of Industrial and Labor Relations, 1967 (1968). Analysis of various guaranteed-income proposals.

Lansbury, George. *The Principles of the English Poor Law.* London: Twentieth Century Press, Ltd., 1897. Criticism of the restrictive effects of the proposals of the 1834 Commission.

MacIntyre, Duncan M. *Public Assistance, Too Much or Too Little.* Ithaca, N.Y.: New York State School of Industrial and Labor Relations, 1964. Brief history of welfare from British Poor Law through Depression, and how AFDC works.

Podell, Lawrence. *Mothers' Education and Employment.* Families on Welfare in New York City series. New York: Center for Social Research, City University of New York, 1967. Statistics on education and work patterns.

Roberts, Samuel. *Mary Wilden, A Victim to the New Poor Law.* London: Whittaker and Co., 1839. Recounts the pitiful story of an old woman condemned to the poor house.

Social Security Amendments of 1971. Report of Committee of Ways and Means on H.R. 1. Washington, D.C.: U.S. Congress, House of Representatives, 1971. Reasoning behind various sections of President Nixon's welfare reform bill.

Social Security Programs in the United States. Washington, D.C.: U.S. Department of Health, Education and Welfare, 1971. AFDC, aid to the aged, blind, and disabled; unemployment insurance and other government assistance programs.

Winston, Marian P. and **Forsher, Trude.** *Nonsupport of Legitimate Children by Affluent Fathers as a Cause of Poverty and Welfare Dependency.* Santa Monica, Calif.: The RAND Corporation, 1971. Facts about extent of failure of fathers who have deserted or divorced to provide child support.

Witness for Survival. New York: United Neighborhood Houses, 1969. Testimony from "hearing" held by community groups to investigate effects of N.Y. state relief cuts.

Articles

"A Negative Income Tax?" *Dun's Review* (August 1968). Comments of businessmen on guaranteed income proposals.

Abbott, Edith. "Abolish the Pauper Laws." *Social Service Review* (March 1934). Influence of Malthus, charity organization societies; principles of English Poor Law.

Abbott, Edith. "Is there a legal right to relief?" *Social Service Review* (June 1938). Rulings about welfare rights in the past.

Abbott, Edith. "The Webbs on the English Poor Law." *Social Service Review* (June 1929). Extent of pauperism in England.

"After 30 Years—Relief a Failure." *U.S. News and World Report* (July 7, 1967). New Jersey county officials say unwed mothers who apply for welfare will face prosecution as adulterers.

"Appraising the Social Security Program." *Annals of the American Academy of Political and Social Science* (March 1939). Series of articles that analyze background and nature of then new law, including problems of relief in the Depression, and debate over direct relief v. work relief.

Branch, Taylor. "The Screwing of the Average Man." *Washington Monthly* (March 1972). Findings of Joint Economic Committee of Congress which show how most government subsidies go to the rich and the middle class.

Cloward, Richard A. "The War on Poverty—Are the Poor Left Out." *The Nation* (August 2, 1965). Ceilings on welfare; suitable home laws.

Cloward, Richard A., and **Piven, Frances Fox.** "Finessing the Poor." *The Nation* (October 7, 1968). How New York City reacted to welfare rights movements special-grant campaign by ending special grants and substituting annual flat payments.

Cloward, Richard A., and **Piven, Frances Fox.** "Migration, Politics, and Welfare." *The Saturday Review* (November 16, 1968). Effect of Southern welfare policies and migration of blacks to the North.

Congressional Digest (February 1939). History of relief measures in the Depression.

"Eight Congressmen Try Welfare Diet." *The New York Times* (July 3, 1969). Senators Mikva, Mondale, and Church spend hungry week on welfare food budget.

Freeman, Roger A. "Aid to Dependent Children." *Vital Speeches* (October 15, 1962). Less than one-fifth of absent fathers contribute child support to AFDC children.

Friedman, Milton. "Social Security, the Poor Man's Welfare Payment to the Middle Class." *Washington Monthly* (May 1972). How social security actually is regressive program that takes more money from poor, relative to their salaries, than from the middle class.

Franke, David. "Newburgh; Just the Beginning." *National Review* (July 29, 1961). The Newburgh welfare reform plan.

Gans, Herbert J. "Three Ways to Solve the Welfare Problem." *The New York Times Magazine* (March 7, 1971). Economy cannot give everyone jobs at living wage; working poor don't get welfare aid; poor ought to get guaranteed income.

FOR FURTHER READING

195

Hill, J. Gilbert. "Federal Relief Will Have to End." *Nation's Business* (October 1939). Relief should be made unattractive and unprofitable so people will seek to get off it.

Howard, Donald S. "But People Must Eat." *Atlantic Monthly* (February 1940). Effects of relief cuts in cities.

Johnson, Harry G. "Approaches to the Reduction of Poverty." In *Inequality and Poverty*. Edward C. Bidd, ed. New York: W. W. Norton & Co. 1967. Proposals by Ad Hoc Committee on the Triple Revolution.

Kotz, Nick. "Welfare: A Human Crisis." *Washington Post* (February 1971). Series of articles about the welfare crisis, with stories of its effect on peoples' lives.

Mitchell, Joseph McDowell. "The Revolt in Newburgh." *Vital Speeches* (January 15, 1962). Speech before Economic Club of Detroit.

"Now It's 'Illegal' for a City to Curb Welfare Abuses." *Saturday Evening Post* (August 5, 1961). Editorial in favor of Newburgh "reforms."

O'Gara, James. "Welfare a la Newburgh." *Commonweal* (August 25, 1961).

"Public Aid in the United States, 1933 to 1939." *Monthly Labor Review* (December 1939). Statistics on government spending for relief in the Depression.

Reich, Charles. "Midnight Welfare Searches." *Yale Law Journal* (June 1963). Challenges constitutionality of midnight raids.

Rein, Martin. "Choice and Chance in the American Welfare System." *The Annals of the American Academy of Political and Social Science* (September 1969). Causes of dependency; women workers.

"Senator Byrd's 'Facts' About Welfare Payments." *New Republic* (December 14, 1968). The "ineligibles" found by Byrd's committee.

Stern, Edith. "Broken Lives and Dollar Patches." *Nation's Business* (March 1950). Relief scandals that "fizzed out."

Stern, Philip. "Uncle Sam's Welfare Program for the Rich." *The New York Times Magazine* (April 16, 1972). Excellent analysis of tax breaks that benefit the rich.

"Subsidies for the Well-to-do: the Case of California." *Trans-action* (September 1970). Middle-class benefits more from educational subsidies than the poor.

"Taking it Out on the Kids." *New Republic* (October 7, 1967). Maryland county attorney general charges welfare mothers with neglect.

"Two Ohio Cities Face Big Crisis Over Relief Funds." *Scholastic* (December 18, 1939). Money in cities running out.

"Welfare—Big Stick, Small Carrot." *Time* (August 25, 1967). HEW officials live in slum environment.

"Welfare Frauds Exposed." *Nation's Business* (June 1965). Local newspaper prints welfare rolls.

"Where Charity Begins." *Life* (July 28, 1961). Editorial in favor of Newburgh "reforms."

Wiltse, Kermit T., and **Roberts, Robert W.** "Illegitimacy and the AFDC Program." In *The Unwed Mother.* Robert W. Roberts ed. New York: Harper and Row, 1966. Results of California study.

Unpublished Papers

Blawie, Marilyn J. "Law and Politics of Welfare Rights Organizations." Paper delivered at meeting of American Political Science Association, Los Angeles, September 1970. Activities of NWRO.

Blong, Adele. "Comment on Revision of New York's Proposed Projects Under Section 1115 of the Social Security Act." New York: Center for Social Welfare Policy and Law, November 19, 1971. On brownie point program.

Dolan, Merillee. "H.R. 1 and the Poverty of Women." Testimony on behalf of National Organization for Women before Senate Finance Committee, February 11, 1972. Says two causes of women going on welfare are sex discrimination in employment and social system that keeps women dependent on men and, when working, paid low wages: opposes forcing AFDC mothers to work for low wages.

"The Gaps in F.A.P." Washington, D.C.: National Welfare Rights Organization, August 27, 1971. Analysis and criticism.

Levin, Judith, and **Vergata, Patricia.** "Welfare Laws and Women: An Analysis of Federal Sexism." Paper; New Brunswick, N.J.: Rutgers University Law School, 1971. Analysis of discrimination against women in welfare—man-in-house rules, WIN program, child care.

Martin, George. "The Emergence and Development of a Social Movement Organization Among the Underclass: A Case Study of NWRO." Ph.D. thesis; Chicago: University of Chicago, 1972.

"The Talmadge Forced Work Requirements." Washington, D.C.: National Welfare Rights Organization, 1972. An analysis.

FOOTNOTES

Chapter 1. The Heritage of Europe (pp. 1–13)

1. Brian Tierney, *Medieval Poor Law* (Berkeley, Calif.: University of California Press, 1959).
2. *Ibid.*, p. 99.
3. *Ibid.*, p. 55.
4. Hilary M. Leyendecker, *Problems and Policy in Public Assistance* (New York: Harper and Brothers, 1955), pp. 22–5; Blanche D. Coll, *Perspectives in Public Welfare* (Washington, D.C.: U.S. Department of Health, Education and Welfare, 1971), pp. 4–5.
5. Tierney, pp. 128–9; Philip Klein, *From Philanthropy to Social Welfare* (San Francisco: Jossey-Bass, 1968), p. 279.
6. Tierney, p. 113; Coll, p. 4.
7. Tierney, p. 130.
8. Marcus Wilson Jernegan, "The Development of Poor Relief in Colonial New England," *Social Service Review* (June 1931), 176.
9. Robert W. Kelso, *The History of Public Poor Relief in Massachusetts, 1620–1920*, p. 45.
10. Tierney, p. 131.
11. Kelso, p. 45.
12. Alexander Johnson, *The Almshouse* (New York: Russell Sage Foundation, 1911), p. 150.
13. Leyendecker, p. 22; Johnson, p. 151; Jernegan, 178; Edith Abbott, "Abolish the Pauper Law," *Social Service Review* (March 1934), 5; Coll, p. 5.
14. Leyendecker, p. 29; Coll, pp. 7–8.
15. Johnson, p. 153; Coll, p. 8.
16. Coll, p. 9.
17. Klein, pp. 280–1.
18. Johnson, p. 155.
19. Frances Fox Piven and Richard A. Cloward, *Regulating the Poor* (New York: Pantheon, 1971), p. 28.
20. Johnson, p. 156; Ben B. Seligman, *Permanent Poverty: An American Syndrome* (Chicago: Quadrangle Books, 1968), p. 4.
21. Thomas Malthus, *Essay on the Principles of Population (1798)*, pp. 341–3, 486–7; Abbott, 4.
22. Seligman, p. 4; Johnson, pp. 156–7; Leyendecker, p. 148.
23. Piven and Cloward, pp. 33–4.
24. *Ibid.*, p. 35.

25. Coll, p. 12.
26. *Ibid.*
27. *Ibid.,* p. 13.
28. Samuel Roberts and Mary Wilden, *A Victim of the New Poor Law* (London: Whittaker and Co., 1839), pp. v, 32.
29. William Gaspey, *Poor Law Melodies and Other Poems* (London: Longma, Brown and Co., 1842), pp. 7–8.
30. Charles Dickens, *Oliver Twist* (New York: New American Library, 1961, first published 1850), pp. 34–5.
31. Edith Abbott, "The Webbs on the English Poor Law," *Social Service Review* (June 1929), 255.
32. Johnson, pp. 146–7.

Chapter 2. Early America (pp. 14–29)

1. Robert W. Kelso, *The History of Public Poor Relief in Massachusetts, 1620–1920,* pp. 50–1, 96–7.
2. Marcus Wilson Jernegan, "The Development of Poor Relief in Colonial New England," *Social Service Review* (June 1931), 184.
3. Kelso, p. 97.
4. *Ibid.,* p. 45.
5. Jernegan, 180.
6. *Ibid.,* 179.
7. *Ibid.,* pp. 179, 182.
8. William Clinton Heffner, *History of Poor Relief Legislation in Pennsylvania, 1682–1913* (Cleona, Pa.: Holzapfel Publishing Co., 1913), pp. 31, 40, 46, 50.
9. Kelso, pp. 107–9.
10. Jernegan, 185.
11. *Ibid.,* 196.
12. Kelso, p. 113.
13. Heffner, pp 74–5
14. *Ibid.,* p. 90.
15. *Ibid.,* p. 138.
16. *Ibid.,* p. 51.
17. Philip Klein, *From Philanthropy to Social Welfare* (San Francisco: Jossey-Bass, 1968), p. 282.
18. Jernegan, 191.
19. Heffner, p. 84.
20. Marcus Wilson Jernegan, "The Development of Poor Relief in Colonial Virginia," *Social Service Review* (March 1929), 7–8.
21. Jernegan, "The Development . . . Virginia," 186.
22. Heffner, pp. 107–8, 124.
23. *Ibid.,* pp. 65, 168.
24. Kelso, p. 51.

25. John Lewis Gillin, *History of Poor Relief Legislation in Iowa* (Iowa City: State Historical Society of Iowa, 1914), pp. 4–18.
26. *Ibid.,* pp. 22–4.
27. Grace A. Browning, *The Development of Poor Relief Legislation in Kansas* (Chicago: University of Chicago Press, 1935), p. 33.
28. *Ibid.,* p. 62.
29. Frederic Veeder, *The Development of the Montana Poor Law* (Chicago: University of Chicago Press, 1938), pp. 7–8.
30. *Ibid.,* p. 12.
31. Blanche D. Coll, *Perspectives in Public Welfare* (Washington, D.C.: U.S. Department of Health, Education and Welfare, 1971), p. 22.
32. Heffner, p. 173.
33. Kelso, p. 118–9.
34. Coll, p. 20.
35. Kelso, p. 133–4.
36. *Ibid.,* pp. 132–3.
37. Coll, pp. 24–5.
38. *Ibid.,* p. 26.
39. Browning, p. 47.
40. *Ibid.,* p. 51.
41. Coll, p. 31.
42. *Ibid.*
43. *Ibid.,* p. 32.
44. Gillin, pp. 104–5.
45. Coll, p. 34.
46. *Ibid.,* p. 37.
47. *Ibid.,* pp. 34–5.
48. Charles Theodore Russell, Jr., *The Disenfranchisement of Paupers* (Boston: Little, Brown and Co., 1878), p. 4.
49. Josephine Chapin Brown, *Public Relief, 1929–1939* (New York: Henry Holt and Co., 1940), pp. 10, 16.
50. Coll, p. 42.
51. *Ibid.,* pp. 42–3.
52. Browning, pp. 77–9.
53. Veeder, p. 14.
54. Gillin, p. 212.
55. Coll, p. 44.

Chapter 3. Charities and Almshouses (pp. 30–42)

1. Blanche D. Coll, *Perspectives in Public Welfare* (Washington, D.C.: U.S. Department of Health, Education and Welfare, 1971), p. 45.
2. Josephine Chapin Brown, *Public Relief 1929–1939* (New York: Henry Holt and Co., 1940), p. 43.
3. Coll, p. 59.

4. *Ibid.*, p. 54.
5. *Ibid.*, p. 61.
6. *Ibid.*, pp. 54–5.
7. *Ibid.*, pp. 64–5.
8. *Ibid.*, p. 77.
9. *Ibid.*
10. Grace A. Browning, *The Development of Poor Relief Legislation in Kansas* (Chicago: University of Chicago Press, 1935), p. 65.
11. Fredric Veeder, *The Development of the Montana Poor Law* (Chicago: University of Chicago Press, 1938), p. 19.
12. Coll, p. 78.
13. Winifred Bell, *Aid to Dependent Children* (New York: Columbia University Press, 1965), pp. 10, 16.
14. Veeder, p. 20.
15. Harry Evans, *The American Poorfarm and Its Inmates* (Des Moines, Iowa: The Loyal Order of Moose, 1926), p. 1.
16. *Ibid.*, p. 6.
17. *Ibid.*, p. 7.
18. *Ibid.*, p. 16.
19. *Ibid.*, p. 13.
20. *Ibid.*, p. 68.
21. *Ibid.*, p. 36.
22. *Ibid.*, p. 9.
23. *Ibid.*, p. 13.
24. *Ibid.*, p. 29.
25. *Ibid.*, p. 64.
26. *Ibid.*, p. 66.
27. *Ibid.*, p. 64.
28. *Ibid.*, p. 74.
29. *Ibid.*, pp. 13–4.
30. *Ibid.*, p. 29.

Chapter 4. Depression (pp. 43–71)

1. Caroline Bird, *The Invisible Scar* (New York: David McKay Co., 1972), p. 28.
2. *Ibid.*, pp. 56–7.
3. Josephine Chapin Brown, *Public Relief 1929–1939* (New York: Henry Holt and Co., 1940), p. 99.
4. Bird, p. 27.
5. *Ibid.*, p. 71.
6. Harry Hopkins, *Spending to Save: The Complete Story of Relief* (New York: W. W. Norton and Co., 1936), p. 52.
7. *Ibid.*, p. 69.

8. *Ibid.,* p. 38 (quote by Myron C. Taylor, Chairman, Finance Committee, U.S. Steel Corporation).
9. Arthur Schlesinger, *The Age of Roosevelt: The Coming of the New Deal* (Boston: Houghton Mifflin Co., 1958), p. 274.
10. Bird, p. 78.
11. Hopkins, p. 74.
12. *Ibid.,* p. 26 (quote from Rudolph Spreckels' letter to Colonel Arthur Woods, Director of President Herbert Hoover's relief committee).
13. *Ibid.,* pp. 26–7 (quote from John B. Nicholas of Oklahoma Gas Utilities Co., Chickasha, Okla.).
14. Brown, p. 116.
15. Hopkins, p. 100.
16. Brown, p. 119.
17. Bird, p. 27.
18. *Ibid.,* pp. 171–2.
19. Hopkins, p. 100.
20. Brown, p. 153.
21. Schlesinger, p. 272.
22. Hopkins, p. 105.
23. Brown, p. 165.
24. Schlesinger, p. 274.
25. Hopkins, p. 133.
26. Schlesinger, p. 264.
27. *Ibid.,* p. 274.
28. *Ibid.,* p. 275.
29. *Ibid.*
30. Brown, pp. 240–1.
31. Frances Fox Piven and Richard A. Cloward, *Regulating the Poor* (New York: Pantheon, 1971), p. 108.
32. Paul Douglas, *Social Security in the United States* (New York: McGraw-Hill Book Co., 1936), pp. 71–3.
33. *Ibid.,* pp. 74–5.
34. Bird, p. 203.
35. Schlesinger, p. 304.
36. J. Douglas Brown, "Some Inherent Problems of Social Security," in "Appraising the Social Security Program," *Annals of the American Academy of Political and Social Science* (March 1939), pp. 1–3.
37. Elizabeth Wickenden, "Sharing Prosperity: Income Policy Options in an Affluent Society," *Toward Freedom from Want* (Madison, Wisconsin: Industrial Relations Research Association, 1968), p. 9.
38. Interview with Elizabeth Wickenden in February 1973 by the author.
39. Douglas, p. 116.
40. Schlesinger, p. 311.
41. *Ibid.*
42. *Ibid.*
43. *Ibid.*

44. *Ibid.,* pp. 311–2.
45. *Ibid.,* p. 311.
46. *Ibid.,* p. 296.
47. Piven and Cloward, p. 109.
48. *Ibid.*
49. *Commonweal* (May 27, 1938), 114.
50. Gilbert J. Hill, "Federal Relief Will Have to End," *Nation's Business* (October 1939), 27.
51. *The New Republic* (June 1, 1938), 86.
52. Brown, p. 341.
53. *Ibid.,* pp. 388–9.
54. "Two Ohio Cities Face Big Crisis Over Relief Funds," *Scholastic* (December 18, 1939), 6.
55. Donald S. Howard, "But People Must Eat," *The Atlantic Monthly* (February 1940), 193.
56. *Ibid.,* 197.
57. *Ibid.*
58. Brown, p. 389.
59. *Ibid.*
60. Editorial, *Collier's* (March 4, 1939), 62.
61. "Work Relief and States' Rights," *The New Republic* (June 14, 1939), 145.
62. "Relief Goes Wrong," *Collier's* (July 16, 1938), 54.
63. "The Fortune Survey," *Fortune* (March 1939), 132.
64. Hill, 27.
65. *Congressional Digest* (February 1939), 53.
66. Brown, p. 10.

Chapter 5.   Postwar Relief "Chiselers" (pp. 72–90)

1. *Saturday Evening Post* (December 10, 1949), 17.
2. *Saturday Evening Post* (September 30, 1950), 25, 114.
3. Edith Stern, "Broken Lives and Dollar Patches," *Nation's Business* (March 1950), 46.
4. "Why 5,500,000 Americans Get 'Relief' Money," *U.S. News and World Report* (April 19, 1957), 48.
5. Winifred Bell, *Aid to Dependent Children* (New York: Columbia University Press, 1965), p. 50.
6. *Ibid.,* p. 118.
7. *Ibid.,* p. 99.
8. *Ibid.,* p. 126.
9. *Ibid.,* pp. 42, 46, 76, 175. Winifred Bell makes several references to discrimination against blacks which existed from the beginnings of the welfare program. "In 1942, the Bureau of Public Assistance studied 16 state programs. The most significant finding was the wide divergence in their attitudes toward assisting nonwhite and illegitimate children. No eligi-

bility condition explicitly excluded them, but where the 'suitable home' philosophy prevailed, their exclusion was endemic."

She adds that the general attitude of white southerners was that the black families were immoral and their homes unsuitable; and that "Indian children, too, received help according to the dictates of local mores."

"Seasonal employment policies emerged in areas where seasonal labor was almost exclusively performed by nonwhite families. In Louisiana in 1943 the state agency adopted a policy requiring all applicants or recipients of ADC to be refused assistance so long as they were needed in the cotton fields. In one parish the policy extended to children as young as 7 years of age."

Substitute-parent policies fell most heavily on black children and the removal of such children from the rolls was a prime function of the policies.

10. *Ibid.*, p. 101.
11. *Ibid.*, pp. 137–47.
12. Gilbert Steiner, *Social Insecurity: The Politics of Welfare* (Chicago: Rand McNally & Co., 1966), p. 101.
13. "After 30 Years — Relief a Failure?", *U.S. News and World Report* (July 17, 1967), 46.
14. "Taking It Out on the Kids," *New Republic* (October 7, 1967), 9.
15. Edgar May, *The Wasted Americans* (New York: New American Library, 1964), p. 159.
16. *Ibid.*, pp. 158–9.
17. *Ibid.*, p. 158.
18. *Ibid.*, p. 156.
19. Hal Bruno, "Birth Control, Welfare Funds, and the Politics of Illinois," *The Reporter* (June 20, 1963), 33; other details here and in Steiner, pp. 225–33.
20. Bell, p. 78.
21. *Ibid.*, p. 86.
22. *Ibid.*, p. 7.
23. Robert M. O'Neil, *The Price of Dependency* (New York: E. P. Dutton and Co., 1970), p. 281.
24. Edward Sparer, Unpublished paper, Center for Social Welfare Policy and Law, New York.
25. Ben B. Seligman, ed., *Poverty as a Public Issue* (New York: The Free Press, 1965), p. 222.
26. *Ibid., see* footnote.
27. Bell, p. 90.
28. *Ibid.*
29. Herbert Krosney, *Beyond Welfare: Poverty in the Supercity* (New York: Holt, Rinehart and Winston, 1966), p. 138.
30. Edward Sparer, "Legal Entitlement Assurance Program," Address Before the Suffolk County Public Welfare Staff (New York: Center for Social Welfare Policy and Law, October 19, 1966).
31. Bell, p. 34.

32. Frances Fox Piven and Richard A. Cloward, *Regulating the Poor* (New York: Pantheon, 1971), p. 128 (footnote).
33. Bell, p. 82.
34. Piven and Cloward, p. 124.
35. Charles Stevenson, "When It Pays to Play Pauper," *Nation's Business* (September 1950), 30.
36. Bell, p. 43.
37. Meg Greenfeld, "The 'Welfare Chislers' of Newburgh, N.Y.," *The Reporter* (August 17, 1961), 37.
38. David Franke, "Newburgh: Just the Beginning?" *National Review* (July 29, 1961) 45.
39. Joseph McDowell Mitchell, "The Revolt in Newburgh," *Vital Speeches* (January 15, 1962), 214.
40. "Where Charity Begins," *Life* (July 28, 1961), 36.
41. "Now It's 'Illegal' for a City to Curb Welfare Abuses," *Saturday Evening Post* (August 5, 1961), 9.
42. James O'Gara, "Welfare a la Newburgh," *The Commonweal* (August 25, 1961), 462.
43. Mitchell, 215.
44. Fletcher Knebel, "Welfare: Has It Become a Scandal?" *Look* (November 7, 1961), 32.
45. "Growing Scandal in Relief," *U.S. News and World Report* (September 11, 1961), 88.
46. "Where Relief Goes and Jobs Go Begging," *U.S. News and World Report* (October 19, 1964), 17.
47. "Welfare Frauds Exposed," *Nation's Business* (June 1965), 94, 98.
48. Charles Stevenson, "Children Without Fathers," *Reader's Digest* (November 1961), 72.
49. Michael Murphy, "The Deceit, Corruption and Scars of 'Relief,'" *Life* (January 31, 1964), 63.
50. "Senator Byrd's 'Facts' About Welfare Payments," *New Republic* (December 14, 1968), 9.
51. Bell, p. 62.
52. *Facts, Fallacies and Future: A Study of the Aid to Dependent Children Program of Cook County, Illinois* (New York, Chicago and San Francisco: Greenleigh Associates, 1960), pp. 9, 55.
53. Lloyd Setleis, "Civil Rights and the Rehabilitation of AFDC Clients," *Social Work* (April 1964), 3.
54. *Facts, Fallacies and Future . . . ,* pp. 41, 56.
55. Piven and Cloward, p. 156.

Chapter 6. Rising Rolls and Reaction (pp. 91–104)

1. Stephen Leeds, "In-Migration: How Important?" *The Welfarer* (New York: New York City Department of Social Services, January 1969), 1–7.
2. Robert M. O'Neil. *The Price of Dependency* (New York: E. P. Dutton, 1970), p. 267.

3. Martin Rein, "Choice and Change in the American Welfare System," *Annals of the American Academy of Political and Social Science* (September 1969), 94.

4. Frances Fox Piven and Richard A. Cloward, *Regulating the Poor* (New York: Pantheon, 1971), p. xvii.

5. *Ibid.,* pp. 345–6.

6. *Ibid.,* p. 348.

7. *Ibid.*

8. "Nixon's Big Decision on Welfare," *Business Week* (June 21, 1969), 110.

9. Rein, 103.

10. Gilbert Steiner, *Social Insecurity: The Politics of Welfare* (Chicago: Rand McNally & Co., 1966), p. 29.

11. Rein, 107.

12. National Center for Social Statistics Social and Rehabilitation Service, Department of Health, Education and Welfare (Washington, D.C.: February 1973).

13. Joel Handler, *Reforming the Poor* (New York: Basic Books, 1972), p. 23.

14. House and Senate Committee Report on HR.1 (Washington, D.C.: The Committee, 1972).

15. *Witness for Survival* (New York: United Neighborhood Houses, 1969).

16. Handler, p. 42.

17. Nick Kotz, "Welfare: Taxpayers Rebel," Washington, D.C. *Post* (February 8, 1971), A1.

18. "Poverty Amid Plenty, The American Paradox," The Report of the President's Commission on Income Maintenance Programs (Washington, D.C.: The Commission, 1969), 29.

19. Letter from Ronald W. Park, Director, Office of Information, Manpower Administration, U.S. Department of Labor, Washington, D.C.: December 13, 1972.

20. National Center for Social Statistics, (Washington, D.C.: May 1973).

Chapter 7. Welfare Rights (pp. 105–124)

1. Interview with Johnnie Tillmon, March 8, 1973.

2. George Martin, Unpublished Ph.D. thesis, University of Chicago, 1972.

3. *Ibid.*

4. *Ibid.*

5. Frances Fox Piven and Richard A. Cloward, *Regulating the Poor* (New York: Pantheon, 1971), p. 294.

6. The information here and throughout much of the rest of Chapter 7 comes from the National Welfare Rights Organization, Washington, D.C., and the Center for Social Welfare Policy and Law, New York, N.Y.

7. Robert M. O'Neil, *The Price of Dependency* (New York: E. P. Dutton, 1970), p. 277.

8. Winifred Bell, *Aid to Dependent Children* (New York: Columbia University Press, 1965), pp. 34–5.

9. Interview with Faith Evans, board member. National Welfare Rights Organization, Washington, D.C., April 25, 1972.

10. Interview with Nancy "Duffy" Levy, attorney, Center for Social Welfare Policy and Law, New York City, November 16, 1972.

11. "U.S. Asks 8 States for $10.2 Million," *The New York Times* (November 21, 1972), 39.

12. Interview with Evans.

13. O'Neil, p. 254.

14. "Eight Congressmen Try Welfare Diet," *The New York Times* (July 3, 1969), 27.

15. Herbert Krosney, *Beyond Welfare: Poverty in the Supercity* (New York: Holt, Rinehart and Winston, 1966), p. 25.

16. *Ibid.*, pp. 136–7.

17. *Brief Against New York State Work Rules* (New York: Center for Social Welfare Policy and Law). 16.

Chapter 8. Guaranteed Income (pp. 125–136).

1. Robert Theobald, *Free Men and Free Markets* (New York: Clarkson N. Potter, 1960).

2. Robert Theobald, ed., *The Guaranteed Income* (Garden City, N.Y.: Anchor, 1967), p. 29.

3. Theobald, *Free Men . . .* , p. 157.

4. Theobald, *The Guaranteed . . .* , p. 101.

5. Theobald, *Free Men . . .* , p. 147.

6. Milton Friedman, *Capitalism and Freedom* (Chicago: University of Chicago Press, 1962), p. 192; George H. Hildebrand, *Poverty, Income Maintenance and the Negative Income Tax* (Ithaca, N.Y.: New York State School of Industrial and Labor Relations, 1967), pp. 13–30.

7. James C. Vadakin, "A Critique of the Guaranteed Annual Income," *The Public Interest* (Spring 1968), 58–9.

8. Vadakin, 55–7; Hildebrand, pp. 37–41.

9. *Ibid.*, 54; *Ibid.*, pp. 31–6.

10. Hildebrand, p. 46.

11. Vadakin, 61.

12. Harold Watts, *Hearing Before the Joint Economic Committee* (Washington, D.C.: U.S. Congress, June 1968), p. 110.

13. Vera Shlakman, *Children's Allowance* (New York: Citizens' Committee for Children), pp. 7–8.

14. Sar A. Levitan, Wilbur J. Cohen, and Robert J. Lampman, eds., *Toward Freedom from Want* (Madison, Wis.: Industrial Relations Association, 1968), p. 183.

15. *Ibid.*

16. Shlakman, p. 17.
17. Elizabeth Wickenden, "Sharing Prosperity: Income Policy Options in an Affluent Society," in Sar A. Levitan *et al.,* eds., *Toward Freedom from Want* (Madison, Wis.: Industrial Relations Association, 1968), p. 24.
18. Interview with Elizabeth Wickenden,
19. "A Negative Income Tax?" *Dun's Review* (August 1968), 39.
20. *Ibid.*
21. Larry L. Orr, Robinson G. Hollister, and Myron J. Lefcowitz, *Income Maintenance* (Chicago: Markham, 1971), p. 29.
22. *Poverty Amid Plenty, The American Paradox,* The Report of the President's Commission on Income Maintenance Programs (Washington, D.C.: The Commission, 1969), p. 7.

Chapter 9.   Issues—Subsidies and Women (pp. 137–152)

1. Taylor Branch, "The Screwing of the Average Man," *Washington Monthly* (March 1972), 10.
2. *Ibid.,* 12.
3. *Ibid.*
4. *Ibid.*
5. Dorothy Haener, "Who Is on Welfare," (fact sheet; Detroit: United Auto Workers, April 1971). Author is the international representative of UAW.
6. *Ibid.,* 16.
7. *Ibid.,* 25.
8. Bernard J. Friedan. *Improving Federal Housing Subsidies: Summary Report* (Washington, D.C.: Committee on Banking and Currency, U.S. House of Representatives, June 1971), pp. 11–16.
9. Haener, 18.
10. "Work and Welfare," *New Republic* (January 15, 1972), 6.
11. Branch, 11.
12. *Ibid.,* 18.
13. *Ibid.,* 13.
14. *Ibid.*
15. *Ibid.,* 22.
16. *Ibid.*
17. Eileen Shanahan, "276 with Income Over $100,000 Paid No Federal Tax in 1971, A Study Shows," *The New York Times* (April 2, 1973), 26.
18. This material comes from statements in the NWRO files in Washington, D.C.
19. Milton Friedman, "Social Security, The Poor Man's Welfare Payment to the Middle Class," *Washington Monthly* (May 1972), 11–16.
20. Ibid.
21. Alan Keith-Lucas, *Decisions About People in Need* (Chapel Hill: University of North Carolina Press, 1957), p. 76.

22. Kermit T. Wiltse and Robert W. Roberts, "Illegitimacy and the AFDC Program," in Robert W. Roberts, ed., *The Unwed Mother* (New York: Harper and Row, 1966), p. 228.
23. See footnote 18.
24. Edgar May, *The Wasted Americans* (New York: New American Library, 1964), p. 155.
25. Louis Kriesbert, *Mothers in Poverty* (Chicago: Aldine Publishing Co., 1970), p. 147.
26. Gilbert Steiner, *The State of Welfare* (Washington, D.C.: The Brookings Institution, 1971), pp. 54–5.
27. See footnote 18.
28. *Ibid.*
29. Johnnie Tillmon, "Welfare Is a Woman's Issue," *Ms.* (January 1972), 111–16.
30. Judith Levin and Patricia Vergata, "Welfare Laws and Women: An Analysis of Federal Sexism" (paper; New Brunswick: Rutgers University Law School, 1971), p. 31; Gilbert Steiner, *Social Insecurity: the Politics of Welfare* (Chicago: Rand McNally & Co., 1966), p. 51.
31. National Center for Social Statistics, Social and Rehabilitation Service, Department of Health, Education and Welfare (Washington, D.C.: May 1973).
32. "Fact Sheet on the Earnings Gap" (Washington, D.C.: Women's Bureau, U.S. Department of Labor, 1971); "Pay Gap Widens Between the Sexes," *The New York Times* (December 28, 1972), 34.
33. Nick Kotz, "Welfare Tide—A Human Crisis," Washington, D.C. *Post* (February 7, 1971), A21.
34. *Ibid.*
35. "Fact Sheet . . . ."
36. Marian P. Winston and Trude Forsher, *Nonsupport of Legitimate Children by Affluent Fathers as a Cause of Poverty and Welfare Dependence* (Santa Monica, Calif.: The RAND Corporation, 1971).
37. Interview with New York City regional office of U.S. Department of Manpower Administration, 1972.
38. Shelley G. Thorn v. Elliott L. Richardson (Secretary of Health, Education and Welfare) in U.S. District Court for Western District of Washington, D.C., Northern Division, November 1971.
39. "Fact Sheet . . . ."

Chapter 10. Workfare (pp. 153–172)

1. Explanations and analyses of the Family Assistance Plan are found in the hearings of the House Ways and Means Committee, U.S. Congress, and in papers distributed by the National Welfare Rights Organization and the Center for Social Welfare Policy and Law. Of special interest

are: Center for Social Welfare Policy and Law, "H.R. 1: The Social Security Amendments of 1971: A Critique" (New York: The Center, June 1971); and *Welfare Law News* (November 1972).

2. "Workfare: Reforming the Welfare System" (Washington, D.C.: Domestic Council, Office of the President, 1971).

3. National Welfare Rights Organization, "The Gaps in F.A.P." (Washington, D.C.: The Organization, 1971).

4. Elizabeth Wickenden, "H.R. 1: Welfare Policy as an Instrument of Coercion" (New York: Center for Social Welfare Policy and Law, 1972).

5. Merillee Dolan, "H.R. 1 and the Poverty of Women" (Chicago: National Organization for Women, 1972). Testimony before the Senate Finance Committee, February 11, 1972.

6. National Welfare Rights Organization, "The Talmadge Forced Work Requirements" (Washington, D.C.: The Organization, 1972).

7. Interview with Ken Niemond, an attorney at the Center for Social Welfare Policy and Law, November 16, 1972.

8. Adele Blong, "Analysis of Proposed New York Projects in Public Assistance Programs" (New York: Center for Social Welfare Policy and Law, 1971); Adele Blong, "Comment on Revision of New York's Proposed Projects under Section 1115 of the Social Security Act" (New York: Center for Social Welfare Policy and Law, 1971).

9. Peter Kihss, "City Is Sued to Stop Giving Unpaid Work-Relief Jobs," *The New York Times* (August 31, 1972), 1, 20.

10. "6% Eligible Given Training or Jobs," *The New York Times* (September 6, 1972). Statement by Jules Sugarman.

11. Report of the Survey of New York City Public Works Program (New York: Community Council of Greater New York, May 1972).

Chapter 11.   The New Law (pp. 173–183)

1. Marjorie Hunter, "Senate Unit Puts 'Must Work' Plan Into Relief Bill," *The New York Times* (April 29, 1972), 1.

2. James Welsh, "Welfare Reform: Born Aug. 8, 1969; Died Oct. 7, 1972," *The New York Times Magazine* (January 7, 1973), 16.

3. "Excerpts from Platform Approved by G.O.P. Resolutions Panel for the Convention: Welfare Reform," *The New York Times* (August 21, 1972), 21.

4. Welsh, 22.

5. Robert B. Semple, Jr., "President Scores 'Welfare Ethic,' " *The New York Times* (September 4, 1972), 1, 16.

6. Peter Kihss, "Welfare System Over U.S. Scored," *The New York Times* (January 2, 1973), 23.

7. Richard D. Lyons, "Welfare Reform or Curb In Funds Faced By States," *The New York Times* (December 5, 1972), 1, 20.

8. "President's News Conference on Foreign and Domestic Matters," *The New York Times* (March 3, 1973), 12.
9. Interview with Arthur Schiff, Assistant Administrator, Office of Policy Planning, Research and Evaluation, New York City Human Resources Administration, November 27, 1972.

FOOTNOTES

INDEX

Page numbers in italics indicate glossary definitions.

Inflation, 94, 102
  Nixon and, 139, 167
  See also: Cost of living increases; Need standards; Poverty line
Insurance companies vs. Social Security program (1930's), 61-62
Internal Revenue Service, 139
  See also Income tax
"Involuntary servitude" argument (vs. N.Y. work law), 171
Iowa:
  poor farms in, 40
  poor law (19th century) in, 25
  veterans' aid (19th century) in, 28
Irish immigration, 16-17
Italian families, mother's aid discrimination vs., 36

Jefferson v. Hackney (U.S. Supreme Court decision), 114
Johnson, Lyndon B., 133-134
  See also Antipoverty programs
Joint Economic Committee (U.S. Congress), 137-138

Kansas:
  binding out policy in, 20
  grasshopper plague of 1874 in, 27-28
  mother's pensions in, 35, 36
  poorhouses in, 23
  relief (1930's) in, 49
  welfare cuts in, 102
  See also: Kansas City; St. Louis
Kansas City, Mo.:
  coal mining areas (1932 riots) of, 48
  relief (1930's) in, 48
  welfare rights movement in, 112
King v. Smith (U.S. Supreme Court decision), 120
Kriesberg, Louis, *Mothers In Poverty*, 146

Labor Department:
  and H.R. 1, 164
  "poverty line" of, 94-95
  priority orders of, 150-151
Ladies of the Maccabees, 38
LaFollette, Robert, 47-48
Lampman, Robert, 130
Lanham Act (World War II), 147
Las Vegas, Nev., welfare rights movement in, 113
League to Improve Family Emphasis (Toledo, Ohio), 111
"Less eligibility" principle, *185*
  COS movement and, 34
  in early U.S., 26
  in English poor law, 10-11, 13
Life magazine, 85, 88
Little Rock, Ark., welfare rights movement in, 115
Lone Star Steel Company, 134
Lonergan, Senator (Conn.), 61-62
Long, Huey, 59
Look magazine, 87
Los Angeles, Calif.:
  postwar welfare in, 87, 96
  welfare rights movement in, 105, 107
Louisiana:
  postwar welfare in, 76, 80-81, 83, 84, 98
  voting denied paupers in, 27
Low, Seth, 29
Low Income Welfare Rights Organization (Nevada City, Calif.), 161
Lowell, Josephine Shaw, 31
Loyal Order of the Moose, 38
Lundeen Bill (1934), 59

MacArthur, General Douglas, 49
McGovern, George, 177, 179
  See also Presidential election (1972)
Maine:
  mother's pensions in, 36
  voting denied paupers in, 27

in colonial America, 14-18
in England (*see* English poor laws)
and guaranteed income debate, 125-126
postwar attitudes toward, 72-91 passim, 182-183 (*see also* Work ethic)
"Poor People's Platform" (1972), 123-124
Poverty (Robert Hunter), 34
"Poverty line," 94-95, *186*
and guaranteed income proposals, 125-126, 129, 130-131, 134-135
H.R. 1 and, 162
and 1972 law, 175
Ribicoff amendments and, 178
welfare rights movement and, 108
women vs. men below, 151-152
See also Need standards
Poverty-Rights Action Center (Washington, D.C.), 107-109
Presidential election (1972), 175, 176, 177, 179-180
national political conventions preceding, 123-124
President's Commission on Income Maintenance Programs (Johnson's), 134-135
President's Commission on Population Growth (Nixon's), 145-146
President's Organization on Unemployment Relief (Hoover's), 45
Price ceilings, during World War II, 71
Price supports (for farmers), 138
See also Farm subsidies
Prince Georges County, Md., unwed mothers in, 77
Property taxes, tax deductions for, 139
Prostitution, in Nevada, 113

Protestant ethic. *See* Work ethic
Protestant Illinois Council of Churches, 78
Providence, R.I., welfare rights movement in, 114, 117
Proxmire, William, 137-138
Public housing. *See* Housing programs (federal), for poor
Public Service Work Opportunities Program (PSWOP, N.Y.), 168-169, 170
Public works projects (1930's), 52-55
See also Works Progress Administration (WPA)

Quota system (Ga.), 83

Reader's Digest magazine, 88
Reagan, Ronald, 119, 149, 168
Recessions:
1938, 67-68
1950, 74
1958 and 1961, 99
See also Depressions
Reed, Daniel, 62
Regulating the Poor (Piven and Cloward), 93-94
Relative-responsibility laws, 108
Relief (1930's), 49-51
ending of, 66-69
opponents of, 56-59, 62-63, 69-71
See also: FERA, Work relief (1930's)
Relief (postwar):
attacks on, 86-88
increase in, 91-104 passim
Truman's proposal for, 73-74
See also Social Security program, changes in
Reno, Nev., welfare rights movement in, 113
Rensselaer County, N.Y., poor farm in, 41
Rent allotments, 116

Rent strikes, 116
Republican party:
  in 1930's, 45, 62, 65, 69-70
  1972 platform of, 177-178 (see also Presidential election [1972])
  and welfare rights movement, 112
Resettlement Administration, 55
Residency requirements:
  in ADC program (1935), 64
  H.R. 1 and, 158, 159
  in 1972 law, 176
  for old-age insurance, 63
  for relief (1930's), 38, 55
  U.S. Supreme Court on, 119, 120-121
  welfare rights movement vs., 108, 164
  See also Immigrants
Revenue sharing bill (1972), 181
Rhode Island:
  in 1930's, 45
  state infirmary in, 42
  voting denied paupers in, 27
  welfare rights movement in, 116, 121 (see also Providence)
Rhys-Williams, Lady Juliette Evangeline, 126
Ribicoff, Abraham, amendments (1972) of, 178-179
Roberts, Samuel, Mary Wilden, A Victim of the New Poor Law, 11-12
Rochester, N.Y., welfare rights movement in, 115
Rockefeller, Nelson, 93
Roosevelt, Franklin D.:
  vs. Lundeen Bill (1934), 59
  and relief, 49-50, 66, 67 (see also Relief [1930's])
  and work relief, 52, 53, 61, 70 (see also Work relief [1930's])
Roosevelt, Theodore, White House Conference on Dependent Children, 34-35

Sacramento, Calif., Welfare Department, 78
St. John Chrysostom, 2
St. Paul, 6
St. Louis, Mo.:
  outdoor relief abolished in, 25
  welfare rights movement in, 119
Samuelson, Paul, 134
San Francisco, Calif.:
  outdoor relief abolished in, 25
  postwar welfare in, 96
Sanders, Beulah, 149
Sandusky, Ohio, poor farm in, 41
Saturday Evening Post, 72, 73, 85
Savings banks, vs. Social Security program (1930's), 61-62
School clothing campaigns, 114-115
School lunch programs, 111, 115-116
  See also: Food stamps; Surplus food
Schorr, Alvin, 132
Schwartz, Edward, 129
Sears, Roebuck and Co., 56
Seasonal employment, home relief and, 100
Seattle, Wash., sex discrimination in, 151
Security Benefit Association, 38
"Security wage" system (WPA), 53
Senate Committee on Aging, 97
Senate Finance Committee, welfare reform bill in, 165, 173, 174
Settlement-house movement, 31
Settlement laws (early U.S.), 18-19
Sex discrimination, 58, 137, 141-152
  in AFDC, 148-152
  banned (1971), 123
  and H.R. 1, 164, 165
  in jobs, 76, 141
  and Talmadge Amendment, 166
  in WIN Program, 101-104, 123, 150-152, 166

Supplemental assistance (for working poor), 34, 117, 142, *187*
  H.R. 1 and, 157-158, 159-160
  in New York City, 95, 100, 142
  in 1972 law, 176, 179
  opposition to, 182
Support payments, 89, 150
  H.R. 1 and, 157
  1972 law and, 174
  welfare rights movement and, 112
Supreme Court. *See* U.S. Supreme Court
Surplus food:
  in 1930's, 47, 51
  in postwar period, 83, 100
  welfare rights movement and, 109
  See also: Food budgets; Food stamps
Surprise visits, 81-82
  U.S. Supreme Court on, 122
  welfare rights movement vs., 105, 108
"Survivors'" insurance, 65, 69, 97, *187*
  See also Old-age insurance
Sutter County, Calif., welfare rights movement in, 118

Taber, John, 62
Talmadge, Eugene, 53, 57
Talmadge Amendment (1971), 166-167, *187*
Tax breaks, 138-139
  See also Income tax
Tennessee, sterilization for unwed mothers in, 146
Terrel County, Ga., poor farms in, 40-41
Territories (U.S.), poor laws in, 19-21
Texas:
  day care in, 181
  mother's pensions in, 36
  voting denied paupers in, 27

welfare cuts in, 102
welfare rights movement in, 114, 122-123
See also Houston
Textile industry (England), child labor in, 8
Theobold, Robert, *Free Men and Free Markets*, 126-128
Thirteenth Amendment, 119-120
Thorn, Shelley, 151-166
Tillmon, Johnnie, 105, 140, 148-149
Tioga County, N.Y., poor farm in, 41-42
Title I (Elementary and Secondary Education Act, 1965), 114-115
Tobin, James, 129-130
Toledo, Ohio:
  relief (1930's) in, 68
  welfare rights movement in, 111
Townsend Plan (1934), 58-59
Townshend, The Reverend Joseph, 7
Transportation, federal aid to, 138
Travel, constitutional right to, 120-121
  See also Residency requirements
Truman, Harry, federal relief proposal of, 73-74

Unemployed Father (UF) provision of AFDC, 90, 95, 97, 100, 102, *184*
Unemployment compensation:
  adoption of (1935), 60, 61-62, 65, 72
  Lundeen Bill (1934) and, 59
  in postwar period, 99-100
United Fund, 181
U.S. Chamber of Commerce, and relief (1930's), 56-57
U.S. Civil Rights Commission, 83
U.S. Conference of Mayors, and relief (1930's), 70
U.S. News and World Report magazine, 74, 87

ABOUT THE AUTHOR

Lucy Komisar became concerned about the inequities of America's social welfare system when she served for a year as a special assistant to the deputy administrator of the Human Resources Administration—the agency that ran the anti-poverty program—in New York City. She is the author of *The New Feminism* and the forthcoming *The Machismo Factor;* her next book for Franklin Watts, Inc. will be a history of the Equal Rights Amendment. She has also written cover stories for *Saturday Review, New York Magazine,* and the *Washington Monthly.*

Ms. Komisar was graduated from Queens College of the City University of New York in 1964 with a B.A. in history. She has worked as a reporter and associate producer for National Educational Television on news features and documentaries and has been a writer, reporter, and producer for WBAI radio in New York City. She now has her own program of feminist news and commentary for WBAI.

In 1970–71, she was elected vice-president of the National Organization for Women, and lectures nationally on the subject of women's rights.